About the Author

Kath Shorrock was born in Blackburn, Lancashire in 1950. She has been married twice. Her first husband, Ian, died in 1993 and she married her second husband, Keith, in 2004. She has three grown-up children, two stepchildren and ten grandchildren, and now lives in the Ribble Valley. Now retired, her occupation spanned twenty-two years as a receptionist for the NHS. Her love of writing began when she was just eight years old, telling the story of her beloved dolly, Carol, who is now sixty-seven years old!

Today, Tomorrow and Forever

Kath Shorrock

To. audrey

with Love & Best Wishes

Today, Tomorrow and Forever

from

Kath

xxx

Vanguard Press

A CIP catalogue record for this title is
available from the British Library.

ISBN 978 1 78465 758 1

Vanguard Press is an imprint of
Pegasus Elliot MacKenzie Publishers Ltd.

www.pegasuspublishers.com

First Published in 2020

Vanguard Press
Sheraton House Castle Park
Cambridge England

Printed & Bound in Great Britain

Dedication

This book is in loving memory of Ian Michael Abbotts
Born May 22nd 1946
Died November 23rd 1993
Aged forty-seven years

It has been an absolute pleasure and a privilege to write this book. I am so lucky that I have been a Daughter, Sister, Auntie, Wife, Mother and Nan to my lovely family and this is my legacy to each one of you. I have been truly blessed with two wonderful husbands: Ian Michael, the one who loved me unconditionally to the very end of his short life and who gave me my three beautiful children, Andrew Richard, Mark Ian and Laura Katherine whom I have loved beyond all measure; and my second darling husband, Keith John who has given me my life back again. Nearly every day since December the 18th 1996, we have laughed mostly with tears falling down our cheeks. Keith is the most wonderful, loving and amazing person, and I thank God for the day he came into my life and changed it forever. No words could ever describe just how much I love and treasure this man of mine.

Some people did not approve of our relationship: they thought it was too soon to live together after we met but we knew we loved each other, and we have proved to them that life is for the living. We have been happily married now for over fourteen years and we would not have changed a thing. Thank you to all of you who have contributed to this book and you know who you are. Widowhood is a very, very lonely life. May all of you who read it take heart that there is a new tomorrow after tragedy, and I thank God from the bottom of my heart for the second chance of a love beyond compare.

Keith, you are my world and I love you my darling with all my heart.

Yours Forever and Always, Kath xxxxxxx

ONE

Kate stood in the dining area of her lounge looking out towards the back garden. She knew without a doubt that she wanted to spend the rest of her life in this house, she loved it so much. This beautiful home was more than just a house; it was a sanctuary to her, somewhere where no one could frighten or tease her about her fears any more. She had endured them for most of her life and as far as she was concerned, they would probably be carried with her forever. She had been very happily married for four years and this was her second home. She shared it with Michael, her wonderful husband who was her saviour, her lover and most of all her very best friend, the only person in fact on whom she could totally depend upon for all the love and support she so desperately needed. She knew that no matter what happened in their lives together that he would never ever let her down.

Each night after he had finished work at the brewery, and because he was on the road for most of the day, he had driven around the housing estate off Pleckgate Road in Blackburn, Lancashire to find them this new home. They had discussed it over and over again and decided they must find one on the back row of the estate where there were rolling fields, as they had the most beautiful views to the rear and also, they were nearly new, being built only four years ago. On a clear day you could see across the fields towards Yorkshire, a view they both wanted desperately, and after much searching Michael had found them a semi-detached house that had come up for sale at the right price. It was perfectly suitable for them and they moved into their new home on August the 15th 1975. It was just over a year since Kate had lost her mother to secondary cancer. Although it wasn't the ideal way to be able to afford a new house with her inheritance, it was a good investment for them and a step up from their two-bedroom semi-detached house in the Redcap area of Oswaldtwistle, near Accrington, where they had lived since they were married.

Michael and Kate had a lovely little boy; his name was Richard and he was just two years old. He was the apple of their eyes, and they loved him beyond words. Kate had longed for a little boy when she had found out she was pregnant nine months after her wedding day, the 14th of August 1971. Her two sisters both had children. Jean, her elder sister had given birth to a little boy in November 1971, and they already had a little girl who was five years old. Now their family was complete. Her eldest sister Glenda had two little girls, but Kate had always dreamt of having a little boy and here he was. They were the perfect family. Kate would often stand by the window at the back of the through lounge, and just drink in the beautiful views. Cows grazed lazily in the newly mown fields by the fence at the end of the garden and whether it was a miserable rainy day or a gloriously sunny one, the fact remained that no matter whatever the season, Kate was blissfully happy and settled in her lovely home. Living there each day as a family was perfect. Sadly, life had not always been so idyllic for Kate and she knew that her past had contributed greatly to the nervous disposition that she found herself in right now and which she had to contend with daily. She was born on Revidge Road in Blackburn on the 28th of February 1950. When she was just ten weeks old her father, Rob Walsh, had a very serious accident at work. He was a cabinetmaker and joiner by trade and he was working for a firm in Blackburn. Being a foreman did not stop Rob from helping his colleagues at work and whilst they were building a new mill in Darwen, a terrible accident happened. The weight of a double decker bus fell onto him, badly crushing his pelvis. Rob was in hospital for many months and when he eventually did recover enough to return to work he was not bodily fit to resume the heavy joinery work that he had been doing before his accident.

After months of being in terrible pain, Rob was to find out that arthritis had unfortunately set into his hip. It was decided by the orthopaedic consultant surgeon at Blackburn Royal Infirmary that he would need to have an operation for a total hip replacement. Rob was taken into theatre and fitted with an artificial steel hip as the plastic hips used today were not available then for him, but soon he realised that he would never be able to work on the building site again. He would have to find some other means of work, but as his whole life had been in the building trade, it was very hard for him to find an alternative occupation. Kate's mother Mary and her two older sisters, Glenda and Jean, and Rob, had many long discussions together and eventually they decided the only solution to the problem was to buy a grocer's shop; fortunately one had come up for sale in the nearby town of Darwen. It was hard for Mary and Rob to give up their lovely terraced house on Revidge Road, but there was no alternative for them. They had to survive and that meant a new career and a new way of life.

They moved into the shop in the winter of 1954 when Kate was just four and a half years old. It was not what she had imagined it to be; in fact she was not impressed by the shop at all. There was never any time for family life any more. From Monday through to Saturday her parents were so busy she hardly ever saw them. She felt it even more at meal times when they were at their busiest serving people and it didn't help any when Rob said to her, 'Kate, the customers must come first. They are our bread and butter.' 'I know, Daddy,' she said tearfully, 'but what about our family life? Are we not important too?' Her little mind could not understand that Mary and Rob needed every penny they could earn to keep their heads above water, to feed their children as well as themselves. The little friends the two youngest sisters had made since moving to Darwen were all sitting down to eat their meals with their mums and dads, and Jean and Kate would patiently wait in the dining room for a lull in the never-ending stream of customers who came into the shop every day on their way home from work. Eventually, when it was a bit quieter, Mary would break away to go into the little kitchen and make them all a meal. Oh, how she envied those friends of hers. Their lives were normal, and it soon became apparent to Kate that she hated this life altogether. The shop, with its constant demands on her mum and dad, made her hate it even more. She wished that if only she too could have a normal life like those living down the road then it would have been heaven. On the other side of the coin were her friends. They were always wishing that they could live in her shop with all the goodies to eat, and Kate told them she would swap their lives anytime. They were more than welcome to it all; the toffees, chocolates and anything else they wanted. She would have changed places with them at the drop of a hat. The shop itself was quite a large business but it needed some time and money spending on it – time that Rob did not have at the moment. All his energy and strength went into the shop, welcoming his customers every day with a smile and a cheery hello. Mary and the children were told the decorating would have to wait and bit by bit he would modernise it over time. They would just have to be patient.

The dining room was quite small compared to the one they had lived in at Revidge Road. It led into a very small, pokey, cramped kitchen, which was not big enough to house a fridge or a washing machine. It overlooked the small garden which had a very high, dark wall and there was a small yard with a path leading down to the garage. To the left near the garage wall was a tippler toilet; this had no chain to flush as it was connected only to the sewer in the back street. Kate had often dropped keys down it by mistake and got a good telling-off from her mum as it was a bottomless pit and they were lost forever.

The wash house and coal store were situated beneath the kitchen window and this could only be accessed through the yard as there was no direct route through the kitchen itself as it was on a floor below. You could only peer into it over the kitchen windowsill. It was so bitterly cold in there that Mary could put a jelly onto the window shelf and it would be set in no time, even in the summer months. Everything on the shelf kept fresh so there was little need for a fridge. The sitting room however was a much larger room. It had a nice dark mahogany fire surround with an oval mirror in the centre and a real coal fire. In the corner stood the nine-inch black and white television, with a magnifying glass over the screen making it appear larger. Fortunately Rob had been able to buy this screen from his brother's electrical shop and it made viewing much more pleasant. There was a beautiful 'Sames' highly polished, dark mahogany piano that Mary played, positioned on the back wall. Mary could not read sheet music, but she would listen to the radio in the dining room, then go into the sitting room and play the same piece so perfectly on the piano. It was a privilege to sit and listen to her play. She had only heard someone sing once on 'Sing Something Simple', a radio programme broadcasted on a Sunday evening, but she would play the tune perfectly. Kate loved music and so did all the family but there was only Mary who could play the piano, it was her pride and joy. There was a cherry-red coloured three-piece suite in the sitting room which had been newly re-covered, and a deep-pile blue patterned carpet. Rob would sit comfortably in his favourite armchair on a Saturday afternoon when they had closed the shop for the weekend, watching his beloved wrestling on the BBC television channel.

Sometimes Mary would go shopping to Bolton or Preston on their half day closing and she would walk around for hours on end, always bringing a little treat home for everyone; mainly it would be a pink and blue trinket box for Jean's and Kate's bedrooms, or a new brush and comb for their dressing tables. They were not spoilt children by any means and they had to pay for their sweets from the shop with their spending money. There was only one exception to the rules and that was on a Saturday evening when they were allowed to choose a bar of chocolate for free from the shelves in the passageway that led from the dining room through to the shop floor, where all the confectionery was kept. They would eat them sitting with their parents whilst watching the television around a warm cosy fire.

Upstairs were four good sized bedrooms and Kate shared hers with Glenda. Jean had a room of her own. Both bedrooms were on the front of the property facing the main road. Jean's was decorated in a lovely powder-blue colour. She had a single bed and a kidney-shaped dressing table which Rob had made for her. Mary had made a cream floral frill to go all the way around it, making it very girlie and there was a small wooden shelf underneath for Jean to put her rollers, hairspray and perfume on.

Rob had put in a three-bar electric fire for her as there was no central heating in the property. Jean was told she only had to put on one bar at a time as it was expensive to run and if Mary came into her room and caught her with more than one bar on at a time she would get a severe telling-off. Like everyone else in the fifties they were watching their electricity bill like a hawk. Glenda and Kate's room was next door to Jean's and theirs was painted rose pink. They had a double mahogany wardrobe, a three-quarter bed which they shared, and a highly polished mahogany dressing table. On it was a pink crocheted mat with a pink brush and comb set and a mirror to match. A pink trinket box was also on the table which housed all of Kate's little treasures.

On the bed was a pink eiderdown and quilt cover with roses on it and the floor was covered in a beautiful cream and pink floral carpet. The electric fire was to be used the same as in Jean's room, one bar at a time, but all the girls disobeyed the rule, especially in the height of winter when they sneaked on an extra bar! Rob and Mary's bedroom was facing the side street. It was decked out in dark green and lavender which were Mary's favourite colours. The fourth bedroom was at the back of the house and this one was nicknamed the 'Glory Hole'. It was the room where Mary did her ironing and used it for her sewing. Basically, it was a junk room and both Rob and Mary were notorious for keeping things year after year instead of having a sort-out of old and used clothes. If they had thought to decorate the room properly, it would have made a decent fourth bedroom saving Glenda and Kate from having to share. The landing leading to all the bedrooms and the bathroom was the scariest place in the house mainly, Kate felt she would fall down the stairs through the spindles. Her Mum had tried to tell her that she was far too big to fit in-between them but Kate would walk along brushing the wall until she got to the top of the stairs where she then felt safer. It truly was a rambling place to live in and she never settled despite all the years she had to live there.

TWO

In 1954 Kate started at her infant school St Barnabas in Watery Lane, Darwen. Miss Bentley was her first teacher in the reception class. She was a very kind lady who liked Kate and helped her to settle into her new surroundings.

Home life was not all doom and gloom despite Kate hating the shop. Carol was Kate's beautiful dolly and she loved her more than anything else in the whole world. She had been bought for her as a Christmas present when she was only two years old when they had lived on Revidge Road in Blackburn. Rob had said it was a crazy present to buy for such a tiny child, but Mary had insisted that Kate needed a dolly of her own as she would have tormented the life out of Jean who also had a new doll for Christmas and she had called hers Ann. Now that Kate was six years old, each day after school she raced home to play with her. The clothes that Carol wore were all made for a real baby; a terry towelling nappy, some little white rubber pants, a real baby's safety pin and a beautiful dress and coat with knitted pants to match, all in rose pink. Mary bought Kate a baby feeding bottle for Kate to feed her dolly with, and she put some shoe whitening into it for pretend milk. The teat had to be blocked up, so she put some glue in the hole to stop the spillage and there she had her very own pretend bottle of formula milk looking just like the real thing. Some days Kate would come home from school and her mum would say to her, 'go up to your bedroom, there is a surprise waiting for you', and sure enough, there was Carol sat on the ottoman, dressed in a beautiful white christening gown which had belonged to Kate's father. It was a lovely surprise indeed and she ran downstairs to thank her mum. She knew how busy Mary had been in the shop all day, but she always made time for little surprises.

On a Saturday, Kate would take Carol out in her doll's pram. Sometimes she would walk down Bolton Road to the town centre. She was trusted by her parents not to cross the main road and she must turn around at the George Hotel Inn before she actually reached the centre. If she walked to the cemetery she had to turn around at the gates and she knew she had never to go inside where it was very lonely. It was the highlight of her week and she never tired of the walks with her dolly. The pram was a hand-me-down from Jean. It was dark grey in colour and although Kate had begged her parents for a brand new dolls pram of her own, they said she had to make do with the old one as they thought there was nothing wrong with it, but Kate knew it was because they probably couldn't afford one. Her other precious possession was her teddy. She went to choose him at Littlewoods store in Blackburn with her mum and dad for her sixth birthday.

He was the one with the warmest smile and a big royal blue bow around his neck. At her birthday party Kate remembered getting told off by her dad for not sharing him with her little friends and she had sulked and had to apologise to everyone for being so possessive, but she still wouldn't share him. She thought he was the best birthday present she could ever have wished for. Being the youngest in the family often meant having toys and clothes passed down to her from Jean, but these two toys were different; they belonged to her from new. They were hers and hers alone. Her roller skates were the next present given to her for Christmas and she also got a tambourine. A lot of Kate's friends were in the Morris dancers and they used to dance for the Darwen team. She didn't want to join them, but she did want to be the same as them and learn how to dance.

Jean and Kate also had a shop to play with up in the attic. It was a replica of the real one downstairs and the envy of all their friends. They would go to the shop further up the road and ask the lady for empty stocking boxes for their drapery department. They carefully folded some old stockings of Mary's into them, so they looked like a brand-new pair and they hid the ladder if there was one underneath the cellophane. Mary would also save them empty, used jelly and cereal boxes, and empty cans of beans and peas which had been opened upside down, so they looked like new ones. They were washed and turned upright on the shelves. They had a café and a clothes department and it really was authentic. The girls played for hours up there in total harmony with each other. Although Kate hated the real shop downstairs, she really enjoyed playing with Jean and she had made it lovely for them. It took them weeks to complete and they spent many happy hours enjoying it and sharing it with their friends.

***

In 1957 Rob Walsh decided to change the shop into a Spar shop. It was the second Spar shop to be opened in Darwen at 439 Bolton Road. It turned out to be a very big success and everyone was excited about it. Supermarkets were very few and far between in the fifties and early sixties, and Rob and Mary were delighted to find that the business was doing exceptionally well. The idea was for their customers to buy the Spar products which were cheaper and could well have been made by one of the big named manufacturing companies but with the Spar label on them. There were promotions quarterly and special offers, balloons for the children and plenty of free gifts for all. Customers were eager to try these new products as they were considerably cheaper, and Rob and Mary were very happy with the profits they were making.

***

In July of that year, when Kate was seven years old, the family went on their main summer holiday. Glenda was seeing Tom now as she was nineteen years old. He was a local man and they were going out for day trips. Mary, Rob and the two girls set off for a week-long holiday to Colwyn Bay in North Wales. It was to be a holiday Kate would never ever forget. They stayed in a small family-run hotel on the promenade overlooking the sea. They shared a family room with two single beds, one for Jean and the other for Kate and a double bed for their mum and dad. They had only been there for two days when Kate, Jean and Mary went down with a sickness and diarrhoea virus which quickly swept through the hotel.

The only person who was well and did not get it was Rob, and so began the terrible phobia for Kate and for which, although she didn't know it at the time, was to plague her for the rest of her life. From that week on, she was terrified of anyone feeling sick or, God forbid, actually being sick. For people with this phobia they seem to have a built-in antenna and if anyone around her looked in the slightest off colour, immediately Kate would be terrified in case she saw them vomit in front of her, but little did she know what a devastating effect this illness they had all suffered in Wales was to have on her. They returned home at the end of the holiday totally drained and then came the same repetitive dreams for Kate. She would go off to bed perfectly all right, only to be woken up suddenly. She would be sweating and shaking with a pounding heart. She would get up and dive out of bed, run down the stairs two at a time, fling the lounge door open and say, 'Mum, I'm going to be sick.' Mary would look at Rob and say, 'I'll go to bed with her, she will be all right'. Ironically, most times she was not sick at all.

THREE

When Kate was just eight years old her mother was diagnosed with advanced breast cancer. Mary was seen by their family doctor, Dr Lavery. It was one lunchtime when he came into the shop for his ground coffee and a few other bits and pieces. Rob had asked him would he kindly look at Mary's breast as they were both worried it did not look all right. After he had examined her, he immediately got on the phone to the Christie Hospital in Manchester and the next day she was admitted. The diagnosis was not good, and the doctor told Mary that she had to undergo a full mastectomy operation. Fortunately, it was a straightforward operation but inevitably she had a terrible scar leading from her shoulder right down to her navel, which of course Mary was very conscious of. It affected her very badly, both in mind and body. She had seen so many bad cases of people with cancer in the hospital and she needed a lot of tender loving care when she returned home. As the year drew to a close she was on the mend and she tried very hard to make her life as normal as possible for herself and for her family.

***

In 1958 Glenda announced her forthcoming wedding to Tom. He was a nice friendly chap who was devoted to her. They had been seeing each other for quite a few months and were married on Kate's ninth birthday, February the 28th 1959 at St Barnabas Church, Darwen. Jean and Kate were both bridesmaids. They wore their favourite colours, pink for Kate and blue for Jean. They each had a little white fur cape around their shoulders which Mary had made to keep them warm and which they were so glad of, as it was a bitterly cold day. Despite the weather, the sun shone on the happy couple and everyone who attended their wedding enjoyed sharing in Glenda and Tom's special day. They spent their honeymoon in Blackpool for a week and then it was back to the paper mill for Tom, and Glenda returned to help her father in the shop. They had only been married for three months when much to everyone's delight Glenda announced that she was pregnant. Rob and Mary were overjoyed to hear the news. Fortunately, it was an easy pregnancy for her and she worked alongside her dad until nearer the birth.

On the 20th of February 1960, a beautiful baby girl arrived, and Glenda and Tom were delighted with her. She had a full head of ginger hair and they called her Jeanette. Kate and Jean were very proud aunties and they loved her dearly. Jean started to help more in the shop now as she was nearly fourteen and Mary was feeling much better since her operation, so she too helped out when she could. It wasn't easy looking after a family and still having to work in the shop. Kate went to play with the baby each Saturday and they took her out in her pram down to the town centre. This was what Kate had always dreamed of, a normal home life, tea on the table at the right time and no interruptions from the endless stream of customers. They watched the television together and had lovely walks in Bold Venture Park. Some Saturdays they went to watch Tom play football for his firm and life was bliss. Kate had never been happier. Tom was a wallpaper printer at the local wall-coverings mill in Darwen town centre and he loved playing football. Glenda, Kate and the baby waited for him after the match had finished and they all walked home together. Tea was usually a delicious homemade steak and kidney pudding or potato pie that Glenda had made, and which Kate thoroughly enjoyed. This was usually followed by a homemade apple pie. She loved Saturdays: her mum saw her across the main road from the shop around eleven o'clock in the morning and she was put on the Ribble bus to be met at the end of Ratcliffe Street by Glenda, so they could spend the day together.

***

In 1961 it was time for Kate to go to her secondary school. She settled into a more grown-up way of life although she was still a little girl at heart. She still played endlessly with her dolly and her Saturday walks were now shared with Glenda. Rob spent long days in the shop and long evenings in the attic, painting and putting new brakes on an old bike passed down from Glenda to Jean and now to Kate. Her friends were getting brand new ones for Christmas but Kate had to make do with the hand-me-down one. Nevertheless, she was excited to have a bike of her own to ride on, no matter what condition it was in to begin with. She was a grateful child; she never kicked up a fuss and accepted everything that was given to her. It was how her parents had brought her up and she appreciated everything she had, whether it was new or not. The bike was painted blue, the same colour as her father's car. He had used some of the paint that he had bought to touch up the bonnet and he fitted it with new tyres. It had a three-speed Sturmy Archer gear on it and he painted the spokes with bright aluminium paint. He even fitted a new silver bell on the handle bar for her. By Christmas morning it was finished and ready to ride. Kate was so pleased with it she went to call for Lynne her friend, who lived in Maria Street. Lynne had just got a brand-new lilac and purple Raleigh bike that morning from her mum and dad and it shone like a diamond, and together they went up and down the side streets near their homes. It was a freezing Christmas morning, but they never noticed the cold as they were both so delighted to ride together and enjoy themselves.

As Kate was now eleven years old, her parents let her go to the socials on a Saturday evening in the hall of her old junior school. They were held on alternative Saturdays, one held in the school room at St Barnabas on Watery Lane, and the other one was held at St Mary's Church at Grimehills on the Roman Road going towards Bolton. Jean and Kate were picked up along with the other parishioners in the back of a cattle truck. The farmer was called Mr Robinson and he used to clean out his truck on a Saturday afternoon and put clean hay on the floor for them to stand on. He came down from his farm in Hoddlesden, on the outskirts of Darwen, to collect them all from the school door at seven p.m. prompt. They all filed into the back of the cattle truck, each one holding tight onto the gap where the cows usually looked out. When the truck was going through the village area Mr Robinson would knock on the cab to tell them all to be quiet, so he would not get fined by the police for carrying unlawful passengers. When they got to Grimehills, Jean and her friends and Kate and her friends went downstairs to the cloakroom to put on their make-up and perfume and to change out of their Wellingtons which sometimes had cow dung on them and then they stepped into their dancing shoes. Upstairs in the school hall the band was playing and they waltzed and did the quickstep all night long. There was an interval where everyone was given a small meat pie, a cake and a cup of tea and they all had a wonderful time. The week after, on the Saturday evening all the people from Grimehills would come down to do the same thing at St Barnabas school, and it continued throughout the winter months. Kate learned to dance at all these events with Eric Jackson, her school friend's dad and he taught her the foxtrot and the barn dance and many more. The congregational church, which was situated across the road from the shop, also held dances frequently and Eric would take Kate in his arms and dance the night away with her. Fortunately, Jean, Eric's wife, was not a lover of dancing and this gave her the opportunity to dance most of the night with him. She thought he was the best dancer in the whole room and she was grateful to be taught by him. Unfortunately, the weekends sped by too soon, but she looked forward to all the socials as dancing was her favourite pastime.

FOUR

It was in the autumn of 1963 that life changed so drastically for Kate and the family. The first thing Kate knew of anything was when she came home from school one day in September. There was a big discussion going on in the lounge at the shop and she could hear her parents' voices along with Glenda and Tom's. Jean meanwhile was serving in the shop. 'Why don't you want them to go, Mary?' Rob was saying,

'It's too far away from here.' she said.

'We can visit them, we have a car.' he protested. 'It's only about a four-hour journey up to County Durham.' Kate was astounded. What on earth were they all talking about and she listened as they continued. 'It's a chance in a lifetime.' Rob continued. 'These job opportunities don't come along very often, Mary, and when they do you have to seize them whilst you can.' Kate stepped into the room and asked them what they were all talking about. She nearly died when they explained that Tom had been offered a better job in a new town called Peterlee in County Durham. It was at a paper mill that had just been newly built and he was offered a position as a wallpaper printer which was the job he did now. Glenda ,with Tom and Sheila, their second child who was only four months old, and Jeanette her big sister, now three, were contemplating leaving Darwen. How could they even think of moving to a new house when all the family wanted to share their lives with them here, not one hundred and twenty miles away in another town? It was a devastating thought and she prayed that they would hopefully think of the consequences to Rob and Mary and to the girls if they moved away. She hoped that they would change their minds and stay. The devastating truth was, it wasn't to be. They decided they wanted to go to Peterlee and start a brand-new life together in a brand-new town. They had decided they were going to put their house on Ratcliffe Street in the hands of an estate agents and move to the north east of England. Day in and day out Kate hoped and prayed that they would change their minds and realise just how much they would be missed, that they would put a stop to their plans, but her prayers were not to be answered and she was distraught with it all beyond all reasoning.

***

In April 1964 Glenda, Tom and the little ones left Darwen and headed to the North East to begin their new lives. The incomprehensible had happened and there now was no turning back. Kate and the family travelled up the following weekend and they were still getting straight from the move. There was concrete and rubble everywhere to be seen as the town was so newly built. It had been developed out of acres and acres of lush green fields and now in the early spring it was just a mud bath and most of the land was water-logged. The town centre had a few new shops built, but it would be years before it flourished into a beautiful town and the contractors took all their machinery away. Glenda and Tom's house was thoroughly modern with a flat roof. The kitchen was beautifully fitted out and the three bedrooms were quite spacious. The bedroom windows were a problem though as they were so high up you could only see out of them if you stood up. The sky was the only part to be seen if you were in bed and it was only when Kate stood up to get dressed that she could see out at all. The lounge had a nice tiled fireplace and the dining area was comfortably housed with a highly polished new dining room suite. All the windows downstairs were from floor to ceiling making it ultra-modern, and Kate thought it really was lovely. It was just the fact that she didn't want to be there, or for that matter for Glenda and the family to be there either. All too soon it was Sunday afternoon and the weekend was nearly over. With a four-hour drive home they all said a very tearful goodbye to Glenda and the children and they wished Tom all the best in his new job which he was starting the following day.

The journey home was one of a few which found Kate crying silently in the back seat of her dad's car. She had purposely taken a writing pad with her and she began to write Glenda a letter as soon as they got on the road home to Darwen. Tears stained the pages where she wrote the miss you words. She tried to come to terms with the fact that they all, through circumstances, had to be apart and she felt her heart break again and again. They had hardly spent a day without seeing each other in all of Kate's fourteen years of her life and she was struggling to try and understand the way she felt. It was so very hard to be brave and she knew it was a losing battle. She would miss her big sister forever. They arrived safely home back to the shop, and the day after, Kate went back to school. She told her friend Joan about the weekend she had had and Joan said how sorry she was for her. She knew how much Kate loved her sister, and she said she would not be able to cope if had it been her sister that had moved away. Joan was as close to her sister as Kate was to Glenda. Jean was happy working in the shop with her father. She and Kate missed being hands-on aunties, but they got on with their lives. After all, what else could they do? By now Jean was courting with Peter and she was blissfully happy and looking forward to getting engaged soon. Easter came around quickly and the shop was closed from Good Friday to the following Tuesday. Kate knew she had a long weekend up at Peterlee with Rob and Mary and she even looked forward to the journey. When they arrived at Glenda's house after four hours of travelling from Darwen they relaxed together in the lounge, chatting and catching up on each other's news. Kate played with the two children; she had missed them so much. It was a nice break for them all and Rob and Mary said they would like to come up again for their main holiday if that was okay with Tom and Glenda. It would be the second week in July when the shop would be closed for the wake's week. Wow, a whole week together, now that was something to look forward to and Kate couldn't wait!

They closed the shop at lunchtime on the first day of their July holidays and the three of them headed up to the North East. Kate was so excited she willed the miles away, and after the usual four-hour journey they arrived safely but tired, looking forward to a good rest and a week of fun. The week sped by all too quickly and poor Rob and Mary had a tummy bug. By Thursday evening they were on the mend and they decided to have a ride out to see Durham Cathedral with little Jeanette. Tom said that he would like to go along too. Kate and Glenda put baby Sheila to bed and Glenda asked Kate if she would like to put some rollers in her hair. She loved hairdressing and jumped at the chance. The night crept in and it was getting late. There were no signs of Mary and the rest of them coming up the road, and it was now quite dark even for a warm summer's evening. Glenda said to Kate that she thought the four of them would be home by now when suddenly a police car with blue flashing lights came speeding up the road and screeched to a halt. Kate and Glenda thought they were going to the house next door, but to their horror the two police officers opened the gate and were coming up the path. They both went to the door to be confronted by two solemn-faced policemen and instantly they realised something was dreadfully wrong. 'Are you Glenda Yates?' the first officer said.

'Yes I am,' she said. 'Whatever is the matter?'

'I am so dreadfully sorry to tell you,' he said, 'there has been a terrible road traffic accident and I am afraid your father and daughter are critically ill in Newcastle General Hospital,' he continued. 'Your husband and your mother are both in a stable condition in County Durham Hospital. She has a broken collarbone and your husband is being treated for shock, but you need to get to Newcastle General as soon as you possibly can.'

'Are they going to pull through?' Glenda said, her face ashen with the terrible news that the two men had just given to her and then the tears spilled gently down Kate's and Glenda's cheeks as they both tried to take it all in.

The officers' faces gave them the agonising answer they were dreading, and they prayed that he was wrong when he said, 'Let's just hope so.' It was incomprehensible. What he was telling them was like a scene from a nightmare. One minute they were having a hairdressing session, the next they were hardly able to stand up with the sheer shock of it all.

Apparently, a drunken driver had ploughed into Rob's car at some crossroads just outside of Durham town. He should never have got behind the wheel in that drunken state, but he had done, and this was the consequence of it. They would be told more details later and Glenda said they should get to the hospital as soon as possible. The police officers said again how sorry they were to bring such devastating news and so late at night and she thanked them both. They left the two girls gently crying in each other's arms and quietly closed the door behind them. Glenda turned to Kate, who was crying harder now that the officers had gone, and she told her they had both to be very brave. She would have to go and get someone to babysit Sheila who was now fast asleep in her cot, whilst they went together to the hospitals. 'How long will we be gone?' Kate asked,

'I don't know,' Glenda replied. 'It's going to be a very, very long night,' and it was. The babysitter Glenda brought to the house was called Miriam Aspinall. Her husband George had been one of the men who had first introduced Tom to the new job at Peterlee and he offered to drive Kate and Glenda to both hospitals. Firstly, they were to go to Newcastle General which was thirty miles away from Peterlee and afterwards onto the hospital in County Durham. George did not know what to say to the girls during the journey, they were all so shocked and numb. He felt helpless for them. He wished Miriam was with him, but she was looking after the baby and so he drove them quietly and carefully to Newcastle and he prayed the news would be better on arrival than had first been predicted.

The news was not good. Rob was still in the operating theatre. He had taken the brunt of the crash, as had little Jeanette who had been sat behind him in the back seat next to her grannie, and they were both critically ill. Jeanette had a fractured skull and cuts all over her little face. She looked like a patchwork quilt with all the black stitches. She was in a cot, even though she was four years old, with the sides up for safety. At first glance Glenda and Kate did not recognise her. She was so small, she looked so weak and the doctors said it was because of the shock to her body that she looked that way. They stayed with her through the night, hoping and praying she would pull through, although the doctor had said it was touch and go. 'Please God, let her be all right, she is so precious.' Glenda said, and Kate silently prayed for her to wake up so that she knew she was going to survive. By the early hours of the morning there was no change in the little girl's condition but at least she was putting up a good fight. At around three a.m. Glenda and Kate turned towards the door as they heard footsteps behind them. It was the surgeon who had operated on Rob. Looking at his solemn face said it all, and they braced themselves for what he was going to say. 'I am so terribly sorry,' he began. 'We did all we possibly could for your father, but he died on the operating table after undergoing a massive brain operation. He never regained consciousness and he died peacefully.' They both looked at each other in total disbelief and broke down sobbing incoherently. Their prayers had been in vain, their father had gone forever to another place far away and they knew they would never ever be able to see him or talk with him again, not in this life anyway, and as they looked at one another with unbearable pain written across their faces they clung to one another sobbing, with inconsolable grief as if they never wanted to let go of each other again.

Rob had been driving at the correct speed of thirty miles per hour through the built-up area, but the other car driver had been doing seventy and he had hit them head on, overturning the car and sending it into the air, spilling the four occupants out onto the road below. The driver of the other car had been to a twenty-first birthday party. He knew he had had too much to drink and he told his friends that he was going to get some fresh air to clear his head, but his head was anything but clear. He ploughed into the Ford Prefect car at speed. They were found by the residents of the housing estate who were making their way up to bed.

The driver was named as a twenty-four-year-old local miner to the area. He was the man responsible for killing Rob Walsh and for injuring his beloved family. He knew he had had too much alcohol, yet he chose to drive his car and took the life, in that one night of hell, of a much-loved husband, father and grandfather. He had devastated forever the lives of the ones that Rob had left behind, and seriously injured the ones he had deeply loved. The surgeon advised that none of the family should see Rob again as he was so badly disfigured, especially for Glenda to identify him, and so his only brother, George, came up from Accrington in Lancashire and went to the mortuary at Newcastle General Hospital to identify him instead. George sadly looked at the brother he had loved and lost, and he told the girls he could not believe what a sad, tragic and sudden end Rob had come to.

FIVE

Their next visit was to see Mary who, along with Tom, had been taken to Durham County Hospital. Tom was very shaken up and dazed and Mary had a broken collarbone. They were both very badly bruised but at least they were alive. Mary had to stay in hospital for a week or so, but Tom was allowed to go home the next day. When he arrived home, he was in a state of complete despair. He had come to like and respect Rob as if he was his own father. Tom had been brought up in a one-parent family, and although he had lots of brothers and sisters, a father figure had always been missing from his life. When he had married Glenda, he had found that father figure in Rob and the two of them could be found decorating rooms together or tinkering under their cars. They were the best of friends. Tom was the son that Rob had never had, and Rob was the father that Tom had never known. The house at Westmorland Rise, Peterlee, that had had so much laughter in it for the whole of the week, was now silent. Each person was deep in their own thoughts, trying desperately to come to terms with the whole sorry and sad situation they found themselves in. Kate dressed the baby for Glenda, whilst she and Tom waited for the arrival of Jean and Peter, who were travelling up in the car from Darwen. It was Friday the 18th of July and the three of them should have been on their way home to the shop today, but now Rob would never see the shop again, and Kate would be returning without both her parents, one of them dead, the other one very poorly.

Jean and Peter were going to see Mary at the hospital first and then they were to come back to Peterlee to be with the rest of the family for the day to share in each other's sorrow and to plan the next move. There was nothing anyone could do to bring Rob back but they all needed to be together for support and to grieve with one another. Jean and Peter had been to Scarborough the day of the accident and they had had a lovely day together. It was their annual holiday too and it was a terrible shock as they were greeted by the police on arriving back home in Darwen, telling them of the terrible accident. The news given to them was that Mary was dead and that Rob had survived. The officers soon corrected the situation by ringing and apologising and saying it was, in fact, Rob who had died and Mary who was hurt and could they go up to Peterlee as soon as possible. They had set off early the following morning and drove the four-hour journey to be with the rest of the family. There was very little they could do except to visit Mary and Jeanette and to try and organise some cover for the shop, which needed to be opened the following Monday.

The staff at Spar Ltd, Preston had kindly stepped in and managed to employ a temporary manageress, a lady called Valerie. Valerie said she would stay at the shop and run the business until Mary was fit to come home and take over the reins. Later, it could be decided what would be the best for the three of them who were left, as to whether or not they would continue with the running of the shop or if it would have to be sold, but for now it was the least of their worries, and so for the moment Kate stayed up at Glenda's house and Jean, Peter, Glenda and Tom all visited Mary each day followed by a visit to little Jeanette who was still desperately poorly but clinging to life in Newcastle General Hospital. After a very harrowing week there was some slight improvement in both of the two still in hospital, but Mary was still not fit to travel a four-hour journey to attend the funeral. Glenda, Kate and Tom came down to Darwen and with Jean and Peter now home, the funeral took place. The customers who came into the Spar shop, neighbours and the staff at James Hall Ltd in Preston where Spar was based, were shocked and horrified by the news.

Everyone was so very sorry for the whole family. It was such a friendly family business and Rob Walsh was a much-liked grocer and friend to many. It showed by how many people had sent funeral flowers for him and the many cards and messages of condolence to the family. His grave was covered by the width of two, as there were so many sprays and wreaths. He would have been so touched by the outpouring of grief expressed by so many of his customers, neighbours and friends, to Mary, Jean and Kate, and to Glenda and Tom and their little girls, and for offering their support and love to them all in their hour of need. Mary came home in the middle of August from Glenda's house where she had been recovering from the accident. She had been away from the shop now for several weeks and was still in a great deal of pain. She was very quiet and withdrawn. Naturally Kate felt bad leaving her during the day, but she had to go back to school as it was the beginning of the new term. It was difficult facing her friends and peers as they all knew of the terrible accident and that her father had been killed. Their hearts went out to Kate, the teachers were very understanding, and they gave her the time and space she needed. She was in her fourth year now, her last year at Spring Bank Secondary Modern School. It was not an easy time for her or them. They didn't know what to say to her, but their faces told of their sorrow for her. She was very lucky in that she had so many good and loyal friends both at school and at home and they admired her for her strength and courage. The problem was she felt like an outsider. Kate knew of no one in her predicament. She knew life had to go on, but she wished for all the world that she could be like them with a mum and a dad.

Each night after school she would go to her friend Jean's house and together they would go up to Darwen Eastern Cemetery where Rob was buried. 'Dad,' she said to his grave, 'I shall come up here every day and be with you,' but as she said it she knew that it was not possible to do this forever, but she did continue to go often, not every day but several times a week. After a few months struggling to run the business and not in good health, Mary decided to sell the shop. She had regained some of her strength after the accident but the shop was too big a business for her to cope with, especially without the help and guidance of her husband. They had had their ups and downs during their marriage like everyone else does, but Mary, at fifty years old, realised that she had to give up the shop and make a new life for Kate and herself. If it had been under any other circumstance Kate would have been elated, but she knew that Mary was struggling to cope with herself and her loss, never mind the business with all the books to balance and the orders to see to, plus with more demanding customers it was all getting too much for her, so reluctantly the 'For Sale' sign went up outside the shop. Kate had recurring dreams about her dad. He would be standing at the bottom of the stairs at Glenda's house at Westmorland Rise and she called out to him, 'Oh, Dad, you are alive, where have you been?' Then he would fade away out of the hallway and she would wake up and realise it had only been a dream. It took Kate a very long time to understand just what the dream meant but she had never said goodbye to her dad. She had never seen him dead as he was so badly hurt, and her mind was playing tricks on her in her sleep. It was like a film, where a person was trying to swindle an insurance company for money and they weren't dead at all. As much as she wished it was not true he really was dead, and she had no choice but to come to terms with it, like the rest of the family. She never told anyone of her dream. What was the point when each in their own way were dealing with the grief themselves, and to her this was just another part of it?

Jean got married to Peter on January 14th, 1965 and they went to live with her father-in-law in a lovely house across the road from the shop. She still worked in the shop whilst it was up for sale and then another grocer who lived further up the road said he was interested in buying it and running the two businesses. Jean could still work in the Spar shop and she would be helped by the gentleman's son and that suited everyone. The deal went through and the shop, which was so hated by Kate for more than ten years, was finally sold. The next problem was, what was Mary going to do with herself and where would Kate and her going to live? There was a council house available at the other end of the town in Birch Hall Avenue and Mary went to view it. It wanted a lot of work doing to it, but it was only cosmetic, nothing structural and Kate's Uncle George helped Mary to make it nice for them both. It was still possible for Kate to come home from school for her lunch although it was a very fleeting visit, but her mum looked forward to it and had a meal ready for her each day.

When Kate left school, she went to work at Boots the Chemist in Church Street Blackburn. She didn't really know what she wanted to do for a job and a lot of the girls from school were going to take an apprenticeship in hairdressing. Kate thought she might give it a try but unfortunately there were no vacancies in Darwen or Blackburn at the time that she left school, so she took the job in Boots until one came available. She really should not have gone for shop work as she had hated their own, but it seemed a sensible move, and as it was only temporary, Kate thought she could manage. After all, she had had a very good grounding over ten years of looking after Rob's customers, but she still hated it at Boots. She remembered the first few days when at break time the girls would be crowded around a table together in the canteen and she was hurt to think that they never included her with them; they never even asked her what her name was, and she felt left out. The girls continued to do their own thing and that was why Kate decided she would go home for her lunch. It was a real push as she only got a one-hour lunch break and she had to get on the bus at the Boulevard to Darwen, then run all the way up Birch Hall Avenue, get her dinner, and then run back to catch the bus back to Blackburn. She knew Mary looked forward to seeing her at lunchtime as it broke up her day. Kate was happy. She felt she now had a mum who was always there waiting for her and it was a nice feeling. There were no interruptions any more from demanding customers, just Kate and her mum. Mother and daughter looking after each other just as she had always longed for, except of course there was no dad.

It was a problem for Mary though, because after so many people coming into the shop all day she felt very cut off and lonely at Birch Hall. On reflection, it would have been better if they could have found a house nearer the shop then at least she would still be in touch with the people she had seen every day for the past ten years, but there were no council houses near there and the insurance money being paid out for Rob's life was not through yet. The house they were renting was only temporary until the money was sorted, and Mary knew what she could afford to buy and where she wanted them to live. During the week, she would go into the town centre and the market, and she tried to keep busy, but it was an adjustable time for everyone concerned, even for Glenda and her family up in the North East, who were all still trying to come to terms with the death. They had talked about coming home from Peterlee now that the shop had been sold, and to buy a house somewhere back in the Darwen area. Tom could go back to the paper mill where he had worked before and Kate was thrilled to bits. Now after all the sadness of the past few months she was finally able to look forward to being reunited with her sister and her family. Was it really possible that some good had come out of all this heartache?

What a terrible sad turn of events it had taken to bring them all home to Lancashire to start their lives again. All too soon yet again her hopes were dashed as Glenda and Tom could not decide one hundred percent to return to their old lives. The home they had bought which was still amongst all the concrete with workmen and rubble everywhere was indeed their castle and even after the short time they had lived in Peterlee they had grown very fond of the area. Tom was enjoying his new job and Glenda had made new friends. They felt obligated to come home on the one hand, but their hearts were not in it, and they sat down together and told Mary and Kate of their decision that they were definitely not coming back. It was a very bitter blow, but they had to acknowledge that it was their lives and the lives of their children which were at stake and they had to do what was best for themselves and not to consider Kate and Mary who would soon have to settle down in another house and get on with their own lives without Rob and without them.

SIX

Kate really did not like her job at Boots. The girls were aloof still, and she was looking forward to a hairdressing job being available soon. Unfortunately, the nearest apprenticeship was in the next town to Darwen in Bolton, but she decided to take the position anyway. If anything any nearer came up she could always transfer back to Darwen and she hoped that maybe something would come up soon. Up with the lark she was each morning and away at eight o'clock sharp, down to the bus stop. It was nice to feel her independence at last. Even though she was only fifteen she started to feel grown up. She got on the bus to the circus (a part of Darwen town centre) and walked up School Street to the railway station and she boarded the train for Bolton. 'Be sure not to sit in a carriage alone,' warned Mary. 'You have to go through the Sough Tunnel and you never know who might be prowling around.' Kate took heed and did as Mary said. It was a pleasant journey to Bolton and she enjoyed the freedom especially going into the bakers down the road from the hairdressers where she got some lovely sandwiches and cream cakes for her lunch. Her boss was a very nice lady, but Kate soon realised that hairdressing was not for her. If she had been allowed to leave five minutes earlier she could have caught the six thirty p.m. train home, but the hairdressers shop did not close until six thirty p.m. and she was not allowed to leave her position any earlier. This meant another hour to hang about on the lonely platform in the train station whilst she waited for the next one, then a long journey home followed by a bus ride from Darwen town centre to Birch Hall Avenue. This meant that she was not getting home every night until nearly nine p.m. It was not ideal. She had no social life and so she gave her notice in. It was during her fourth weeks' notice that Kate was asked to rinse off a lady's hair colour. By mistake, and with wearing rubber gloves, she did not realise the temperature of the hot water. The lady jumped from one sink to the other as her head scalded with the heat. Kate was so embarrassed, but the lady was a good sport about it and they all saw the funny side. Yes, hairdressing was not for Kate, as she confirmed to herself that day and she couldn't wait to leave.

'Right,' said Mary. 'What next then, madam? Where are you going to get a job now?'

'I think I will try at Walpamur Ltd, Mum,' she said. 'There are a lot of the girls from my old school who have gone there and although I can't type I would like to see if there is a job there that I can do.' Fortunately, Mary knew the personnel manager at Walpamur. His name was Jack Woods and so here came job number three. This was in the accounting machine department but with Kate's history of maths it soon became a big challenge. The lady who was to teach her the job was a pinched-nose woman who loved to hear her own voice. Her name was Anne and she put the fear of God into Kate. She would bellow for all to hear in the office as Kate desperately tried to understand her instructions for using the comptometer machine. Soon it became evident that Anne had a distinct dislike of Kate and Kate had a distinct dislike of her. As soon as Kate saw her coming along the corridor in the morning, she would start to shake, her hands were trembling, and her knees felt like they would buckle underneath her if she had to stand up. She was totally petrified of the woman. Soon it took its toll on Kate's health and Mary took her to see their family doctor, Dr Lavery. He sent Kate to see a specialist as a precaution and after many tests on her, the specialist said that he could find nothing wrong at all. He did not think it was advisable to put Kate on tablets and he wrote to Dr Lavery and told him so. Kate just had to grin and bear it and hope she could cope with Anne until she knew how to do the job. Despite the fear of the woman whom she felt hated her, Kate enjoyed her life in the paint industry, even going out in the evenings with some of her old school friends. They started going to a youth club one evening a week. That was where Kate met her first boyfriend.

His name was Wayne and she thought he was wonderful. He was very handsome with jet black hair and a smile that melted her heart. His best friend, called Harry, unfortunately took first place in his life. Kate persevered to win his affection and eventually she did so. He was the love of her life and she would have done anything for him. Wayne's mum, Elsie, liked Kate and treated her as if she was her own daughter. She let Kate stay over at the weekends occasionally, unlike Mary, who on the other hand was having none of this relationship. Wayne was not allowed into their house and the only excuse Mary could come up with was, he is 'not our type', a typical and bigoted remark probably made through jealousy because Mary was so lonely she couldn't bear anyone else having a life, and no matter how much Kate protested, the answer was the same. She would say, 'He is not welcome here,' so they had no alternative but to do their courting inside bus shelters or telephone boxes and in the winter months it was really miserable for them. They felt that they could not keep going to Wayne's house although they did spend a lot of time there, but they loved each other so much that they just had to abide by Mary's rules. Mary was not a forgiving type of person at all. She stood her ground making sure that Kate was in the house by ten p.m. each night and she was allowed to stay out until eleven p.m. at the week-end. The summer months were heaven as they went into Bold Venture Park or SunnyHurst Woods and if the weather was warm enough they would walk for miles together and lay on the newly mown grass up near the moors. Wayne never complained about Mary; he knew she gave Kate a hard time and he made no demands on her either. They loved each other and that was enough. Kate was very much under her mother's thumb throughout her teenage years but when Mary went to Glenda's house for the six-week school holidays to see her grandchildren, Kate let Wayne stay over at her house at the weekend. They told Wayne's mum and dad that he was staying with Kate's friend's boyfriend, but the real truth was that Kate's friend told her parents the very same thing and they both hoped that neither couple ever found out. It was a risk they both took but they felt they had no alternative. It was the only time that they could be alone together.

It wasn't an ideal situation for them both to be in, having to tell lies, but Kate thought that when you love someone so much, it doesn't really matter how you get through things, and Mary had forced them to be deceitful anyway with her keeping such a tight rein on her. They just had to get on with their lives whilst she was out of sight and out of mind and anyway she knew that Mary would be away for at least the six weeks holidays so Wayne and Kate took advantage of the peace and quiet. 'What the eye doesn't see, the heart doesn't grieve,' Kate said to Wayne one night in bed. Thank God they had no telephone in the house so neither of them could be contacted. Kate and Wayne got engaged after eighteen months together. She fretted and was ashamed that she had never let him make love to her. It wasn't that she didn't want to, she so desperately did, but it was the terrible fear of an unwanted pregnancy and the wrath of Mary's tongue that she kept her virginity. The contraceptive pill was in its early stages in the sixties and she had heard so many stories of split condoms that she would not let him go all the way. Bless him, he never complained because he loved and respected Kate and he knew only too well what sort of a life she had now with Mary's dominant behaviour since Rob had been killed, let alone an unplanned pregnancy and then a baby to contend with, so for now it was enough that they loved each other so much, but the frustration felt by both of them took its toll on their lives together. Kate at nearly nineteen, felt ready to get married but Wayne was more immature. They viewed houses together with a view to buying one, but after looking at a good number, the alarm bells started to ring, and Kate felt that he was just not ready for such a big commitment.

Eventually with all the pressure on both of them they were starting to argue with each other, something they had never done before and finally both of them, now nineteen years old, broke off their engagement. Kate was devastated by the break-up and her weight dropped down to seven and a half stone. She told everyone that it felt as if he had died. There was no consoling her although her friends had tried to. Mary said very little and Kate thought she probably was secretly pleased it had turned out that way in the end. Mary would never know of the nights they had spent together or of the love they had shared in her bed. They may have only been petting but they had found so much fulfilment in each other that no one could ever take that away from them both.

Weekends and weekdays rolled into one and she was grateful for the Sunday nights to come as she knew she would be at work in a few hours and her mind would be occupied. Kate had made some new friends at work and one was a very special friend in particular. Her name was Chrisanna. She was such good fun to be with and she worked in the pricing department. The staff in her office were mostly men and quite a few were young. It was nice for Kate to be wolf-whistled at sometimes when she went in to check on an account, but some of the guys were a bit too old for her. She was desperately trying to get over her break-up with Wayne. He was seeing someone else now – a girl she used to play with when she lived at the shop and it broke her heart. She imagined them making love together and him telling her how Kate never would. She hoped and prayed he would not betray her because then people would get to know about their sex life as well as her mother's overbearing snobbish ways that had led them to behave the way they had. It was bad enough him finding someone else, never mind her being the laughing stock of them as well. Kate tried to win Wayne back; she wrote him a letter and explained why she needed him so much and just how much he meant to her, and they did see each other once for a date, but the magic had gone. She turned her work instead into her whole life but even after months apart she was still pining for him and wishing things could have worked out for them. She knew that, no matter however long she lived, he would always be in her heart, her first love, the one she had hoped would become her husband and the father of her children, but it was never to be.

'Any toffees today, love?' Barry would shout from the back row of the pricing department and Kate was very flattered to be even noticed by him especially as he called her love as well. He was a good-looking tall guy at that! Unfortunately, he was not really interested in going out with her, he just wanted her sweets. Nevertheless she had a big crush on him anyway. After all now she was footloose and fancy-free, why should she not do! Kate tried to look forward to going with the girls from work for a night out in Blackburn at the Mecca dancing, but as she was so shy and reserved she didn't drink alcohol (probably because of what had happened to her dad). She did smoke cigarettes, although not in the house; Mary would have gone crazy. The girls who worked alongside her were far more outgoing than Kate and it was hard to fit in with them. She knew she had to get on with her life now there was no Wayne any more. She had to move on.

Life was pretty miserable for a time but then one of the men in the office where Chrisanna worked called Michael Abbotts asked her to go out with him for a drink one lunchtime to the George Hotel down the road from Walpamur. Most of the lads from his department frequently went in there, especially on a Friday lunchtime to wind down for the weekend ahead. Kate had only just finished in a long-term relationship and did not feel ready to go out with anyone yet, but Michael knew she had finished with Wayne because it was common knowledge in the office. Gossips especially, were high on the agenda.

She didn't really want to go with him, but he was very patient with her and persuasive too, so she accepted his offer to go and have a dinner-time drink with him. Kate ended up pouring out the whole story to him over lunch. She told him how Mary would not accept Wayne as her fiancé even after two and a half years together, and how their lives had been one long battle with her constant dislike of him just because he was not from a posh area of the town. The laugh of it was that they lived in a council house until Mary had sorted out the money from Rob's estate and it was a pure snobbery issue with her and now finally they had split up. He listened to her talking as they ate their lunches together as slowly she told him everything, and she knew from the sympathy in his voice that he really understood and cared for her. He was a tall, lean-looking guy, always dressed in immaculate suits. They had chatted before at work in the offices, and although she was very nervous with him and felt out of her comfort zone at first, they got on like a house on fire. He told her that he had lived for a few years in Leeds and now his family had moved back to live in a semi-detached house in Salesbury, a lovely area of Blackburn.

Kate felt it was too early to be seeing someone just yet, but she desperately needed a friend, someone she could confide in and who would not judge her, more so she needed someone who would be impartial to it all. Michael, on the other hand, desperately wanted her as his girlfriend but she didn't know that then. Apparently, she found out later that he had liked her since they had first been introduced by their mutual friend Chrisanna. Everybody loved Chrisanna, how could they not do? Before Kate knew it, she was seeing Michael regularly, much to the delight of the lads and everyone in the pricing department, especially Chrisanna as Michael was one of her closest friends. It wasn't an easy start for Kate to be dating again as it was for Michael. She felt like he was waiting in the wings for her and she was still hurting for Wayne. Unmercifully she messed him about, went on dates with him and then decided she didn't want to get involved yet she was lonely and mixed up, but he would always be there waiting for her. He would bring her flowers and boxes of chocolates and treat her like a lady. He opened doors for her, something Wayne had never done, and he was such a gentleman, even opening the car door and closing it as she was safely sat inside. He made her feel like a princess but even that wasn't enough.

SEVEN

Kate kept finishing with Michael, and then he would wait for a while and ask her out again and she would go. Finally, after yet another finishing fiasco Chrisanna took Kate to one side. 'Kate,' she said, 'For God's sake stop messing Michael about. If you don't want him, let him go and find someone else.' Kate was shocked by what Chrisanna had said to her. It was a wake-up call. She could not let him go. No, at the moment she wasn't crazy in love with him because he was so different to Wayne, but she knew that he loved her more than life itself and he would have walked to the ends of the earth for her. Could she not see she was breaking his heart? 'Yes,' Kate said, 'I know I have messed him around and believe me I do like him a lot. I promise I shall get my act together. Do you think he will give me another chance, Chris?'

'I am sure he will do, the guy would marry you tomorrow if you would have him,' she said. 'Don't waste your life, Kate, on memories of yesterday.'

Kate had felt different with Michael; he was such a steady, level-headed man, four years older than her, and she felt ready for a complete relationship now. She was still nineteen years old and Mary's hold on her had made her more defiant than ever. She felt she had possibly lost Wayne partly because of their lack of lovemaking but she told herself she was a woman now, not a child, and this time she would not hold back her true feelings for Michael; she wouldn't risk losing him too. She so much wanted to make the final commitment with him. One night after they had been out for a drive in his mother's car they took their love further. It was a scary thing for Kate with her strict upbringing, but she loved Michael and she needed to show him that she did. There was no pressure at all from him; her kisses told him she was ready. He gently took her in his arms that starry night parked in a secluded lay-by and they made love for the first time in the back seat of the Triumph Herald car. After that night, they made love whenever they could, although the times they were alone were few and far between. Michael's mother and father were more diplomatic than Mary and they used to leave the couple in the lounge together, put the dog to bed and then go upstairs themselves, unlike Mary who never let them out of her sight when they were at Kate's house. She watched them like a hawk. On May 22nd 1970 they finally got engaged. It was on Michael's twenty-fourth birthday. He bought Kate a beautiful single stone diamond ring in yellow gol,d and she bought Michael a lovely nine carat gold signet ring. They exchanged their rings in Sale Wheel Woods near Ribchester, a couple of miles from Michael's home in Salesbury. His parents George and Norah, along with Michael's brother Andrew, went for a celebration meal at the Yew Tree pub in Charnock Heath near Chorley.

Michael and Kate bought a house together on Avondale Avenue, Redcap near Accrington. It was a small semi-detached house with a main lounge, a lovely dining kitchen, two bedrooms, one large one on the front and one smaller overlooking the back garden and there was a nice three-piece bathroom suite. There was a massive garden to three sides of the house as it was the last on the avenue and there was also a good-sized garage. It was nice inside and they did not need to do very much work to it. It wanted decorating to their liking, but there was nothing structural to do at all. They saved up for some furniture and they got the keys at the end of July 1971. Their wedding was at St Cuthbert's church in Darwen on the 14th of August 1971. Mary and Kate had moved from the council house on Birch Hall Ave in 1969 to a lovely semi-detached house near the Blackburn/Darwen boundary. They were now in the parish of St Cuthbert's. Kate was glad that Mary had settled in this house better than the one on the estate, but she was still not easy to live with.

It seemed to Kate that there was an element of jealousy from Mary as Kate had had two boyfriends and now she had a fiancé. She still made damn sure that Kate had to be in at eleven o'clock each night even on a Saturday and Michael had said to Kate how he thought she was being unreasonable given the fact that Kate was now nearly twenty-one.

It was a terrible rainy day, but the wedding was a lovely one. Kate was given away by Tom, her brother-in-law, and her little nieces were her bridesmaids. There was Jeanette and Sheila who were Glenda's children and little Michelle who was Jean and Peter's little girl. They wore beautiful tricel crepe turquoise blue dresses trimmed with matching lace. The junior bridesmaids carried pomanders of small pink roses and mixed white flowers, whilst Jeanette, the chief bridesmaid, carried a shower bouquet of pink roses and white chrysanthemums. Mary looked lovely in a bright cerise dress with a matching coat and hat. She wore black patent shoes with a bag to match. She had accepted Michael better than she had done so with Wayne, probably because he came from a lovely semi-detached house in Salesbury. His mother did not work, and his father had a good job at the brewery. Mary hadn't always been nice to Michael. One Saturday evening Kate and Michael had been to Jeffrey Hill and, after a kiss and cuddle and whilst listening to the radio they had both fallen fast asleep in the front of the car. Michael woke up first and said to Kate, 'God it's nearly one o'clock, your mum will go mad. Let's get you home.' He drove like a madman through Ribchester to get her back quick, but unfortunately it was too late. Mary was pacing the living room floor at Birch Hall Avenue with a face like thunder. They tried to explain why they were so late, but Mary wouldn't listen. 'Look here, Michael,' she said, 'If you can't do whatever you have to do with my daughter before this ungodly hour you will not take her out again.' Michael started to apologise but she interrupted him. 'I didn't have any trouble when she was seeing Wayne and I'm not having any with you.' Michael apologised again then said to Kate, 'Here is sixpence. If you need me, call me from the pay phone and I will come straight back for you.'

There were many more incidents with Mary but after she realised that they were serious about each other she backed off. It was obvious the woman was affected badly by Rob's death and her miserable life. Kate thought her mind was obviously less than normal. Before Kate went for her wedding dress in February 1971, Glenda and Kate heard her talking in her sleep. Mary was asking for an accident to happen over a terrible road to Bolton, the A666 over Bull Hill, and that Kate would have to go down the aisle in a wheelchair, and Michael would not want to marry her if she was crippled. It was a very scary night, with Kate wondering if Mary hated her so much that she may want to harm her. In the morning Glenda approached Mary and confronted her about the incident the night before but Mary said she didn't know what Glenda was talking about and denied she had ever said it. Kate couldn't wait to get away now, and she knew she would never forget that night as long as she lived.

Jean was pregnant with her second child at the wedding and she looked very elegant posing for the photographer. Glenda also looked really classy in a short cream and blue dress with a matching cream hat. Kate looked radiant. She wore a beautiful empire line gown of white crystal satin trimmed with guipure lace and pearls. She carried a shower bouquet of pink roses and white carnations. Michael wore a new navy-blue suit, looking very smart as always and his best man, Tom Jones, also wore a navy suit. They had their wedding reception at the Whitehall Country Club in Darwen, followed by a week's honeymoon in Weston-Super-Mare. When they returned from their honeymoon to their new home, Michael decorated the bathroom for them and he made a brilliant job of it to say it was his first attempt at wallpapering.

They had no car at first to get to work in Darwen, but they were offered a lift each day to Walpamur by Christine Crook, a girl who worked in the offices upstairs and who lived near them farther up the road. It was a big help to them and they were very grateful, but they soon realised that they needed some transport of their own.

They found a little Volkswagen Beetle in a nearby garage. It was a pale-yellow colour and they both fell in love with it. It was super to be independent again, and they happily continued to enjoy their newly married life. Kate and Michael both wanted a family, but the wages were not very good at the time for either of them, and Michael was desperate to find a better paid job. He particularly wanted to get into the Whitbread Brewery Group, where his father George Abbotts worked. George promised his son that as soon as a suitable job came up in the office he would let him know, but until such time, Michael would just have to continue to stay where he was. They used to have their lunches together at work and then they would steal kisses and cuddles in the lift. They worked as a team in the pricing department now, as the accounting machine department where Kate had worked had closed, and the work was now being computerised.

Chrisanna told Kate there was a job coming up on the switchboard soon where she now worked, and Kate was delighted. She applied for it and got the job. Chrisanna taught her all she knew. She had previously been trained in the GPO at Oldham, Greater Manchester, as a telephonist, and she was excellent at her work. She was Kate's best friend now and they got on like a house on fire. She was so witty and full of fun. Each day they used to fall about laughing together. Although they did their job,s they also shared lots of fun. Now it really was a pleasure to go to work but in truth, the damage had been done; Kate was now having problems with her nerves. Although she loved the switchboard, she still trembled a lot, and she could not go on buses or mix comfortably with crowds of people. Strangely though no one would have thought it. Kate hid her fears so well. Nevertheless, it was becoming a big problem to her, but she still kept it very much to herself. There was really only Michael, who truly knew her inside and out, and he knew just how much she was suffering. Even on their honeymoon she found that one day she could not go down into some caves that Michael had taken her to. She just freaked out when they got inside. 'Come on, sweetheart.' he said,

'I can't, Michael. I feel sick and my heart is pounding, you go, I am okay here.' He took her outside and sat her on a bench in the gardens very near to the entrance of the caves. She told him to go down on his own as she would be okay, and also she didn't want to spoil it for him as she knew how much he had been looking forward to it. The truth was she felt terrible, even though he had brought her back into the fresh air; her heart was still pounding, and she felt faint and sick. She was trembling totally from head to toe. She was suffering from agoraphobia, a fear of open spaces, but she didn't know it was that. At the time, she had never heard of the word but a few months later when she went to see her doctor

49

and she told him of her symptoms on their honeymoon, he diagnosed it. It was such a relief to know that she was not going crazy and that this was an illness that she was suffering from.

EIGHT

Early in 1972, Michael got the news that he had been waiting for. There was a job at the Whitbread Group becoming vacant for a stocktaker, and excitedly he applied for the job. He went for the interview and was determined to get it on his own merit, and not because his father George had a senior position in the company with many years of loyal service. Michael came home elated; the job was his. He gave one month's notice the following day to his boss Eric Crook in the pricing department. Eric said that Michael would be sorely missed by himself and all his colleagues and friends as whenever Eric was on leave or off sick Michael would take over the reins.

He wished him well in his new job, and friends and colleagues had a collection. They bought him an electric drill for his DIY work at home. As his last day appeared everyone at the firm wished him all the very best of luck for the future, and he promised to stay in touch with them. Kate was also delighted for him. Did this mean there was going to be a baby next? She really hoped so! She knew he would have to get used to the job first, and then they would need to work out how best Kate could get to work, as now he needed the car to get to Shadsworth, where he would be working from, and she couldn't drive anyway. Soon he would have the use of a company car and their car would be at home in the garage. The job was everything Michael had hoped for. He was out on the open road every day. He went from Blackburn to as far as the Wirral in Cheshire and even up to Cumbria. He particularly liked going up into the Lake District, and it was even better when he did not need to share a company car with someone and he was given one of his own. Kate decided after a few months to take the bull by the horns and she asked Michael about them trying for a baby. To her delight he said yes. They would try for one soon and so after only a few weeks, it was confirmed she was expecting their first baby at the end of February 1973.

Kate continued to work at Walpamur Ltd until Christmas 1972. She was overwhelmed by the gifts presented to her when she finally left her job. There was no maternity leave, then and so Kate had to give in her notice. Her friends and colleagues had collected enough money to buy a navy-blue carrycot and a chrome Silver Cross transporter pram for the new baby, along with enough clothes to see it through for many months to come. It was a lovely farewell for her and a very tearful one. She desperately wanted to be a mum and she was touched by all of their thoughtfulness and their generosity to herself and to Michael, and for the baby growing healthily inside her. Chrisanna promised to ring her every day to keep her in touch with all the goings-on at work and she did. Kate felt she was still in touch with everyone, as each person chipped in daily to say 'Hello.' she knew she would miss everyone as they were like one big happy family to her, but the need for a baby outweighed it all. She looked forward to the rest which was much needed now, for the pregnancy was nearing its end. The 23rd of February 1973 finally arrived. It was Kate's due date and she still had not delivered her baby. Her mother-in-law cruelly insinuated that she was pretty hopeless not to have delivered on time, and Kate thought to herself did the woman not know that babies came when they were ready and not on demand. That was nothing new for Norah Abbotts. She had never liked Kate, not since the day that Michael had told her that they were going to get engaged. Kate thought that she thought she was not good enough for her son, and there was certainly no love lost between the two of them through the years.

Norah was a difficult woman with a lot of people; neighbours and family alike found her to always be indifferent. She once asked Michael if he was getting enough to eat. It happened after a particularly bad stomach bug he had contracted, and naturally he had lost some weight. She implied that perhaps Kate wasn't feeding him well enough.

Kate had heard her ask him that one day when she had called at their house. She was absolutely fuming and, when she had gone, she asked Michael why he hadn't stood up to her, but he said he didn't want to upset her! Kate absolutely detested her, and she frequently had a row with Michael after she had left their home, saying why did he not stand up to the woman when she tried to belittle his wife so much. The trouble was that Michael hated to upset her, although he knew what she was like and so Kate had to put up with years of nasty and insinuating remarks from her. His father George on the other hand, was a truly lovely man, so gentle and so kind, and she felt he was the father she had never really known and that she was the daughter he had longed for but never had after the birth of his two lovely sons. Their relationship was born out of love and respect for each other. They would share jokes together, sometimes funny and sometimes rude, but they always laughed together, and she knew that Norah was a hard woman to live with and she hated the way she belittled him. Kate felt so sorry for him as he was picked on by her, especially when he said that he was feeling the cold. Norah would mimic him, she had very little patience, but little did she, or any of them realise that the reason he was feeling the cold so much was that he had hardening of the arteries and a very bad heart and that he would only live to see his grandchild when it was born for the next four years.

On the evening of Friday the 9th of March 1973, Michael and Kate were sat in the lounge watching a late film on the television. She was already overdue by nearly two weeks and was told by the gynaecologist at the hospital that day, that if the baby was not born by the evening of Saturday the 10th of March, then she was to be admitted and induced in the hospital and that the planned home birth could not go ahead. All of a sudden at 12.40 a.m. that very night, well early morning, her waters broke, and they soon realised the baby was well on its way. Michael rang for the midwife on duty, but she did not rush to the house as usually first babies take quite a long time to arrive, but no, not this baby. By the time she came to the front door she rushed upstairs to see what all the noise was about. After examining Kate, she told Michael to pull the plug out of the bath as there was no time to bathe; this baby was well and truly on its way. Richard was born at 2.50 a.m., two hours and ten minutes since her waters had broken, and Kate and Michael were delighted with their beautiful new-born son. Secretly, Kate had wanted a little boy, but in those days scans were not even heard of. There were only X-ray machines, and to know the sex of a baby was still light years away. He was gorgeous. He weighed in at eight pounds and even though they had planned him and created him themselves, they could not believe that he was finally here in their arms. He had jet black hair and a very long body with long fingers. He was going to be tall like his daddy, and bonny like his mummy, they had both decided. What a wonderful gift he was, and they were over the moon. They couldn't wait until it was daylight to ring and tell the family of the safe arrival of Richard, their beautiful bundle of joy.

First to arrive at the house was Norah and George with Andrew (Michael's brother). They were asked to come in the afternoon just to let Kate have a little rest after a long night, but they came in the morning anyway. The doctor who had been sent for to stitch Kate was not very obliging .It was the middle of the night and he was tired and to top it all, he did not believe in home births.

He gave Kate no local anaesthetic and it had been pretty traumatic for her. The midwife apologised for him and said he was very unreasonable in his behaviour, but Kate told her not to worry as it wasn't her fault. Next to arrive was Mary, with Glenda and Tom and the two children. They had travelled from the North East that morning and picked Mary up en route. She was delighted to be a granny again and the children loved their new baby cousin. Glenda could not believe her baby sister Kate had had a baby of her very own, and she hugged her and Michael and nursed her new little nephew. Jean and Peter arrived later in the afternoon with their two children, Michelle and John, and they thought he was like a little doll. Jean and Peter were pleased for them both and they nursed little Richard who slept blissfully in their arms. After they had all left Kate and Michael sat and looked at their new baby son cradled in his mummy's arms. They had so much love for the little treasure that had been given to them twelve hours ago, and together they thanked God for his safe delivery.

NINE

Soon it was time for Michael to go back to work and for Kate to look after little Richard. He was a hungry baby and she was unsure why he kept crying when he had not gone a full four hours since his last feed. When she was told by the midwife that he probably was hungry and needed more food, she increased his bottle and he settled to be a good little baby. She felt guilty for not realising why he cried so much. It was after all his only way of saying, 'Mummy I am hungry'. Kate struggled taking the baby out for walks because she was so bad with her agoraphobia. She so much wanted to stroll out with him in his new beautiful two-tone green Silver Cross high coach-built pram, but there were so many times when she had to turn back, or cut it short instead of taking him for a longer walk. It became increasingly hard. Some days she would be okay and others she would be so afraid she would just sit and cry. If only those walls could talk. They witnessed the agony of her dilemma and she realised this phobia was indeed ruling her life. Something needed to be done to help her and bravely she made another appointment to see her GP. He was very kind to her and he confirmed her fears again that it was indeed agoraphobia. He gave her some anti-depressant tablets and told her it would pass eventually but that it wasn't going to be a quick fix. Gladly she took the tablets every day and she tried to have as normal a life as possible. She didn't realise however just how much she would become reliant on them, not only for the present time to see her through the worst, but for a lot of years still to come.

In the spring of 1974 it was confirmed that Mary Walsh had got secondary cancer. This time it had attacked her lungs. She had never smoked a cigarette in her entire life, although Rob had always smoked a pipe for all their married life together, so passive smoking could have contributed to it. It was a very difficult time as Glenda had told both Kate and Jean that Mary should not be told that she was dying. It would have served no purpose at all and besides Mary would have gone to pieces. They were all to keep up the pretence that she had a bad chest infection. Telling her that she was going to die, would have spelt disaster, both mentally and physically. It was for certain she just could not have handled it, and the specialist agreed with them to keep up the pretence. Mary had been on holiday with two of her cousins, Betty and Peggy, down to Bournemouth in Dorset. She had come back home very breathless and she thought it was a bad chest infection, and everyone let her believe this right through to the end. Mary would stay with Jean for a few months during her illness and then with Kate, and in-between she was admitted to the chest hospital.

It was at one of those times when it was Kate's turn to nurse her that Mary was vomiting a lot. This was due to the high doses of tablets that she was taking, and it was also her poor condition which by this time was vastly deteriorating. Kate was absolutely terrified having to look after her. If she mentioned the word sick, that same fear came back again. Mary would ask for a bucket and Kate would start shaking and her heart would pound. Many times however, Mary would manage to get to the toilet in time and Kate thought, bless her. She knew how frightened Kate was of her vomiting in front of her. On the 7th of August 1974 Mary lost her brave fight for life. She was staying at Jean's house at the time and the district nurse was coming early that morning to get her ready for her hospital outpatient appointment. The nurse realised when she arrived at Jean's house that Mary was not fit enough to make the half hour journey by ambulance to the hospital. She told Jean to help her to lay Mary flat out on the bed where she gasped her last breath, and gently without a word to anyone closed her eyes and died.

The phone was ringing in the lounge when Kate came downstairs to get Richard his breakfast. Jean told her that Mary had died that morning and she said she had rung through to Glenda and Tom, and that they were on their way down to Jean and Peter's house straight away.

Kate and Michael arrived half an hour later with Richard, and when Glenda and Tom arrived they all discussed the funeral arrangements to be made for Mary. The funeral was finally organised, and Mary was to be buried with her beloved Rob in Darwen Eastern Cemetery, ten years and one month after the fateful accident that had taken him away from her. She had endured ten lonely years without him. If only Mary could have met and found happiness again with another man, her life would not have been so sad, but it was not to be. They would be together again in 'Heaven' this time, and this is what the girls decided to write on their parents' gravestone 'Together Again'.

Kate realised now that they were all orphans; they had lost both of their parents and all too soon. Glenda was only thirty-six-years-old, Jean twenty-eight years and Kate twenty-four years. The older grandchildren would remember Mary with love. She used to call them her little 'chucky jewels', but Jean's little boy, John, and little Richard, were far too young to know what was going on, but they would both be told about their grandparents, how they had lived and died when they were a little older. It took time to adjust to life without Mary. They knew now she was at peace, and fortunately each of the girls had wonderful husbands. When Mary's estate was finalised, and her house was sold, the girls and their husbands planned how they were going to change their lives now that they had their inheritance. Jean and Peter decided to build an extension to their home and Glenda and Tom decided to move to a new house as did Kate and Michael. Although Kate and Michael's house was adequate for the three of them, it was their intention to have more children and they needed extra bedrooms and space to do so. They decided that to invest the money into property was the most sensible idea.

The three-bedroom semi-detached house that Michael had found for them off Pleckgate Road in Blackburn was only four years old and there had been only one owner before them. This meant that the decorating was minimal. There was so much scope to make it their ideal home and they said they thought that Mary would have been really pleased with their choice. There was a lovely entrance hall with a small window on the gable end. The hall led to a small but adequately fitted kitchen. The lounge was twenty-three feet long and had a massive picture window at both ends. The front window looked onto the ample front garden and the back one overlooked the spacious garden, some of it with vegetables, and a well-kept lawn went straight down to the open fields beyond. There was a serving hatch from the lounge into the kitchen which was very handy, and there was a lovely teak-framed gas fire on their neighbours' adjoining wall. The décor in the lounge was not to Kate and Michael's taste but it would do for the time being. The upstairs was lovely and very spacious. Three good-sized bedrooms, one for little Richard and the other for Kate and Michael. They decided to put Richard in the front bedroom next to theirs until he got a bit older. He was nearly out of his cot now so the spare bed that used to be Michael's would easily fit in there. The back bedroom could be used for any guests who might come to stay. There was a good-sized bathroom: it had a yellow suite with grey tiles halfway up the walls. The toilet was separate and that was yellow with grey tiles too. The wardrobe in the guest room was a built-in one next to the cylinder cupboard so they didn't need to buy one, and the landing could fit a good-sized chest of drawers still with plenty of room to spare. All in all it really was a beautiful home, and Kate and Michael could not believe their luck in finding it, and eventually buying it. They knew they could make it perfect given a little time and money.

The agoraphobia continued to dominate Kate's life. One Saturday morning whilst they were out shopping Kate suddenly felt faint and sick. Michael took her back to the car and then he carried on with the shopping, taking Richard with him. The following week they went down into town shopping again and the same thing happened. Kate was terrified now, and she started to avoid each place she had had the panic attacks in, until eventually she felt unable to shop at all. Michael paid all the bills, and although to some people this was a mistake it was so very necessary. Kate found people were quick to judge her, especially her friends and neighbours who would not be able to cope themselves with the way that it was affecting her and the family. Everyone felt helpless and most of them tried to understand but one friend said, 'I could not cope with her, Michael' to which Michael replied, 'Perhaps it's a good job it's not your wife then or where would she be?' Kate was so proud of him.

'How can people be so cruel?' she said. 'Do they think this is a game?' 'I would give all I had to rid myself of this terrible fear,' she said. 'I just can't',

'I know sweetheart,' he said. 'We shall fight it together, take no notice of other people. This is us and we will get through it. I love you, Kate, so much and I can't make it go away for you, but you know that, and I will do all that I can to make your life as easy as possible.'

'Thankyou I don't know how I would manage without you, sweetheart,' she replied.

When Richard was nearly three-years-old, Kate felt he needed to go to playschool. She wanted him to mix with children of his own age. She made enquiries and got him a place in the local playgroup. Each Tuesday and Thursday she had to take Richard nearly half a mile to playschool and the stress of it nearly killed her. She cried all the way there through the panic attacks, and after leaving him she had to go back home only to turn around half an hour later and walk all the way back for him again. To top it all, Richard cried each time she left him and so she told him she would just be sat on the steps outside waiting for him and he was not to cry as she wasn't very far away at all. One day the lady in charge asked Kate, 'Did you tell Richard you were waiting outside on the steps for him?'

'Yes,' said Kate, 'I thought it would comfort him.'

'Well,' she said, 'please don't do that again, he will start to mistrust you. You are in fact lying to him.'

Kate was flabbergasted. 'I did it to comfort him not to lie to him,' she said, 'but okay I won't do it again.' When Michael came home she told him what had happened.

'What harm did it do?' he said. 'You were only thinking of him crying and what is a little white lie to a little boy if he played contentedly for a few hours?'

The panic attacks happened time and time again. Kate held onto the pram handle gripping it like iron. How long was this nightmare going to go on for she continually asked herself. Michael continued to be supportive, but he had to go to work and he felt so helpless and sorry for the situation that she was in. He wished for all the world he could do more but what? One night after a particularly bad day, Kate and Michael were talking after Richard had been put to bed. Kate said, 'How would it be if I learned to drive?' The car after all was not being used during the day as Michael had the use of a company car. 'It may help me.' What do you think?

'I think it's a great idea.' he said. 'How will you cope if you have one of your panic attacks when you are out with a driving instructor? You can't just say stop the car, I want to go home,'

'No, I can't,' she said, 'but you could teach me, couldn't you?' Michael had no hesitation in saying yes. He loved her so much he would have given his right arm to help her through this pain she had to endure each and every day of her life. 'Yes, why not, let's give it a go,' he said and the next day he went to the post office at Shear Brow to get her a provisional driving licence form. They both prayed that she would be able to cope doing it. If anyone could help her and teach her to drive properly it had to be Michael her rock, her sweetheart and her saviour.

TEN

They went out driving as often as they possibly could with Richard in his car seat playing in the back. He was a good little thing. It was as if he knew this was the most important task his mummy had to do, something which would benefit everyone, and he sat there as good as gold. There was only one time when Michael lost his patience with her as she could not get the car off a small incline and she panicked. She stormed at Michael, 'You do it if you know better.'

'I can and I will, as I have passed my test,' he said calmly, and they both laughed and she got herself together, knowing that he would be with her all the way. What a patient and perfect man he was. Michael was always there for her and for everyone whoever it was that needed his help.

Kate took her driving test on July 19th, 1976 and she passed the first time. The driving examiner was ironically called Mr Walsh (no relation) but he was renowned for only passing one person per week and he was nicknamed 'once a week Walsh'. The weather had been less than kind to her on that Monday morning and Michael had smeared the rear car window with Johnson's baby oil to keep it from steaming up and it was a tremendous help to her. What a relief that was, for now she had four wheels under her and she was no longer trapped in her home. If she felt unable to cope outside with the panic attacks she could now come home without being beholden to anyone. A new life lay ahead of her. She knew people would say that this was the easy way out instead of forcing herself to go and catch a bus, but to Kate it was the only way out and she didn't care a toss about other people or their opinions. They had no idea what her life was really like. Another friend's husband had once remarked to Michael saying, 'How do you put up with her?'

'I don't put up with her, I love her,' he replied. 'all I can say to you is, it's a good job it's me who she is married to and not you.' She had proved one thing; she could now drive a car and the outside world was not going to be as frightening to her as it was now. She knew she was not out of the woods with this phobia and probably never would be, but at least this was an opening and she was not stuck indoors any more without hope. People are so quick to judge without thinking things through. It was very hurtful to Kate and she would have given the world not to be like this, but life had dealt her a cruel blow and she had to live with it. That, or be housebound which was totally unacceptable for a woman of twenty-six years of age. No, she would fight on, forever if necessary. There was no alternative and she had no one except Michael who could help her through it and her self-belief.

Around the end of October 1977 Michael suggested they should try for another baby. Richard was now over four and a half years old and Michael said it was the right time. He needed a baby brother or sister to play with and they had always wanted two or more children. Kate wasn't sure though. She would have loved a new baby, but how would she cope? Ante-natal appointments, possible hospital appointments, and shopping trips to buy new maternity and baby clothes; the thought was daunting, but the thought of a new baby persuaded her to say yes, they would try. After all she had gotten pregnant right away with Richard and it could take a lot longer the second time around. It was Christmas time and Kate thought she may be pregnant again, but she decided to wait until early in the New Year before going to the doctors for confirmation. When she went to see her GP, she was surprised to say the least. She asked Kate if it was a good idea to get pregnant with her history of anti-depressant tablets and Kate told her that she had had her own misgivings too. Kate had weaned herself off the tablets before trying for the baby, and that had been very hard. She told the doctor that Michael had suggested they try for a baby sooner rather than later and she had conceived straight away.

Dr Walsh said she would help her all she could, and she proved it by having a sympathetic ear whenever Kate needed her. It was ironic that Kate had a driving instructor called Walsh, a GP called Walsh and it was also Kate's maiden name. Yes surely someone, somewhere was watching over her, a guardian angel perhaps, and she really hoped so. Besides it was comforting to her anyway. The pregnancy went well, and Ian Abbotts was born a healthy weight of eight pounds on Bank Holiday Monday August the 28th 1978. It was not an easy birth, although Kate was not long in labour. When Richard had been born she was in labour for only two hours and ten minutes and this time it was a little longer; two hours and twenty-five minutes. The telephone in the hall rang constantly with enquiries regarding the delivery, and the midwife told Michael to take the phone off the hook or he was going to miss the birth. The midwives clearly did not want to be there. They seemed short of patience, and though Kate was not causing a fuss or anything, she was glad when the baby was born, and she looked forward to them going back to their Bank Holiday Monday. 'I am sorry you were inconvenienced on your day off,' she thought. The baby, a lovely little boy, had his daddy's sandy-coloured hair and he was a chubby little soul. He was a delight for Michael and Kate, and little Richard thought it was ace to have a new baby brother to love. He was already five and a half years old now and at infant school. He had not liked it at first, and when Kate left him he had cried and so did she. It was awful leaving him, and she missed him terribly. She let him come home for his dinners so that she could see him, and they could spend some time together, even if it was only for an hour. It was no problem to go for him now that she had the car all day.

On the third day after Ian was born, Kate was worried about him. He was taking his feeds all right but after she lifted him up to burp him, he would vomit the feed back. It was not just a dribble – it shot across the floor. When the doctor called in to see them he said he would like a second opinion from a leading paediatrician at the local hospital. Kate and Michael were mortified. What on earth could be wrong with their new baby boy? Fortunately, he was a good birth weight and he wasn't looking poorly at all, but Michael said they would have to wait to see what the consultant had to say. It was arranged that after he had finished work at the hospital he would call on his way home. He only lived on Lammack Road, so it was not far out of his way. He checked the baby over and told Kate and Michael he wanted a second opinion with his colleagues. He wanted Kate to go into the hospital the following day and stay with baby Ian whilst they did further investigations on him. Dr Fossard had asked Kate to feed the baby and he took the bottle fine, then when he was ready for burping the doctor held him himself and Ian vomited all over the poor man's suit, and Kate apologised to him. 'That is exactly what I wanted him to do,' he said. 'Please do not worry, it will soon dry clean. Now let me please use your phone so that I can make some arrangements for admission for you both to go into the hospital tomorrow,' he said again.

'Hospital, oh no, please can we see if he improves tomorrow?' Kate said.

'No, I am sorry. He needs admitting tomorrow morning first thing and I need to let Mr Claude Brun the tummy specialist have a look at him.' They both thanked him for coming so quickly and Michael saw him to the door. So, on the Wednesday morning the 30th of August, Kate, Richard and baby Ian were taken by Michael to the children's ward in Blackburn Royal Infirmary. There were a sea of faces greeting them when they arrived, along with Dr Fossard and his team. They proceeded to feed baby Ian and then they started prodding his little tummy. Again back came the feed. They all had a short discussion and it was confirmed that the little mite was suffering from a condition called pyloric stenosis, a muscle in the tummy which in Ian's case was too tight.

The milk the baby drank was only seeping slowly into him. It did eventually go down into the bowel, but the majority of the milk sat on top of the muscle, and when there was some movement like sitting the baby upright, he vomited the surplus back as it had nowhere else to go.

The good news was that it was operable, and they made plans to go to the theatre with him as soon as possible. Kate looked at Michael in dismay. How could this be happening to them? It was only forty-eight hours ago that he had been born, and now they were facing a life or death operation. The nurse took the baby in an adjoining room next door to Kate's and all they could hear was him crying. Kate and Michael did not know what they were doing to him, so Michael went to find a nurse to ask her. Apparently, she said that with such a small baby, a drip was impossible to be put into his hand, and so a small part of his hair needed shaving, so they could put a drip into a vein in his scalp. This was then secured by a small cap made of Plaster of Paris. Michael was then called again by another nurse and when he returned to the room Kate asked what she had wanted. He said it was nothing, but Kate demanded to know what she had said to him. 'The nurse asked me if we wanted him Christened,' he said

'What did you say to her?'

'I said no we didn't thank you.'

'Michael, we do,' she cried. 'If anything happens to him he has to have a name. Please go back and tell her yes, we do want him Christened.' She pleaded with him so much that he went back to ask for the arrangements to be made.

The vicar from their church came and performed the service for them. It was very moving with Kate crying through most of it, and Michael trying to keep his tears at bay. Little Richard was as good as gold. He could not make out what on earth was going on. The vicar asked God to watch over little baby Ian through his operation, and to guide the surgeon's hands in what would surely be a very delicate operation given the size of him, and his very young age. He then asked God to take the baby into his Heaven if the operation was not successful, and Kate reeled at his words. No wonder she cried the whole way through, it was so upsetting for them all. The vicar left them and soon the baby was taken to theatre for his operation. After what seemed like an eternity they brought the baby back to the special mother and baby room where Kate and Michael were waiting. Mr Brun and Dr Fossard announced that the operation had gone very well. The baby was to have only boiled water for his first feed, and then half-strength formula and water for a few more feeds. Finally, he would be put onto full-strength formula if all went well and he kept the other feeds down. Thank God he did keep the feeds down, and baby Ian went from day to day gaining weight. Kate did not cope as well. She was so frightened of the children vomiting in the ward next door, she could not eat. The food was not very good to start with, so

Michael brought her in a sandwich and she ventured into the nearby kitchen to make some toast and a cup of tea in-between feeding and changing the baby. They came home after four days in the hospital, and Kate was relieved to be back to normal. The baby was doing really well although he could be a sickly baby after his feeds, but he was not vomiting like he was before. Ian proved to be a very lively baby and when he started to crawl he would put keys into plug holes in the lounge and he continued to be a handful, although Michael and Kate and Richard all adored him. When he began to walk he would put his dummy through the letter box, or get a cup of water from the toilet. Thankfully Kate caught him before he started to drink it. He needed watching from morning until night. Sometimes it was a relief when he went to bed. In fact the health visitor even asked Kate if she would like him to go to a nursery school to give her a break, but she said, 'No thank you I can cope with him. He is just so very active and inquisitive.'

ELEVEN

In January 1981 Kate found out that she was pregnant again, and this baby was a very big shock to both of them. She found it hard to come to terms with the pregnancy. The trauma of Ian's birth, and the operation that followed had taken its toll on her; all she could think of was what sort of a birth would this one be, and would this baby suffer the same as little Ian? Would this baby need an operation too? She decided she needed to discuss it with her midwife. Apparently, it had been discovered that pyloric stenosis was more common in the second-born son, and hopefully the next child would be all right. They both hoped and prayed it would be, although she continued her pregnancy in total fear. When the time came for the baby to be born Michael rang her midwife straight away. With both her babies being born at home and with the length of her labours lasting only two hours ten minutes with Richard, and two hours twenty-five with Ian, they were not taking any chances of a delivery without a professional being there. Jean her midwife said, 'Why did you not tell anyone you are so scared?'

'What could anyone do for me? I have to deliver this baby and no one can help me.' Kate replied.

'No, we can't have the baby for you, but because of your past bad experience with Ian's birth, and in view of the midwives' attitude we can talk it through, and I wish you had said something to me before now, as you have suffered in silence for nine months,' she said.

The labour was only three hours from beginning to end and Kate sailed through it. She thought of all the months of worry she had coped with when all the time she wished she had known it was not going to be so bad. She openly said that she could have done it all over again, but here was the icing on the cake as the midwife announced, 'It's a little girl.' 'Are you sure?' Kate asked her in total surprise. Both she and

Michael were expecting the baby to be another boy and the midwife laughed.

'Oh yes I am very sure.'

'Oh Michael, little pink dresses and pink frilly knickers,' said Kate. She was absolutely ecstatic. What a wonderful gift this little girl was to them. The boys would be delighted with her. She had black hair and beautiful blue eyes. She weighed in at a healthy seven pounds fourteen ounces and was born at 6.29 a.m. on the 1st of October 1981. Michael was just as thrilled as Kate. The thought of a little girl had not been imaginable, as both Kate and he had expected the baby to be another boy. The health visitor who had called in to see little Ian a few days before the birth had said that usually after having two little boys, the odds of a little girl would be pretty slim, and so they took that on board. They chose the name 'Christian'. They had spoken loosely of a little girl's name and decided if a miracle did happen, then they would call her Katherine. Kate said she wanted the name to be a part of hers and this was a perfect match. The midwife left the house after a well-earned cup of tea and a biscuit which Michael had made for all of them and they sat looking at this perfect little baby, newly bathed and smelling of baby powder. Michael went into the boys' room to tell them that their mummy had had the baby.

Richard came in first, looking very sleepy and peeped into the carry-cot. His first words to the baby Kate knew she would never forget.He bent down and said, 'Hello I am your big brother Richard.' He had always loved babies and it was clear to see how much he already adored his new baby sister. Little Ian came toddling in next, rubbing tired eyes, and he looked at her in amazement. He could not believe it. He had never seen such a tiny baby, and his gentle smile and love for her were absolutely priceless. Their family was now complete. 'Do you want to stay at home today or go to nursery?' Kate asked Ian, and 'Would you like to go to school, Richard?' They both decided to go to their schools and Michael got their breakfasts ready.

Kate rang Jean her sister, to tell her of the news. When Jean answered the telephone Kate said, 'Born 6.29 a.m. this morning, a little girl, Katherine,' Jean took a second or two to register what she had just heard. 'Oh, what lovely news.' Jean said. 'Congratulations to you all.'

'Thanks,' said Kate. 'It went so well I can't believe she is here. Do you know what, Jean, I could do it all over again if I had to. It wasn't half as bad as when I had Ian.'

'I am so pleased for you,' she said. 'I know you were terrified and now you can relax and enjoy her. How did the boys take it? No little brother for them?'

'Oh, they are over the moon with her. It was lovely when Richard said 'hello' to her. He was so gentle in his voice. He has gone to school now and Ian has gone to nursery. They weren't staying at home today they want to tell their friends the lovely news.'

The midwife came back again at lunchtime and she gave Kate and Michael a little package. Inside were two beautiful pairs of frilly knickers, one pink and one white. She said she remembered Kate saying after the birth, 'Are you sure it's a girl?' and 'now we really can buy little frilly knickers,' so here are your first pairs.'

'Thank you so very much,' Kate said, 'We are so very grateful to both you and Janet the student midwife. You have made the birth a pleasant experience when I expected it to be hell.'

'I am glad it went so well this time for you and I managed to get some sleep before you rang at 3.45 a.m. Also, it wasn't a long labour either, so well done you!' This time there was no trauma, no hospital or operation to cope with, just a peaceful time enjoying a new baby and being a complete family. Life had turned around again, and Michael and Kate knew their family life was going to be the most important thing to them both. The boys adored their baby sister and she adored them too. She soon recognised their voices and watched them as they played. There was no jealousy from the boys; they were delighted to be with her and to come home from school to see her. After a week off work Michael went back to the brewery. He was doing well in his job there and he was now made deputy head stocktaker, He went all over the county from Lancashire to the Wirrall in Cheshire, and up to Carlisle. His days started early and finished late. He was a good worker and had a company car now which helped Kate immensely, so she had the use of the Volkswagen

Beetle when she needed it. It was a bright orange colour called 'Clementine'. The agoraphobia was still there, but not as bad, and Kate enjoyed taking little Katherine out in her big pram which was a beautiful raspberry-coloured corduroy with a chrome frame. She had a lovely rose-pink eiderdown and pillow case to match. It looked really girly and Kate felt better in herself than she had done in a long time.

In October 1983 when Katherine was two years old Michael lost his grandmother. She died peacefully after a short illness and she left some money to him in her will. It was totally unexpected as he thought his mother would get the money, but his grandma had not got on with Norah. In fact did anyone? The money amounted to £2,500 and Kate and Michael decided to buy a caravan with it. Jean and Peter had one, and so did Glenda and Tom, so they knew what it was like to go caravanning, as they had visited both couples at different campsites. They started to look for one in the spring of 1984 and they couldn't find one that they could afford. However, one Saturday morning as they were passing a petrol station near West Houghton, Bolton, Kate spotted a caravan which was for sale. It was a Sprite five-berth van and they decided to take a look at it. The manager at the petrol station said he was selling it for his friend who had had the caravan repossessed. Michael and Kate could not believe their luck. It had never been used except for the hob where workmen had boiled a kettle on it. The plastic sheeting was still on all the settees and tables, and there was a tiny bathroom with a wash basin which folded up whilst travelling. They would have to buy a chemical toilet but that was all it needed. It had a good-sized fridge and cooker, both brand new.

The children were so excited they were already making plans for the holidays. Michael had to change the car to a Ford Cortina so that they could fit a tow bar on it. It was an automatic, making it easier to drive and to pull the caravan. They were looking forward to their main holidays and one night after the children had gone to bed, Michael and Kate started to look at the map. 'Shall we go to Cornwall?' Kate said. 'Well if you like we can do, but it's an awful long way,' Michael said. 'Yes, let's go there, I have never been that far down the country with my mum and dad, but I know you have with your parents. It was Falmouth you went to, wasn't it?'

'Yes, let's settle on that then.' They decided on a trial run and Michael did exceptionally well driving, especially with a six-foot caravan and a big car to contend with. They had a few weekends away just to get used to the feel of things and by the July holidays they were ready for Cornwall, although they had to empty their kitchen cupboards to take pans and cutlery to use. They knew they would have to build up the caravan utensils at a later date. It was not cheap to buy everything all over again. Towels and toothbrushes would have to be transferred from the house until eventually they had duplicated five of everything.

They set off down the M6 motorway and it took them seven hours to arrive in Newquay. Kate was nervous. She wished they had gone somewhere nearer to home, but they hadn't, and she knew that she had to cope. One day, when she was walking down a narrow street in Newquay with Michael and the children, the same fear came over her: racing heart, palpitations and the old familiar feelings. She was nearly scraping the walls of the houses she was so near to them. Michael, as usual, was lovely with her, he was so understanding, and he offered to take her home. She would not hear of it saying that she had suggested the holiday and she would see it through, so they continued to the end of the week. As the days passed she got more used to the idea of being away from home and Michael told her to think of this as her home, only this one had wheels on it. Bless him, he was so patient with her and she wished for all the world she wasn't like this. It was a good philosophy when she felt out of her depth. She would cuddle up to Michael and he would wrap her in his arms. He was ever the protector and ever the comforter; she needed him so much. They had a good time despite Kate's fears and returned home rested. The children thought caravanning was the best thing since sliced bread and they couldn't wait to go away again. During the year they went to several sites. Sometimes they met up with Glenda and Tom at Thirsk. Tom taught Ian to fish and Richard played alongside with his ball. Little Katherine had her dolls pram, and they enjoyed being together. They had a barbecue each night which Tom cooked, and they sat and chatted until it was dusk.

TWELVE

By now the family were growing up fast. Richard was at his secondary school, Pleckgate High and Ian was in the juniors at St James'. Katherine had been to John Smethurst Nursery School and was now in the infants' class, also at St James'. Kate was glad they were all settling into their various classes and she and Michael were very proud parents. The children all had good reports and life was easier than it had been for a while. In 1986 Ian joined the Cub Scouts and became a member of the church choir. He was also having guitar lessons and enjoying them. Richard was doing well at swimming; he had won endless badges and he was going to learn to be a lifesaver. The teachers at both their schools said each child was a pleasure to teach and any parent couldn't ask for more.

One afternoon in March, Kate had to take Richard to the orthodontist practice in Preston. When they got home she noticed that Michael's car was on the drive; he was home from work early. Thinking he was ill, she ran upstairs to find him. His face was ashen as he slowly told her why he had come home in the middle of the afternoon. Apparently, he had done his stocktake at a pub near Haslingden and then returned to the office after lunch, which he often did. His manager had then asked him to step inside his office away from the other workers. He was asked various questions on what he had actually done during the course of the day. Michael explained to his boss that he had done his work at the pub, had quickly called home, then gone to the bank and returned to the office. Without a warning his boss dropped the bombshell. He told Michael that a certain amount of money had gone missing from the pub where he had been working, and Michael asked what that had got to do with him. 'I am sorry to have to tell you,' he said, 'We are accusing you of the theft.'

'That is ludicrous,' Michael said. 'why would you think it was me?' 'We have our reasons,' he said, and he told him there and then that it was company policy to suspend him until further notice. He would be kept on full pay, and he could take the company car home immediately and return to the office the following morning.

Kate stared at him in total disbelief. 'It's impossible Michael.' she was crying by now. 'They know you so well there must be some mistake. How could they even think it was you?'

'I don't know, I can't believe it myself,' he replied. 'I have been going over it and over it in my mind.' 'You have the job of head stocktaker in the palm of your hand when your immediate boss retires. Why would you jeopardize that for a few hundred pounds?' Kate said, tears pouring down her face. They went downstairs together in total silence. Kate knew there was some mistake and tried to be positive if only for Michael's sake. They talked it over and over again all evening. Michael traced his day through his mind and still he came up with nothing. The following day he returned to the office again at nine a.m. as he had been asked to. Kate waited for him to call her. When he finally did he was crying down the phone hysterically. 'Please come and get me, Kate' he said. 'I am in the bus shelter near the hospital.' 'Ok, Michael, hold on sweetheart,' she said. 'Don't cry, darling, I will be there as soon as I can.' 'I am setting off straight away, I love you, I won't be long.' When she arrived at the bus shelter she found him slumped down by the glass, his face as white as a sheet. 'Where is the car?' she said,

'They told me to leave it in the carpark and I handed them my keys. I now have no job and no company car,' he sobbed 'I haven't done anything wrong.'

My God. How could this be happening, thought Kate. It was like living in a nightmare and there was no way out of it, not at the moment. They would have to contact a solicitor in the morning, but for now there was only one place to go, to cancel the beautiful G Plan furniture they had ordered to be delivered when Michael had finished decorating their lovely lounge.

All their plans and dreams had been cruelly shattered in twenty-four hours and all because some thief had taken some money and poor Michael had taken the blame. Kate knew that he would never have taken anything that did not belong to him. He had been brought up better than that. If only George, his dad, had been alive. he would have known what to do, been able to get to the bottom of it for his son's sake who now had to face the world branded a thief. Only Kate and Michael knew different and she hoped and prayed that their family and friends would see the wrong that had been done to him. This beautiful pure-minded person, who had had his name tarnished forever. The shame he had to endure, the talk of the brewery, George Abbotts' son, taking money that did not belong to him. She couldn't bear it for him. She turned their car around and headed down to the town centre to cancel the furniture that they had ordered, and she hoped that the manager would accept her apology and understand their predicament. Kate parked the car on the car park at Edmundsons and went into the shop in floods of tears. The manager thought she was going to collapse and sat her on a chair. The furniture was cancelled, and Kate thanked the manager. She truthfully told him what had happened. It was pointless to lie, soon it would be in the Telegraph and on every news bulletin on the radio. He said he was so sorry for them as he knew the couple well. They had always got their furniture from them and he offered her a cup of tea as the tears rolled down her cheeks. She thanked him and said, 'You have been so kind. I promise you, we will come back to you and order again when this mess is sorted out. Thank you from us both. My husband is in the car park crying, a broken man.'

The following morning they went to see a solicitor. He was helpful and truthful by saying they needed someone who could represent them at a tribunal, and that his fees would be extortionate, and it was not a forgone conclusion, but that the brewery might win. A close friend did represent Michael at the industrial tribunal which went on for three days. Kate and her friend Liz listened as they tore Michael's evidence to shreds. It was a terrible ordeal for all of them and unfortunately, they lost the case. The tribunal panel apparently were only there to observe if the correct procedure had been adhered to. Firstly being accused, then being suspended, and finally being sacked. The jury at the tribunal were not interested in whether the person in the dock was guilty or not guilty of the crime in question. It was their job to decide if all the procedures had been followed and they had. Despite his plea that he had done no wrong, and after three days of humiliation, Michael admitted defeat. He was told by a very reliable source that in fact the money had turned up in the banking, but for Michael it was too late. They would never have told him so and he had lost his job, his dignity and his career, and all for what? He truly was a broken man.

The children got on with their lives although there had to be changes. Ian had to stop his guitar lessons, and Kate and Michael drastically cut back on everything they could. It took its toll on their relationship as a couple and they had bad days, very, very bad days. There was a time when even Kate asked him had he done it. She was at her lowest ebb. She pleaded with Michael to tell her the truth. She knew by his face she had stepped too far, and immediately she asked him to forgive her for ever doubting him. If she had for one minute ever thought that it was true, would she have ever given her total support to him?

She knew it was a silly thought in a very tired mind. A few weeks went by when there was a knock at their door. There stood a neighbour from farther up the road. She asked Kate if it would help them financially if her and Michael wanted to deliver some Yellow Pages for her. They said yes, they would be happy to help her, and Michael said it would at least pay the electricity bill which was now due. They walked down all the side streets and main roads near Audley Range in Blackburn, methodically posting each directory through the letter boxes. Each morning for a week they dropped the children off at school and started the long trek until they had delivered them all.

'How can we thank you?' Kate said to Margaret when they had finished. 'We are so deeply grateful to you for giving us the job. We will do anything that will help us to bring in some money.' It was degrading for them both as they knew people enjoyed gossiping and Michael had to go down to the jobcentre to sign on the dole. He would not let Kate use the clothing tokens they were allowed, but all the three children needed new winter coats and Kate told Michael that he must swallow his pride and get the children fitted out.

It was nine months before Michael eventually got another job. A friend and neighbour who lived a few doors away from them called at their house one evening after work. 'Michael, my firm Training 2000, are looking for a development officer. I wondered if you would be interested?' Dave said. 'The pay will not be as good as at the brewery, but we could help you if it's what you are looking for.'

'Yes, I would be so grateful, please could you arrange an interview for me?' Michael said. So, someone, somewhere believed in him, someone really knew he was not a thief and Kate saw a glimmer of hope in Michael's eyes that she had not seen for a very long time. Soon one of the parishioners at church asked if he would work on a Sunday at their petrol station on Livesey Branch Road, manning the till. Now people were really believing in him. Maybe they always had done, and Michael and Kate had presumed otherwise, but they hoped and prayed that the dark days of late were now behind them. After Dave had gone they called the children downstairs and told them of their hope of Daddy getting another job and they were delighted.

The interview went well for Michael and he was given the job. He was so glad to be off the benefit ladder and back on the road of employment again. There was no company car, so Kate had to let Michael use their car and she managed as well as she could do. The pressure at least for the moment was off and they slowly started to enjoy their lives again, never taking anything for granted. Money was still tight, and for the foreseeable future it was going to be, but he had his dignity back. The people who did not believe in him were a distant memory, the future was ahead of them once again and they thanked God for the chance that he had been given to be proved worthy of employment again. Not everyone believed he was a thief. Those who truly knew him knew better, and knew that someone, somewhere must have set him up. Kate was so proud of him. He never wavered in believing that somebody would give him another chance, it was just a matter of time. He was happy again meeting new people each day, and when they heard through the grapevine of some distant friend remarking, 'He must have done it, look at the clothes the children have on and look at Kate, she is always so well dressed,' he told Kate, 'Leave it, don't rise to the bait, let them believe what they like. I know I did nothing wrong and so do you. They can go to hell.' But they knew only too well what it was like to go to hell and back as they had already been there.

THIRTEEN

Just after Christmas in 1987 a job was advertised in the evening paper at the local health centre in Blackburn for an Evening Receptionist. Kate read it over and over again and said to Michael she was thinking of applying for it. He was so supportive of her and told her he would help her to write her CV. Michael knew how hard it was going to be for Kate. She was still so bad with her nerves, and yet she knew she had no choice but to help them out financially. She applied for the job and got an interview. It was going to be so hard going back to work after being at home for sixteen years, but Kate got the strength from somewhere and in March 1988 she started her new job. On the first night, she was so overwhelmed she told the senior receptionist she didn't think she would be in the following day. 'I really think this is above me,' she told Dot. 'Give yourself a chance, girl,' Dot said. 'You have been at home for so long you are bound to be scared.'

The night after she met a girl called Fran. She was so lovely to Kate and slowly, with Fran's help, she got her confidence back and she decided to stay. The post was only temporary as the cover was for a girl on maternity leave, but by the time the girl was due back, Kate was finding it hard to leave. She enjoyed the company of the girls, the hours suited both her, the children and Michael. She worked three nights each week. One week it was Monday, Wednesday and Friday, the next it was Monday, Tuesday, Thursday and then Tuesday, Wednesday and Friday. Five p.m. until eight p.m. two nights, and one night until ten p.m.. Kate could not believe it. She had taken to the job so easily, probably because she had been so used to dealing with the public when she had helped her parents' in the shop, and helping people in the health centre there, she just loved it, but there were no more evening posts available so when Sue came back after having her little boy, Kate had to finish. A few months later, after keeping in touch with the night staff she got a phone call from her friend Fran.

'Kate, hi, its Fran how are you?' she said,

'I am fine thanks, but I really miss you guys, how are you all doing?' 'We are missing you and that's why I am ringing you. One of the big practices are looking for their own Evening Receptionist and I wondered would you like to apply?' You know all the doctors down here, so I think you stand a pretty good chance of getting it. What do you think?'

'Oh yes, thank you so much, where can I get an application form from?'

'I'll get one off to you, fill it in as soon as possible and get it back to me'

'I will and thanks a million, Fran. You are a super friend. See you soon give my love to everyone, bye.'

'Michael,' she shouted upstairs, 'guess what? They want a new Evening Receptionist and I am going to apply for it. He was over the moon for her. Was this the start of a new life for them? Yes, money is not everything, but boy did they need it! A few weeks later May 15th, 1989, Kate started her new job. Although she was not working with Fran and the other girls anymore she was in the same room as them and they enjoyed being together again. Soon the practice needed someone to work in the mornings as they were going computerised and Kate was happy to do a few extra hours as they really needed the money and she really enjoyed the change. She loved doing the housework, but this was a nice change. By now Richard was doing well at Pleckgate High School. He was sixteen-years-old, Ian was eleven-years-old and was also at the same school, equally doing well, and little Katherine was still at St James in the juniors. She enjoyed helping her dad in the home whilst her mummy was at work. Every week she went with Michael to the supermarket to get the weekly shopping and she helped him in the house if he asked her to do something. He was a wonderful husband and father and they all appreciated his devotion to them. He very rarely shouted. You could not find a more placid man if you tried.

In the main July holidays, they towed their caravan down to Bournemouth in Hampshire, staying at a beautiful caravan and camping site owned by Basil and Sheila Whitlock. The site was situated in a little village called Hordle, near to Lymington, and was called East Leach on Skye End Road. There was a lovely private swimming pool where the children spent hours splashing around and generally having the time of their lives, if the weather allowed. The beauty of Bournemouth were the beaches, coastline and the countryside too, and the weather was pretty well guaranteed, giving hours of sunshine and cloudless skies. The children were really good swimmers now and even Michael, who had just learnt to swim, was happy playing with them. Kate, who was not a very confident swimmer, preferred to sit on the pool side and watch them. Sometimes she would just have a chat and a coffee with Sheila and they would catch up on each other's news. Basil would let the children ride on his motorised lawnmower whilst cutting the field. It was a very relaxing break for them all and Kate and Michael enjoyed the rest. It was home from home in the caravan and the children looked forward to spending their pocket money in the toy shops in and around Muddiford and nearby Lymington.

Kate spent lazy days reading her books and she told Michael that she would love to write her own story one day. He told her to start it as soon as they went home, but it was many years before she got around to it. (You are in fact reading it now.) Kate continued with her job at the health centre. It was just what she had needed. She learnt a lot about medicine and it gave her a new focus on life. She never would have guessed she'd be so happy and fulfilled. By 1993 her hours were from eight thirtya.m. until one thirtyp.m. and then in an evening she worked four thirty p.m. until seven p.m. Monday, Wednesday and Friday. Michael teased her because he finished at lunchtime every Friday and Kate used to say, 'I really don't want to go back tonight.' 'Heck, Kate, how many times do I have to listen to this?' he said, 'You sound like a broken record.' I really don't want to go he mimicked, and they fell about laughing. He took her in his arms and leaning on the kitchen sink said, 'You know you still turn me on after twenty-two years together,' and he kissed her tenderly. He loved her more than life itself, and she him.

In the autumn of 1993 Michael and Kate decided to change the lounge. The stone fireplace that they had had built in 1987 was dated now and it had cost them a fortune—£700 back then—but Kate had never liked it. Michael said he would pull it down and try to sell the stone. It became a very strenuous task for him to do, but eventually he managed it. They went to Burnley and bought a new open flame gas fire and they ordered a beautiful marble and white fireplace with a white surround from a store in Manchester. They stripped off the old wallpaper and Michael built a new false chimney breast. It was going to be so different from their previous décor as they would now be able to have wall lights in the recesses. Roy, their next-door neighbour came in and plastered it for them and the lounge was slowly but surely being transformed. They had kept their promise to go back to order some more furniture from Edmundsons when Michael began his new job, and they got back on their feet again so the pink, cream and grey carpet was still like new as they never came into the lounge wearing their shoes, as it was so light and delicate. The pink velvet curtains only needed dry cleaning and their grey dralon suite was also still as new. They bought some wall lights and two centre fittings with pink flowers on the edges which Michael put up in the recesses and over the dining room table and the main area making it a totally different room. Kate was so looking forward to it being finished and by November they only had to put up a picture light. They had planned that after Christmas in early 1994, Kate and Michael, Richard, Ian and Katherine were going to have a family portrait taken. It was to be hung on the wall over the mahogany nest of tables by the side of the new fireplace.

It would be the first thing to be seen as you entered the room. Michael had already chiselled out the wall and put in the wiring. He had put some polyfilla in the grooves, and it needed to dry so he could sand it down ready for the wallpaper to be put on, which they still had to choose. Yes, it really was going to have been worth all the hard work and expense, but they deserved it, they both worked hard, and it was nice to be able to keep the house as they wanted it. The last few years had been hard on them both, and although the children had never suffered, Kate and Michael had pulled together because they loved each other so much. They had faced tough times and real hardship, both financially and mentally, but at last they felt that the worst was over, the future was looking good and things could only get better. God willing!

On Saturday the 20th of November 1993 Kate and Michael and Katherine went Christmas shopping. Katherine needed a new outfit for her Christmas party at her school. She was twelve now and had asked if she could have some Rollerblades for Christmas. She also chose a Sylvanian canal boat with figures in it and a white Sony Radio Cassette player. After they had finished shopping they went to the supermarket for something for tea where they bumped into Joan, Kate's friend, and her husband; they were doing their shopping too. It was ironic really as in the next aisle they saw Jean and Peter who were also doing their shopping, and Michael said that after not seeing either of them for ages, it was coincidental to see them both within minutes of each other together in the same store. Monday evening, Michael sanded down the wall where the picture light was to be, and they went to bed happy that things in the lounge were coming on fine. The following morning Kate had plans to wrap a few Christmas presents then do some of her housework. She loved her Tuesdays and Thursdays off so that she could catch up with her chores and have a bit of 'me time', plus it was nice to have time to herself with working most evenings during the week. She was just sorting out the pots in the kitchen when the telephone rang. 'Hi, Kate' the voice said at the other end of the line, 'sorry to disturb you on your day off.' Kate recognised her practice managers' voice.

'Hi Sheila, it's okay, how are you?'

'Oh, I am fine,' Sheila said, 'but I wondered if I could ask you a big favour?'

''Course what can I do for you?' she said.

'Can you possibly come into work all day today please? One of the girls has rung in sick, she is full of a cold and we could really do with another pair of hands.'

'Yes of course I can,' said Kate, I shall have to get ready though and wash my hair, but I will be there as soon as I possibly can.'

'Oh, thanks ever so much, Kate, you are a star. Ring me when you get into work, I'll be in my office upstairs and meanwhile until you arrive I can sort out what time I can give you a lunch break. Thanks again, love. I really do appreciate it. See you later.'

That has really messed up my plans for the day, thought Kate, but the extra money will come in handy especially with Christmas around the corner and with that in mind she went upstairs to get ready for work. She arrived at about nine thirty and the girls were very busy. 'Here she is, they piped up. We had to call in the troops'

'Yes, I know, and I wouldn't give up my day off for anyone but you guys,' she laughed. It was a really busy morning and Kate realised that they would have struggled had she not gone in to help them. Sheila rang down from her office and asked Kate if she could have a twelve thirty to one thirty p.m. lunch, and Kate said yes that would be fine. At 12.25p.m. she got her coat and made her way to the car. She and Richard shared it now between them. When she arrived home Michael was just getting ready to go back to work. 'Hi sweetheart, where are you?' she called

'I am in the kitchen,' he replied. 'Have you had your lunch yet?' 'Yes, thanks I am just going back to work, Are you okay, Michael?'

'Yes' he said, 'except I have a really tight chest.'

'It's probably with you sanding down the wall last night, the dust must have got on your chest. Well if you don't feel okay love, don't go back to work. You never take time off, so take the rest of the day off.' 'No, I will be all right' he said. 'If I'm not I will come home.' 'Promise' she said.

'Promise,' he replied.

'Okay, sweetheart, I'll leave it with you I'd better go and get my lunch now as I have to be back by one thirty p.m..' He kissed her and told her he would see her later. 'Drive careful, Michael, I love you.' 'Love you too, sweetheart, bye.'

83

Kate sat in the lounge and ate her lunch. She was pondering; it wasn't like Michael to be poorly. He never complained, not like Kate. She always said if she didn't feel well, but Michael wasn't one for a fuss and besides he really was never ill. She couldn't remember when he had last seen the doctor. He had, however, been to see the practice nurse recently for a well man check-up, and Bernadette had said his diet needed altering. His cholesterol was quite high at 7.7 and she told him to take it easy on the fried eggs he had at lunchtime. He was also told to cut down on the cheese he was very fond of too. She said she was not unduly worried about him, but she had to point out that the blood results had shown he really did need to watch what he ate. He did say to her that he would try to eat less fat and take a little more exercise. Kate finished her lunch and then set off back to work. It was a bitterly cold day with thick ice on the road. In fact it was like a sheet of glass but that wasn't unusual, for every winter they always had the worst of the ice on their road; with the open fields behind them they were open to the elements.

FOURTEEN

In the spring of 1988 they had been faced with a new housing estate being built behind them and it had restricted their views. They still had a clear view of the hills in the village of Mellor from the boys' back bedroom and they could still see a little in-between the detached houses from the lounge. It had nearly killed Kate to see their beautiful view being taken from them brick by brick, and she would be the first to admit she had cried a lot over it. Michael said she had to pull herself together or she would make herself ill, and they would build on the field behind no matter how much she cried. They had formed a residents' group, and Michael and a few of the neighbours had gone down to sit in on many of the council meetings, but eventually they had lost their fight. The council had won the battle and the houses were built. The good part of it all, if there was a good part, was the new houses had got long gardens, so they were not overlooked, and if anything, the houses and the people who moved in to them were in fact very nice.

The telephone was constantly ringing all afternoon and the receptionists were run off their feet. It was no wonder really with a panel of seven thousand patients and four doctors running the practice. Kate loved her job and the amount of work never fazed her. At four thirty p.m. Richard phoned and asked one of the other receptionists if he could please speak to his mum. 'Hi Richard, are you okay?' Kate asked,

'Yes, Mum, I am, but Dad's come home, he is really ill, he keeps being sick. Can you get some tea bags on your way home please?' 'No, Richard, you go and get some, love, and I will see if I can leave here soon, I will be home as quick as I can.'

'What's the matter, Kate, one of her friends asked?'

'It's Michael, I need to go home now, he's really poorly, Richard just telephoned me, and he sounds worried. Michael's never ill.

'Ring Sheila,' she said, 'we can manage here, it's nearly home time anyway.'

'Okay thanks a lot, I will do, if you are sure,' Kate said. 'Sheila, hi, it's Kate, Richard has just rung me to say that Michael has come home from work and he says he is really poorly. Do you mind if I go home now as its 4.45 p.m. and the girls say they can manage okay for quarter of an hour.'

'Yes of course, you just get yourself off home now and we will see you tomorrow, I hope he is okay.'

'Thank you so much, Sheila, I'll see you tomorrow morning then.'

Kate ran to the car her heart pounding. The thought of him being sick terrified her. She just kept thinking, oh no, not sick, I bet we will all probably go down with it if it's a sick bug he's got. She had passed the trainee doctor on her way out of the main door and prepared him that he might have to come up to the house that evening as he was the duty doctor on call for her practice that day and her employers were also their family doctor. The weather was awful, and the avenue was twice as bad with ice and snow as it had been at lunchtime. She pulled up onto the drive at 4.55 p.m. and ran inside the house. 'Michael, where are you?' she cried. 'He's in the toilet, mum,' Richard shouted to her from inside the lounge. Kate ran up the stairs two at a time and she found him knelt down on the floor with his head bent over the toilet.

'Oh Kate, I am ill,' Michael said.

'I know you are, sweetheart, Richard rang me she said. 'I'll just go and change the bed in case we have to send for the doctor. I won't be a minute.' She turned around and took three steps across the landing towards their bedroom door when she heard a mighty thud. 'Oh my God, Richard, he's collapsed. Ring for an ambulance, quick. No I'll do it,' she shouted, and she ran into their bedroom and dialled 999.

'Emergency services,' the operator said. 'Police Fire or Ambulance?' 'Ambulance, please hurry. My husband has just collapsed in the bathroom.'

'Is he conscious?' the operator asked,

'I don't know. Please hurry.'

'What is his name?'

'Michael Abbotts,'

'What is his age?'

'He's forty-seven please, please, can you send an ambulance right away?' She was nearly hysterical by now.

'Has he been ill?'

'No, but he did complain of a tight chest at lunchtime, he has come home from work feeling ill and he has been vomiting, now he has just collapsed.'

'The ambulance is on its way,' the operator said. 'They will be with you as soon as possible.'

'Thank you.' She put the phone down and went rushing into the toilet. It seemed ages between him collapsing and her returning to him. The door was pushed to and she could not get it open. She shouted down for Richard who was already halfway up the stairs. 'My God, he is trapped behind the toilet door and I can't move it, how can we get to him?' Her voice was hysterical now. Ian and Katherine were bewildered and stood together in the lounge. 'Ian,' Kate said, 'run and get Rita and ask Barbara from next door but one and tell them Dad has collapsed, ask them to come straight away.' She hoped they might know what to do as Rita was an auxiliary nurse at Blackburn Royal Infirmary and Barbara worked in a residential care home.

Richard and Kate frantically tried to get to Michael, but he had collapsed between the toilet and the wall, so he was jammed inside. His feet were blocking the door from opening and because he was over six feet tall and the toilet was such a small room they knew they had to reach him somehow. They didn't know where they got their strength from, but they managed between them to get him out of the toilet and they laid him down on the floor of the landing. His body was lifeless, and he was an awful grey colour. Kate could only stare down at him in total disbelief as Richard started to give him the kiss of life. Suddenly there was a crack and Richard said, 'I think I've broken his rib, Mum.'

'Just keep going,' said Kate. 'The rib will heal, he just isn't breathing. Where is the bloody ambulance. I'll ring them again.' She flew into the bedroom and dialled 999 again. 'The ambulance is on its way, Mrs. Abbotts,' the operator said. 'They will be with you as soon as possible.' 'Okay,' said Kate, but please tell them to hurry he isn't breathing.' Ian came back with Rita and Barbara in tow and they went straight up the stairs. 'What's happened?' said Rita.

'He came home from work sick and he's just collapsed in the toilet,' said Richard. Barbara said she was not sure how to do CPR, but she would give it a go. Both Rita and Barbara and Richard, bless him, took it in turns to try and revive him but still there was no sign of him regaining consciousness, not even a twitch. Kate looked down at him laid out on the carpet and she prayed to God for help. She stroked Michael's face saying, 'Wake up, sweetheart, please wake up.' She knew she was going to become a widow if he didn't come around soon. Working at the health centre had taught her that time was of the essence in cases of a heart attack, as the longer the brain was starved of oxygen the more likely the patient would be brain damaged. It was now going on for more than ten minutes since Michael had collapsed and still no ambulance. Finally, Katherine shouted from downstairs that they had just arrived.

There were two ambulance crew men and they bounded quickly up the stairs. Barbara and Rita left Michael to the professionals then quietly let themselves out of the front door and went home to tell their husbands the sorry state they had left Kate and the children in. The ambulance men asked if they could cut open Michael's jumper and Kate said, 'Yes of course.' Richard and Kate both watched in horror as the ambulance man put the defibrillator on Michael's bare chest, his body writhing off the carpet and then back down again with a terrible thud.

They tried this over and over again. They injected him with adrenaline, but still there was no response. He lay there on the kingfisher blue carpet absolutely motionless and Kate and Richard stepped aside as the crew said there was nothing more they could do here. They would have to take him to Blackburn Royal Infirmary Accident and Emergency Department.

The ambulance man told Kate to follow them in their own car as he said it would be too traumatic to travel inside the ambulance as they had to carry on working on Michael during the twenty minutes or so journey up to the hospital. The roads were very treacherous, especially their avenue, which was notorious for being icy every year. It was never gritted by the council, despite many pleas by the residents. They laid Michael on a stretcher chair and wrapped an orange blanket around him. Gently they carried him down the stairs and out to the waiting ambulance. Kate could not remember hearing any sirens or seeing any blue flashing lights when the ambulance sped away, she could only remember the crunching of their own feet on the ice outside as herself, Richard, Ian and Katherine climbed into the back of the waiting car that Gerald (Rita's husband) had parked outside the house. Gerald had said that Kate was in no fit state to drive herself and the children to the hospital and she gratefully accepted his kind offer of a lift.

Gerald, Rita, Kate and the children drove in silence through the town and up to the Infirmary. On their arrival at the A& E department Kate and the children were taken to a private room. Rita and Gerald said goodbye and told Kate to ring if she needed a lift home. She thanked them for all they had done and said she would be in touch when she knew more of the outcome. She didn't know whether they would be keeping Michael in hospital or if there was to be an operation on him. She would just have to wait until she had seen the doctor who was attending to him. A lady brought in some tea and asked if anyone wanted any biscuits, but nobody wanted anything to eat. They just had a drink each then waited to see the doctor who was on duty. It was a good hour or more before the door opened and a pleasant-looking doctor came in and introduced himself to Kate. She detected nothing as she politely stood and shook his hand. 'Sit down please,' he said gently to her and as quietly as he could, explained to Kate and the children that Michael had suffered a massive heart attack. 'I am so very, very sorry, Mrs Abbotts, we did all we could for him, but I am afraid that Michael has died.'

Kate felt her heart wrench. 'Did he regain consciousness?' she asked him.

'No he didn't,' the doctor replied.

'Would he have been in any pain?' asked Kate.

'No, he didn't suffer either. I am so sorry,' he said again. 'Can you tell me what happened from when you last saw him, Mrs Abbotts?' the doctor asked. Kate told him that Michael had said that he had a very tight chest that lunchtime but that he was okay to go back to work. He had promised her that he would come home early if he felt any worse. The next thing she knew was when Richard phoned her at work, and she told him about the vomiting. 'Were there any heart problems in his family?'

'Yes, his father had a heart attack prior to us getting married in August 1971, just six weeks before actually and then he had another one in March 1977 where he was found dead slumped over his desk at the Whitbread Brewery offices. He had been dead for about half an hour when one of his colleagues found him. That was a total shock for us all as George, my father-in-law had seemed to recover well from his first one in July 1971.'

'Had Michael been ill recently, Mrs Abbotts?'

'No, when he complained at lunchtime of a tight chest and I told him to stay off work this afternoon, he said he wasn't ill enough to stay at home and we thought it was because he had been sanding down the wall in the lounge that we are decorating at the moment, ready to put a picture light up. We were going to have a professional family portrait of us all to be taken in the New Year. He did go to see our practice nurse at the surgery where I work a few weeks ago.'

She told Michael to watch his diet as his cholesterol level was 7.7. He was a devil for having a fried egg on bread at lunchtime and he loved his cheese. He said he would cut down on both and she said she would see him at her next well-man clinic in three months' time.

'What happens now?' Kate asked the doctor.

'Would you and the children like to see Mr Abbotts now?' he said. 'Yes, please we would.'

'Then I think you should go in first, Mrs Abbotts, and come back for the children afterwards.' He led her down the corridor, her heart pounding out of her chest. What would he look like, she thought and how can I live without him forever now? The doctor opened the door and she looked at Michael's lifeless body. He seemed like he was asleep. God, if only he was asleep she thought. She found herself apologising to the nurse for the shoes he had on. Kate was going to get him some new ones for Christmas, which was only a month and two days away. The nurse said it didn't matter and not to worry about anything, then she carried on tidying up in the room. It hadn't sunk in yet. Her beloved Michael laid out on a bed in front of her was dead, not just asleep, but dead. She felt light-headed with all the upset, the shock and the lack of food but she could not have eaten a thing. She never wanted anything else in all the world except to have him back in her arms again.

FIFTEEN

Kate bravely went back to the other room where the three children were waiting. They looked like zombies. Slowly she brought them in to see their dad. It was to have been the very last time any of them were to see Michael. They walked around his body like they expected he was going to wake up and speak to them. They were willing him to really and as Kate watched her lovely children stare at their devoted father's body she could not read their thoughts. She only knew how all of them, shocked and dazed, devastated by his sudden death, wished they all could wake up from this nightmare and face normality again. The doctor who had broken the news to them came back in and asked if Kate would like to ring for the vicar and if so she could use the phone in the adjoining room. The lady who had made them tea offered some more and Kate said no thank you. She offered her condolences again and quietly left the room. Kate asked the nurse for a telephone directory and began to dial the vicarage. Mr Braithwaite answered the phone. 'Mr Braithwaite,' began Kate, 'please could you possibly come to the Infirmary?' she stuttered. 'Michael has had a massive heart attack this evening and he has died. Please will you come up to us,' she said. 'I am so sorry to ask you, but the hospital asked me to ask you to.'

'Oh, Kate, I can't believe what you have just told me,' he said, 'of course I will come up to the hospital right away,' Kate turned to the nurse and said, 'Could I please ring my neighbour now to come for the children? They need to go home and my eldest son will start to ring the family to tell them what has happened.'

They moved Michael into a private room where a black chair had been placed in front of the doorway blocking the entrance. The nurse moved away the chair and opened the door for Kate to go inside. Michael was laid in a bed with an orange hospital blanket covering him right up to his chin. Quietly the nurse closed the door behind her and left Kate alone with him. She broke her heart as she laid her hands onto his chest sobbing incoherently. Her beloved Michael who was only forty-seven years old was as white as the sheet in front of her DEAD. She prayed for the strength to cope with their loss, she prayed for Michael wherever he was right now and for their three wonderful children; Richard who was now twenty-years-old, Ian at fifteen-years-old and little Katherine only twelve-years-old. How on earth were they ever going to get over this night? She prayed reverently in the silence of the room, watching the covers in case he suddenly started breathing again. She felt like she was in the middle of a nightmare and soon she would wake up. She was not afraid of being with him for he had loved her dearly in life and she knew for certain that he would love her the same in death. She had relied totally on Michael for everything in twenty-two years of marriage and two more years of courting with him. How she loved him beyond all measure. He had been her rock, and now that rock had gone she asked God to help her and their children to just get through this night for now, and to help her to try and live without him forever.

As she just kept looking at his lifeless body she wondered where he had gone. 'Oh God, Michael,' she said. 'What happened? Where are you? How can I go on without you? I can't live on my own without your love. Please sweetheart, please wake up.' She knew it was in vain. He would have woken up if he could have done, and with every fibre of her being she willed life into him but to no avail. Mr Braithwaite arrived after about half an hour and she saw the pain he felt in seeing one so young in front of him. Michael had been a sidesman at St James' Church, where Ian and Katherine had both been baptised and where all the three children, including Michael, had been confirmed; his was at the same time as Richard's confirmation.

They prayed together for the soul of Michael, for the strength to carry all of them through the coming days, and for all who loved and would miss Michael besides his family and his many friends, his work colleagues and all at church who knew and respected him.

Kate asked Mr Braithwaite if he would kindly take her home and he said he would. He dropped her at the door and told her he would call tomorrow and they could start to think about the funeral. She thanked him for coming to the hospital and for his prayers for them all and also for dropping her back home. There would have to be a post-mortem on Michael's body as it was a sudden death. He would stay at the Infirmary until then and be released on Friday, the 26th of November 1993. Kate opened the door and went inside. The children were in the lounge with her sister Jean and her brother-in-law Peter, along with Kate and Michael's best friends Chrisanna and her husband Mick who had only just come out of hospital himself after an operation for a cataract. Kate asked him how he was, and he asked her if she would dim the lights for him to ease the strain. Jean looked terrible and so did Peter, in fact they all did. Michael had worked with Chrisanna for many years and she had introduced Kate to him in 1969. They asked what had happened and Kate started to tell them how the day had unfolded. 'Did you ring Nanna, Richard?' Kate asked him.

'Yes, I did, Mum, and she is in a real state, Uncle Andrew said.' Jean asked Kate if she would like her to stay with her overnight, but Kate said no thank you, she just wanted to be on her own. It was just too much to take in and they realised how exhausted the lot of them were. After a cup of tea they made a move to go back to their own homes.

Richard, Ian, Kate and Katherine waved goodbye to everyone then came inside and sat in the unfinished lounge and cried together. The walls were bare, the lovely white fireplace newly put in and the beautiful living flame fire were all there to see, but the wallpaper and the painting was waiting for Michael to finish. Kate sobbed for the thought of him not seeing all his hard work finished and she realised she would have to choose the wallpaper herself now and get someone else to decorate the room. Richard was beside himself, saying how he wished he could have saved his dad's life. He had learnt to do CPR at the swimming baths in Blackburn where he was a lifeguard. Kate said she was so proud of him, how hard he had tried to bring him back and how proud Michael would have been of him too. If he had known, deep in his unconscious state, laid on the landing floor that his precious, first-born son was trying to save his father's life, what more could he have asked for?

Neither of them wanted anything to eat and they had another drink of tea and went up to bed. Ian said on the landing, 'Mum, do you know when someone is dying, and it shows on the television how they have appeared to have come out of their body? Well I bet, if Dad was out of his body up there in the corner of the landing ceiling then he would have been able to see that Richard was really trying hard to save him, wouldn't he?

'Yes sweetheart, I am sure he would have done,' she replied. Bless him, what a lovely thing to think. He was so much like Michael in many ways both physically and mentally. He only needed to be told anything once and he would remember it. Kate made sure that every-one was tucked in bed and then she went into their bedroom. The bed stayed as it was; she couldn't bring herself to change the sheets. She looked at the radio alarm and said out loud, 'Michael, how do I get this alarm to work?' This was the extent to which Michael had done everything for Kate. She had never needed to touch the radio alarm because Michael had always done it. It was the first hurdle of many things she now had to learn to do on her own, and the thought of it all was daunting to say the least.

She remembered she had not told Sheila, her practice manager that she would not be in work in the morning and she went to the phone and dialled her number. 'Hi Sheila, I'm so sorry it's late, only' she couldn't get the words out. 'Sheila, Michael died tonight. He had a massive heart attack and when I got home he collapsed in the toilet and he's dead, Sheila, he's dead.' she started to sob hysterically.

'Oh, darling, I am so sorry, what can I do?' Sheila said.

'Nothing thanks, there is nothing you can do, he's gone. My God he's gone, what am I going to do, Sheila? He is my life, how can I live without him now?'

'I don't know what to say Kate, I am so very, very sorry. I will ring the other doctors and tell them what has happened.'

'Ok love, Sheila, I must go now. The children need me and I am so sorry I shocked you, but I wanted to tell you myself tonight.Please tell the girls at work for me and I'll be in touch soon.Night, God bless Sheila.'

'Night Kate, and Kate, you take care. If you need anything, you only need to ask me.'

'Thanks I will.'

Kate locked up and went back upstairs into their bedroom. She couldn't face another cup of tea and so she got undressed, had a quick wash and climbed into their bed. She looked at the empty place where Michael usually slept and broke down sobbing for the man she had loved and cared for so much for nearly twenty-two and a half years. Her darling husband who she had lost this very evening only a matter of hours ago. How many more deaths could she face? How many more people could this God of hers take away? Did he not hear her prayers each night? When she prayed for her lovely children, her two sisters and their families, their friends and relations and all who had gone to a higher life before. 'God,' she would pray, 'please keep my darling Michael safe, please, take him safely to work and bring him safely home, please God keep him safe, he means everything in the world to me and he is all I have got.' The words rang in her ears. She repeated them over and over again in her mind, as if by doing so Michael would magically walk into the room and take her in his arms, snuggle her close to him as he always did throughout the night. She lay there cold and alone and did not close her eyes all night long. At four o'clock she picked up the phone and rang Jean. Jean said she could not sleep either and asked why had Kate not let her stay with her that night. Kate said she could not bear it if Jean had to go through a time like this and she didn't want Peter and her to have to spend even one night apart.

'Bless you' Jean said. 'I just can't believe this is real, it's just like a nightmare'

'I know,' Kate said. 'Just try and sleep, Jean, snuggle next to Peter and I will ring you tomorrow.'

'You are sure,' she said, 'yes there is nothing you can do for us tonight. Thanks anyway and I am sorry I disturbed you, I just needed to hear your voice.' The night was endless. Kate just cried and cried. She wanted to die too, she wanted to be with him, where had he gone? Only a few hours ago he had thought he had a tummy bug and now he was in a hospital mortuary waiting for someone to cut him open and tell them all why he had died, but Kate didn't want them to do that to him; she wanted him there beside her where he belonged. What was there left to live for now that her precious Michael had gone? She knew, as raw as it was right now, and the pain of losing him was indescribable, that she had three beautiful children that he had given her who were asleep in their adjoining bedrooms and who meant everything to her, and for their sake and only for their sake, she had to carry on as best as she could and face the future alone. They all needed her so much now and she owed it to Michael especially, to do her very best to be a mum and a dad to them for the rest of their lives.

Daylight was a long time coming. It was a freezing cold November day again and the ice was still thick on the pavement and the road outside. The vicar said he would come over around ten thirty a.m. to discuss the funeral arrangements with Kate and the children. First, she must ring her friend Liz. She didn't want her to hear the terrible news from anyone else and as Michael and Kate were well known in the area she knew that news, especially his death, would travel very fast.

'Hi Liz, I am so sorry it's early,' it was only seven a.m. 'but last night Michael had a massive heart attack and he has died.'

'My God, Kate, oh let me just get dressed and I will be down straight away,' Liz replied. She was down at the house within half an hour and took Kate in her arms as they sobbed together like two children. They were very close friends as Liz's children and Kate's three were all the same ages. Slowly Kate relayed the previous day's events to her and they sat together hugging each other and crying at the same time. Liz knew how close Kate and Michael were, and she knew that Kate was really bad with her nerves. She knew it would be a difficult time for anyone to lose their husband, but in Kate's case this was the worst thing in the world that could happen to such a lovely and devoted family. You didn't get a much closer family than these people, and her heart ached for her friend.

After a few cups of coffee Liz said she had to go and get ready for work. She was a school secretary and she promised to ring Kate later in the day to see if she or the children needed anything. 'Thanks for coming,' Kate said, 'I'll speak to you tonight after tea, then I may know a bit more about what the next few days will have in store for us.'

She went upstairs to see the children and their faces said it all. None of them had slept properly and they didn't want any breakfast either. 'You must have something, anything, just to keep up your strength,' she told them and slowly one by one they came downstairs into the lounge. In the light of day, it looked so forlorn. The new fireplace was beautiful, just as Michael had left it. They had only had the new fire on three times if that. The wall lights were in place and the centre fittings were both up and running. There was no wallpaper on the walls as this was to be chosen the following weekend, sadly this was never going to be now, and Kate felt overwhelmed with grief as she thought of the enormity of the task that lay ahead of her. She would have to get someone to finish the lounge now but who would want to help? Suddenly she knew she would ask Peter if he would finish the room for them and she would ask Jean if she would go with her to choose some wallpaper. Yes, she thought, that's what Michael would have suggested to her. All of a sudden, she felt him beside her helping her with her thoughts and ultimately helping her with the plans. She went back upstairs after a small breakfast. She needed to be in their room near their bed, near his clothes, and she opened his wardrobe and took out his shirt and smelt it. It smelt of him, and suddenly from nowhere she thought about the mortgage and if it was due to be paid soon.

She climbed onto the bed and opened the top box where she knew he kept the mortgage book. She looked at it and found that the date was due soon and it was daunting to think she would have to go into town and pay it, something she had never ever done before. He had carried her for so many years, never failing to see to all the bills, and she prayed for him to help her still, as she now took on the role of the bread-winner. He always did the shopping too, taking Katherine with him every Tuesday night without fail. He knew exactly what to buy, what they all liked and didn't like, and now she would have to go and get it all by herself. He would set the alarm clock every night, and now she was responsible for that too. She felt totally overwhelmed with it all.

Why didn't she learn how to manage the finances when he had asked her to? He had said, 'Kate, if anything happens to me you need to know what is what.'

'Yes,' she had said flippantly, 'I will do it, in a hundred years, anyway you do it far better than me.'

'But you ought to know, Kate,' he'd said and now, how she wished she had learnt from him when he wanted her to. What a mess she was in now. She had never paid any bills, never accounted for clothes, she had let him do it all because she knew he would do a better job than her, and she wouldn't go into town anyway without him by her side. Now things had been forced on her and it was awful, she knew if he could watch over her now how distraught he would be, knowing she was not good at coping with everyday tasks, and feeling he had let her down maybe by cushioning her so much for so long. Michael was her everything. She was the cook, the bed maker, the ironer and everything domesticated as a woman could be, and he took on the roles that she could never do. Why beat yourself up, she thought, you were a loving wife and now still a devoted widow; you do everything for everyone so don't be so hard on yourself. He will always be with me, she thought, and broke down again.

SIXTEEN

The vicar arrived at ten thirty a.m. and they sat together discussing the service. The funeral director said Michael's body could not be moved until after the post-mortem which was not going to be until Thursday; that would make it the 25th of November, and then he had to be taken to the funeral home. Kate asked Mr Braithwaite if they could have the hymns 'Great Is Thy Faithfulness' and 'The Day Thou Gave Us Lord Is Ended', both of which Michael and Kate really liked. They had never discussed funerals as Michael was only forty-seven-years-old and Kate only forty-three years. It's not the type of thing up for discussion at such a young age but with the help of Richard and Ian and Katherine they put together a lovely service. At lunchtime there was a knock on the door and there stood Katherine's teacher with six pupils from her class at Pleckgate High School. They had heard of Michael's death through Kate's phone call to the school that morning and they had come to pay their respects and to show Katherine, her mum and her brothers just how sorry they all were for the family. Katherine's tutor told them how that morning he had asked for any volunteers who would like to come up to their house during their lunch break to see Katherine and her family. It was a lovely gesture and Kate thanked him for his thoughtfulness; she would never forget his kindness. He was a very good teacher at the school and the boys had been taught by him also, so he was well known to the family.

One of the doctors who Kate worked for arrived shortly after the vicar had left. She was armed with a beautiful basket of flowers and her sympathy to Kate was very touching. She had a soft spot for her receptionist and she said she would help her all she could. She asked was there anything that Kate needed urgently, and Kate said, 'No thank you.' Her boss felt so dreadfully sorry for her. The children were bewildered and as she was a GP she knew only too well what a devastating time it was for the family of someone who had suffered a sudden death. Death was horrendous for anyone, but an unexpected death was indescribable, especially in one so young as Michael, and she gave Kate a hug and told her if there was anything at all that she needed she only needed to ask. Kate thanked her and saw her to the door. The flowers came fast to the family home. Another doctor from one of the other practices sent a basket, and by the end of the second day when the announcement had been made in the evening paper, the house represented a florist shop. One lady from church brought a lovely chocolate cake and some scones; she told Kate it was something to just nibble on especially when no one could face eating a full meal. Jean and Peter's daughter Michelle helped Kate to sort out her finances; she showed her how to set up direct debits, things that Michael had been totally opposed to. He thought to pay for something before you had used it was sinful, but Kate saw it as a way of knowing exactly where she was with her money, and more importantly, what was left to play with. She was so grateful to everyone who in any small way helped her to cope with the enormity of running a home, and soon she felt she could cope financially. It was a learning process and one that she passed on to her friends who had also let their husbands do the books and run the home. Not a good move; learn now before it's forced upon you she told them.

On Friday the 26th of November, she got a phone call from the funeral home to say they had collected Michael's body from the Royal Infirmary and laid him in his coffin ready for viewing. Jean had come for the afternoon and the boys were both at home. Kate told them that she would go to the home and see Michael and the boys could go later. Katherine insisted on going with them; she was being very clingy as if she were afraid that Kate might die as well.

They set off for the funeral home and arrived after about ten minutes. Jean, Kate and Katherine were taken into a waiting room and the funeral director came in shortly. Kate said to Jean that she would go in first to see Michael and that they could go in afterwards. The director and Kate walked together down a short, dark corridor and the man entered the room first, beckoning Kate to follow him. The coffin was on a stand and the director announced he had done his best to fit on Michael's shoes. 'His feet nearly had to be broken,' he said. 'it was touch and go but we managed to get them on eventually.' It was everyday life to him she realised later but Kate had reeled at his thoughtless words. This was alien to her and although she had seen her mother dead in her coffin she was not prepared for this. She looked down the length of the beautifully polished oak coffin. It was lined with pale blue satin and there inside it lay her 'Sweetheart'. He was immaculately dressed in his best navy blue suit which was a new one bought only a few weeks before he died, he had got it for his inauguration to the 'Masons'. His ice-blue shirt and navy and grey striped tie were just as if he had dressed himself. Michael was always very smart. He even used to decorate the house in a shirt and tie and the whole family would tease him about it, but this was oh so very different, his hands were crossed graciously on his lap and she noticed right away that his bitten nails had gone black near to his fingertips. The greatest shock was still to come when the man slowly lifted the diamond shaped white lace handkerchief from off his face to reveal the rest of him. The director, realising this was an intimate moment for her, quietly slipped out of the room and gently closed the door leaving Kate there alone with him.

Kate could not bear to see him like this. She was absolutely horrified. Why did he look so different now than when she had last been shown him at the hospital? She was frightened now, where was her husband? This man was so white, so unreal and she quickly covered the handkerchief back over his face. 'God bless, sweetheart,' she murmured to him. 'I Love You, Sweetheart, you know I always will,' and with that said, she quickly walked out of the room and quietly closed the door.

It was to have been the last time she ever saw him, and she knew that Michael would have been horrified had he known she was so shocked and so scared of him. How was it possible that she could be so frightened of the man she had loved and made love with for so many years, but unfortunately, she really was. Jean and Katherine were still in the waiting room when Kate walked back in and the look that Kate gave to Jean said it all. No need for an explanation; her ashen face spoke volumes. Kate gently said to Katherine, 'I think it best if you remember Daddy as you last saw him on Tuesday evening, darling. You wouldn't like it if you saw him now.' She nodded and did as Kate had said, no fuss, no tantrums, no pleading. She just knew her mummy knew what was best for her. Kate went to find the funeral director and said to him as nicely as she could, 'Would it be all right please, have I got the right to ask you to put the lid on Michael's coffin? 'You have every right my dear,' he said, 'You are his wife.

'It's just that, I am so very sorry, and I know you have made him look lovely,' Kate stuttered, 'but you see I don't want anyone to see him like that. I want people to remember him just as he was.'

'We shall do it right away.'

'Thank you so much and I am really grateful for all you have done for him. You have dressed him immaculately,' she replied, 'I shall see you on Monday morning.

'Yes, you will, goodbye my dear, take care,' he said. They got into Jean's car and Kate burst into floods of tears.

'He doesn't look anything like Michael,' she sobbed, 'he looked like a ghost.' Jean didn't know what to say to her. Her heart went out to her and the children. What a nightmare they were going through.

They drove back to the house where the boys were waiting for them. Richard was the first to speak. 'Hey, mum, whatever is it?' he said. 'Oh, Richard, he didn't look anything like Dad. He looked so different today than he did on Tuesday.'

'Sit down, Mum,' he said, 'I'll get some tea going.' Jean said she would get off home as Peter would be in shortly for his tea, and Kate kissed her goodbye. She thanked her for taking them down to the funeral home. 'I am so sorry, Kate, that you were so shocked and frightened. Michael would have never expected you to go and see him if he had known how it has made you feel.'

'I know. I will be fine, I am just shaken up.'

'See you tomorrow,' Jean said,

'No,' Kate said, 'you have a day to yourselves, we will be all right, I have so much that I can do and I need to sort myself out for the funeral service on Monday. Really I mean it. Thanks for all you are doing for us. I am sorry I am taking all your time.'

'That's what sisters are for,' she said. 'I'll ring you sometime tomorrow and if you change your mind it's no problem, I can still see you.' Kate waved her goodbye and went back into the lounge, then into the kitchen to see what Richard was preparing for tea. 'I asked them to put the lid on, Richard,' she said,

'Why Mum?'

'He looked so awful, he didn't look anything like Dad and I don't want anyone seeing him like that. He wouldn't have wanted it either.'

'Ok, Mum, you know best. It's our dad and your husband, you did what he would have wanted. Sit down and I will make the tea then we will get out the photographs of him doing the back garden and you can remember him again as he was. Besides it will replace the awful image you have of him today.'

After tea, a knock came to the door. It was Bernadette, who worked with Kate at the practice as the practice nurse and she had seen Michael for his well man check-up. 'I am so sorry, Kate,' she said. 'Tell me what happened.' Kate told her the whole sorry story from Tuesday to now and Bernadette said she should always remember that Michael would have known that they were all with him on the landing. 'How would he, if he was unconscious?' said Ian.

'The hearing is the last thing that dies in someone, so he would have known you were there helping him.'

'So, Dad would have known that Richard was trying CPR on him?' Ian said.

'Yes, he would.'

'So, when it shows someone dying on the television and they have an out of body experience he might have been in the top corner of the landing looking down on us trying to save him?' Ian continued.

'Yes, most probably, sweetheart,' Kate said. 'let's just cling on to that and hope that he did.' Neighbours and friends were a constant stream of visitors to the house. The evening paper had announced Michael's death and people whom Kate and the children had not seen or heard from for years were ringing or calling in to show them all their sympathy.

The hearse arrived on Monday morning the 29th of November 1993. A day Kate and the children would never forget. Kate asked a neighbour to mind the house as they knew it would be a long day and someone had suggested a house minder in case of a burglary. That would really have put the top hat on things and something they did not need. Kate felt numb as the hearse waited outside the front door full of flowers; it was as if this was happening to someone else and she was watching from a distance. She didn't even remember climbing into the car, it was as if she was being carried along by everyone else. St James Church was full to capacity; you could not get one more person through the door. The gallery upstairs was full too, and people were standing in the aisles. It was a beautiful service. 'How Great Thou Art' and 'The Day Thou Gavest Lord Is Ended' were ringing out. The vicar, Mr Braithwaite, spoke with great warmth of Michael, how he was a sidesman at church and a devoted husband and father. He spoke of his work and the colleagues he had left behind, and his enjoyment in the Masons. Most of all he spoke of his untimely death and of leaving his wife and three lovely children who now had to face the rest of their lives without him.

Kate put her arms around the three children as they tried to sing the hymns through their tears. Katherine wore the black velvet hat that had been bought for her by her dad the week before he died and she wouldn't take it off. It was as if he were watching her every move from a distance and she wanted to show him how much she loved it.

Kate was so proud of the way they were coping with their father's funeral, but everyone who witnessed that day in church knew they were looking at a broken-hearted family. The day was bitterly cold with freezing fog and frost. Michael was buried at a cemetery in Blackburn. Kate watched as they lowered her beloved husband into the ground. They had briefly talked together of death, but Michael had said in the past that when he died he wanted to be buried, and Kate was now fulfilling his wishes. The coffin seemed to go down and down and the further down it went the more unbearable it was to watch. Forty-three years old and burying her husband, how cruel could this be. Her family by her side, all feeling bereft and her heart truly and utterly broken. She didn't want him to be buried where the grave was. It was near to the woods and quite eerie but, the truth was, nowhere would have suited her. She just wanted him home, and no matter how much she pleaded with God to give him back to her she knew that this was where he would always be from now on, until she would see him again in Heaven above.

The family and mourners went back to the house after the burial, but Kate only put on tea and biscuits for everyone. As grateful as she was to them all for their support, all she just wanted was for them all to go home and leave them alone. No one could do anything for them any more. The worst scenario had happened and unfortunately, she had the rest of her life to get used to it. People meant well, and she was grateful to all of them for the help she had been given. The lady from church who had made a lovely chocolate cake, the many flowers and a hundred sympathy cards at least which had dropped through the letter box. The post office had to band them together as there were so many, but Kate needed to gather her thoughts together and to be with her children and one by one, they left the house. Most of them promised her they would keep in touch and that she only needed to ask if she wanted anything at all no matter how large or small.

Tuesday the 30th of November saw the children going back to work and school. They had to get back to normal, but what was normal? She had lost all thought of normality. The thought of going back to work was overwhelming and daunting. On the one hand she wanted desperately to see her work friends but she didn't want to face everyone either, especially the patients, many of whom she knew so well. On the following Monday, she did just that and her friends were delighted to see her. Many didn't know what to say and some said the wrong thing, like you need to get a dog then you can go for walks with it. Some never said anything for fear of Kate breaking down in tears. Others cried with her, in particular her boss. One of the male doctors and none of them whoever they were, made her feel she was a burden, as they listened to her endlessly, trying to accept her predicament, and they all offered as much support to her as she needed. Soon it was Christmas and the countdown to it was miserable. Kate got the rest of the presents together for the boys and Katherine, she wrote the Christmas cards to family and friends which was awful, especially having to omit Michael's name on every one of them. She cried so much that she was worn out.

SEVENTEEN

On Christmas morning Kate got up to put the turkey in the oven. It was pitch black outside and she put the lights on under the kitchen units and started to wash the turkey. She got the roasting tin out of the cupboard and stood crying. Michael had always cooked the turkey and she had let him. Now she had no idea how long to cook it for, or even what temperature to put the oven on. Out loud she sobbed, 'Michael, please help me. I don't know what to do.' Suddenly she remembered the turkey foil and surely there on the packet were the oven temperatures and the times for which to cook it, depending on its weight. 'Thank you, sweetheart,' she whispered. 'I know you will always be by my side. You said you would always be on my shoulder no matter what, and you have kept your word to me.' There has to be more than life here on earth, she thought. He is only a whisper away and although I cannot see him I know that he is very near, watching me and guiding me.

Kate had bought Michael a Christmas card. She didn't need to search very far to find it. It read:

---- My Special Christmas Gift to You My Husband ----
MICHAEL

This Christmas I'd like to give you something special
A present no one else could give
But it's hard to find a gift
To express the depth of my emotions
Or my gratitude for all the things we already have
Together, we have created and given the things that are truly important
Our hopes, our dreams, and our shared moments

This Christmas my husband,

I'd like to give you something that will show you how much I cherish us

And the relationship we have together.

My gift to you is

The reaffirmation of my love;

The reassurance that now and forever you have the most precious gifts I could give;

My heart, my soul, and my love always.

Merry Christmas

With Love, Always

Your Devoted Kate xxxxxxxxxxxxxxx 1993

Kate and Ian and Katherine went to Jean and Peter's on Boxing Day for a meal. Richard went to stay with his girlfriend in Wrexham near Wales. It was hard trying to be cheerful when their hearts were not in it. Christmas, after all, was for families and this family was newly bereaved. Kate just wanted to go home, she had to get back there. It was the only place she felt near to him, the only place she could cry and pine without someone saying, come on it will be okay, when she knew without a doubt it would never be okay ever again. They left Jean's house at eight o'clock that night and Kate, Ian and Katherine thanked them both for a lovely meal. Kate couldn't bear to see them together; it cut through her like a knife, but she was glad also that Jean was not going through this hell and that they still had each other. They were as devoted as Kate and Michael had been and Kate knew the depth of love they both felt for their husbands was rare. If only Michael were here she could have coped with anything, but without him she was nothing. He had been her world, her night and her day, her summer and her winter, her everything. How could she explain to anyone just how she felt? All her friends and relations were together, married or living with their partners and the odd few who were divorced or single chose that way of life; she on the other hand had been given this life and she asked God over and over again WHY?

What did I do for you to take my Michael away? She asked in her prayers. She started to hate God and she started resenting the lovely hymns she had sung in praise at his funeral. The anger was developing now adding to her misery. When they arrived home she tore down the Christmas tree and put it outside the back door; she couldn't bear to see it again decorated beautifully and for who to see? Ian and Katherine were dismayed. 'Why have you done that, Mum?' they asked, 'because I can't stand anymore of Christmas,' she replied.

'Please, Mum, put it back up as Dad would have wanted,' said Richard gently, when he rang home. So Kate went outside and brought in the tree and they helped her to re-decorate it. That night she rang the Samaritans switchboard and talked to a lady about how she was feeling. The lady said it was understandable as it had only been four weeks since he had died and that she should just give herself some time. She thanked her and put down the phone. How on earth does she know what I am going through, Kate thought. She probably has a husband at home waiting for her right now.

Bitterness was not Kate's forte, but she found herself feeling it more and more. Someone at work suggested Cruise, the organisation for the bereaved. They met at a nursing home down on Preston New Road and Kate went one Tuesday evening just to see if it would help her. It was no good asking for advice from people if she was not going to take it. When she arrived, she was shocked to see the age group of the people there. They were all old-age pensioners, talking of selling raffle tickets and doing a tombola. This is not for me, she thought and then someone came across and asked her her name. 'Kate,' she said shyly.

'How long have you been widowed?' they asked.

'Two months,' Kate could feel the tears starting to well up in her eyes. 'You must come again next month,' the lady said, 'we are a friendly lot here and you are more than welcome to join us.'

'Thank you very much,' said Kate. 'I will see, as I have got children at home and I don't like to leave them for too long.'

'Very well,' the lady said, 'I shall look forward to seeing you next time.' Kate left shortly afterwards, and walking back to the car she took a deep breath of the cold winter air. She climbed into the silver Ford Sierra and drove herself home.

'How did it go, Mum?' said Katherine when she arrived home. 'Not so good, sweetheart, they are all a hundred and five there, if a day!' They laughed at that and Kate said she would rather be at home with them even if it was lonely without Michael; at least she was with her kids, their kids, and they were her salvation. What on earth would she do without them? They were her reason for living, her reason for climbing in that lonely double bed at night all by herself and for waking up each morning, for she knew the way she felt right now, she would not be here at all if it wasn't for them.

February 1994 arrived and the thought of St Valentine's Day without Michael was unbearable. She did however receive a Valentine's Day card, but only from an insensitive insurance company advertising their goods and whom she had already informed of his death. Angry and hurt, she rang them and gave them a piece of her mind. They apologised for the error, but it was too late; the hurt was already there, eating away at her and with no sign at the moment of any let-up. Her birthday arrived too, the 28th of February, and she had already dreaded the day. It took her over an hour to open the cards sent from her family and friends, all chosen with the right words so as to cause her the least pain possible, and through her tears she gently placed them on the unit. She didn't really want to put them up at all; she just wanted to go back to her bed and waste away the day. She pretended Michael would come home at lunchtime with a lovely bunch of flowers and a card saying: **To My Darling Kate. Happy Birthday Sweetheart, All My Love Today, Tomorrow and Forever Love Michael xxxxxxxxxx**

He had always written those words on every card he'd sent to her; Christmas, Valentine, Birthday and Anniversary cards were all finished with the same loving words. His devotion to her was unfailing and she knew he never would have left her had he had the choice, but there was no card this year and there never would be again.

Grief, she had read in the daily newspaper, is the price you pay for loving someone. How very true that is and what is grief? Grief is wanting to be with someone so badly you want to die too. It is the worst feeling imaginable. It is the aching feeling deep in the pit of your stomach that tells you we were put on this earth to love and be loved, and that now with this person, this will be no more. It's crying constantly for that someone, calling out their name and knowing they can't hear you or comfort you. It's that wondering, where did they go? Are they safe? Do they miss you too and want to come back? In Michael's case that was a certainty; he definitely would have wanted to come back home, or are they so far away in Heaven above that it's impossible to feel anything anymore? Grief, the empty bed, the needing to love and be loved, and then realising those days of lovemaking are now over, and at only forty-four-years-old, no one is there any more to hold you and caress you, to tell you they love you more than anything or anyone else in the whole wide world. Grief is walking down the street and seeing a person wearing a coat or a jacket and thinking and praying it's them wearing it, only to come face to face and realise they look nothing like your loved one, but it was a lovely moment to savour and worth deceiving yourself for. It's playing love songs that keep you ever near to each other, and it's believing against all the odds, that you will see each other again, not in this life but in the next.

Kate would recite in her head over and over again the words from the memoriams in the evening paper. Lonely is the home without you, life to us is not the same, all the world would be like heaven if I could have you back again. She knew them all off by heart and she bought cards to write to him; she put them on the top of the television and read them over and over again out loud.

------------------- For My Loving Husband -------------------
I looked to you for happiness,
And you brought it without even trying
I turned to you for comfort
And your arms were open wide,

I've shared all the joys of life with you,
All the ups and downs, and little pleasures
That make a life together so rewarding,
And through them learned how precious
Love can be between a husband and wife

Michael
I'll always owe my happiness to you
My husband, my lifelong love
I want to be with you, Sweetheart
I don't want to live without you
Wait for me, Sweetheart
Today, Tomorrow and Forever

I love you, Kate xxxxxxxxxxxxxxxxxxxxxxxxxx

They were desperate days. She tried to comfort the children, but they were grieving by themselves. She was struggling to hold herself together let alone cope with them too, but she did her best for them and most of all she loved them with her whole being. They were everything to her and all she had left to live for. The children and Kate talked constantly of him. His memory they knew would never ever be allowed to fade. A bereavement counsellor suggested they bought a treasure chest to keep Michael's things in, like his toothbrush, car keys, glasses, driving licence and anything else that they could just look into the chest and remember him by.

Soon it was the summer July 1994 and the thought of going on holiday without Michael was the farthest thing from their minds. Katherine suggested they got a rabbit to cheer them up a bit. So Kate and the children went to buy a hutch, and the new arrival to the Abbotts family was a white fluffy ball of wool, and Katherine named her Flopsy. The school holidays were upon them now and Kate and Katherine walked together along the riverbank. The birds were singing, and the sky was blue, but it might as well have been pouring with rain as neither of them even noticed the summer at all. They felt totally abandoned and ever so lost. It was a long six weeks. Richard carried on at work, and Ian played out on his bike or hung around with his friends, and they all just got through it the best that they could. The weekends were the worst, as everyone had their husbands and dads with them, and the adjustment was proving very hard.

People suggested what they ought to do and where they ought to go, but Kate was in denial; she realised she was only waiting for a miracle to happen and for Michael to suddenly walk through the door and make everything all right again. How he was loved and missed no one could ever know, except those who had shared a love like theirs and had worshipped a dad so rare.

Kate carried on buying cards. Every time she went into town she would go in a card shop and look under the headings 'Thinking of You'.

YOU'RE ALWAYS WITH ME EVEN WHEN WE ARE APART

Whenever we're apart and I am feeling all alone.
I close my eyes and think of all the happiness we've known...
I think of how your loving smile, is such a precious sight,
And how your arms around me feel so comforting and right,
I think of how I'm free to be myself when I'm with you,
And how you make so much in life seem wonderful and new.
And somehow, I feel better then, because I clearly see,
Since I hold you close within my heart,
You're always here with me

I love you so much my precious Michael.
My World
My Life
My Loss
All My Love Forever
Yours Kate xxxxx

As the first anniversary of Michael's death approached, Kate tried to be strong. She was frightened of losing her friends, not their sympathy, she did not want that; she just wanted to be able to say with conviction, I am okay, don't worry about me, but they read her like a book. They knew she wasn't okay, she was just surviving. 'Please, Kate,' Chrisanna said one day when they were talking on the phone, 'I know you are far from all right so why don't you go and see your GP and see what he says?'

'I don't want tranquillisers again,' she said. 'I had a terrible job getting off them before.'

'I know, you don't need to have anything you don't want, but go and talk to John; you like him, and he may suggest some help.'

'How can anyone help me?' she shouted in exasperation. 'No one knows what the hell to say to me let alone how to help me. I'm sorry, Chrisanna, I know you are trying to help me, but I just want to be with him, can't you understand that?' 'Of course I can Kate. I know you were so close to Michael but it's not that simple. You have the children to consider, you can't just curl up and die too. Life isn't like that. For Michael's sake, you have to keep going. You have done so good, love, and you have an inner strength from somewhere. I am so proud of you and I know I don't know what you are going through right now, but there will be someone else, Kate, in the future.'

'But I don't want anybody else and even if I did there are no widowers my age around.'

'Glenda said that Frank, her partner, said, "tell Kate, 'don't ever close the door, there is always someone for everybody and she will find love again.'

'I'll bear it in mind, Chrisanna, I know you are trying to help me. I wish it was that simple.'

As December 1994 approached, Kate went Christmas shopping and as usual she first found a card for Michael.

A Christmas Wish List

Of all the things, I wish for you,

I would give anything if these wishes could always come true.

To My Sweetheart Michael

I want you to be happy. I want you to fill your heart
With feelings of wonder and to be full of courage
and I want you to have the type of friendship that is a treasure
And the kind of love that is beautiful forever
I wish you contentment: the sweet, quiet, inner kind
That comes around and never goes away
I want you to have hopes and have them all come true
I want you to make the most of this moment in time
And rare you truly are. I want to remind you that the sun
May disappear for a while, but it never forgets to shine
I want you to have faith. May you have feelings that are
Shared from heart to heart, simple pleasures amidst this complex
world and wonderful goals that are in your grasp.
May the words you listen to say the things you need to hear.
And may a cheerful face lovingly look back at you when you happen
to glance in your mirror.
I wish you the insight to see your inner and outer beauty. I wish you
sweet dreams. I want you to have the times
When you feel like singing and dancing and laughing out loud.
I want you to be able to make your good times better and your hard
times easier to handle.
I want you to have millions of moments when you find satisfaction
in the things you do so wonderfully.
And I wish I could find a way to tell you ~ in untold ways how
important you are to me.
Of all the things I'll be wishing for, wherever you are and whatever
I may do, there will never be a day in my life when I won't be wishing
for the best for you.

Wishing you a Merry Christmas and a Happy New Year
God bless you my Darling and keep you safe in Heaven above.
"Wait for me sweetheart"

All my love Today, Tomorrow and Forever
Your Darling Wife Kate xxxxxxxx

Kate thought about what Chrisanna had said to her and she made an appointment the following day to see John. He was a lovely person and a good doctor. He had a perfect bedside manner. 'Hi Kate, come on in. Good morning, how are you and what can I do for you?'

'I am really struggling, John,' she said. 'to be truthful I feel I am getting nowhere. If I could just lift this heavy burden off my shoulders for even a day it would help, but I can't, and I feel like I am sinking fast.'

He looked at her with sadness in his eyes. He liked her; she was a good receptionist, always polite to the patients and everybody loved Kate. He had never heard anyone call her and he knew she knew her job inside out. 'How would you feel about talking to a bereavement counsellor up at the hospital?' he said,

'I could give it a try,' Kate replied. 'anyone or anything if you think it will help.'

'Yes I do, you see that's a counsellor's job, to help people like you through the grieving process. As you know Kate, there are many different stages of grief and you need to go through them all to come out of it at the other end. They may not all be in the order you would imagine them to be, but they all need to be faced.' John sat back in his chair, gave Kate a wink and said, 'I will dictate a letter after surgery and let's get all the help for you that we can.'

'Thanks, John, I really do appreciate this,' she said. 'I will get back to reception now and let you heal the sick.'

EIGHTEEN

It wasn't long before Kate received an appointment to go up to the local hospital. She followed the signs for the outpatients' department which was classed as the mental health team. That alone was un-nerving as she didn't feel mentally ill, but she knew she needed help, and this was hopefully where she was going to get it. In the waiting room, she nearly did a runner. Could she face this alone? What was there to be achieved by pouring out her heart to a stranger? But she knew that she must do it and she waited for her name to be called. Suddenly there was a man standing in the corridor calling her name. 'Good afternoon, Mrs Abbotts, I would very much like to help you if I can? Please come in and take a seat.' Gingerly she sat down in a dark brown, worn-out armchair. She wondered how many other people had felt the same as her on their first encounter with this forty-something gentleman who dressed like he lived in the seventies era. The room was very small, with dark and dowdy walls which needed a good painting. The floor was covered in a red faded carpet with precious little else in the room except an old coffee table.

Kate thanked him for seeing her so soon after he had received the referral from John. He politely acknowledged her and asked her to give him a brief account of her life. Kate started by saying, 'My father was killed in a car crash in 1964, when I was just fourteen, my mother died of cancer in 1974, when I was twenty-four and then last year my husband, Michael, collapsed in our bathroom and died of a massive heart attack. He was just forty-seven-years-old.'

'How old are you, Mrs Abbotts? Sorry could I call you Kate?'

'Of course yes, please do,' she replied. 'I am forty-four-years-old.' She carried on, 'I have three children. Richard aged twenty, Ian is fifteen and Katherine is twelve.' He asked her a few other questions and then said, 'Kate, what an incredibly sad story you have told me. I am so very sorry for you'. Kate could feel the tears well up in her eyes. 'Yes, I am afraid it is,' she said. 'my relations are all dead except I have two wonderful sisters. One lives locally in Darwen but the other one lives in the North-East. My grandparents all died when I was little, and my two aunties from my mum's side died in the eighties. They lived a full life though and they were both old when they died.'

'Michael, you see, was my rock, my nerves have been bad for most of my married life and he was always there for me. He paid the bills, did the shopping and he looked after the children when I worked in the evening at the health centre.'

'Do you still work evenings?' he said.

'Yes, although I have dropped one of the evenings, so I am at work on a Monday evening then off on a Tuesday, working Wednesday evening and off Thursday, back in for Friday evening. The children are so good. I know they are teenagers, but they just get on with things when I am not there. Katherine makes the tea with the help of Ian and Richard if they are around. I am so very lucky to have them; they are the only reason for living and I feel so guilty when I just want to be with their dad. It's difficult to explain why I so much want to die. On the one hand I couldn't live without my kids, but on the other I don't want to be without Michael, and the only people I know who are without a husband are so much older than me. Friends mean well but they go home to their other halves and I go to bed alone.'

'Have you tried going out with your friends, Kate?'

'I don't want to, they ask me all the time, but I always say no,'

'Maybe you should start to say 'Yes, and give it a try.'

The session all too soon was ended and it was one of many sessions that Kate attended, in fact she never missed an appointment with him. He was a very good listener, except the time when Kate caught him trying to stifle a yawn. He didn't realise she had seen him and she felt sorry that he had to listen to this endless misery.

One day she decided to wear her new jacket and best shoes, to get really dressed up and go to one of the sessions; she was sick of them being unworn and left to hang in the wardrobe. When she got to the hospital he asked her why she was so dressed up, and she said she wasn't. She hoped he didn't think she fancied him because as nice as the guy was with her, he certainly was not her type. After many months of these sessions she told him she was not going to go for any more counselling after that one had finished, and he was shocked. 'Thank you, Dave, for all you have done for me,' she said, 'but you can't do the impossible and that's to bring back my Michael for me and that's all I really want you to do. I have cried a million tears for him, brought you the letters to show you that you have told me to write and I think I thought you could work a miracle and make him come home to me. I see now it was all wishful thinking and I was in a make-believe land.' 'Please try to join a club or something, Kate,' he said softly. 'you are too young to sit at home day in and day out. Why not try Cruise the bereavement group?'

'I have done,' she said. 'they were all a hundred and nine,' and she laughed. He smiled too and said to let him know how her life was going in the future, and she thanked him again for his time and patience. 'You help all those who are drug addicts and gamblers. They need you and you will see their achievements. You can't do the impossible for me although I know you would do if only you could,' she said kindly. 'Good luck, Kate, take care,'

'You too,' she said, and she walked down the hospital corridor with a very heavy heart. What did she really expect from the guy she really didn't know, but she knew one thing for sure; she was now on her own and whatever would be would be.

When she went home and in the months ahead, Kate buried her head into more and more bereavement books, desperately looking for an answer. She often went to the bookshop in Blackburn town centre and scoured the shelves where she found some comfort in knowing that the authors who had written these books had also been this way too, that they also understood the depth of her despair. She found herself nodding to the descriptions of the empty bed, she acknowledged the fact that she missed terribly making love with her beloved Michael. She missed his arms wrapped around her in the privacy of their room. She remembered again him saying to her in the kitchen not long before he died, how much she still turned him on even after twenty-two years of marriage. She longed for the warmth of his long body next to hers in their bed, the bed that together they had shared all their married life, the snuggles she had always loved, sleeping in spoons, as well as all the other times of their lives that they would never be able to share again.

The caravan that she had found a haven in had to be sold; she would never be able to tow it, not with it being sixteen-foot-long. One of the girls at work said she would love it, and bit by bit everything that had been in their lives together was now no more. Their car was a silver Ford Sierra, only bought in the March before Michael died. Richard said it was too big for Kate, especially the consumption of petrol and besides, with no caravan to pull she didn't need an eighteen hundred engine. Richard and Kate went to the local Peugeot garage and Kate traded in the Sierra and she bought a new 307 in Pacific Blue.

When she picked it up the following weekend with Katherine, they went down onto the market car park. The electric window came out of the socket on the outside of the car instead of on the inside, and that was the start of all the problems with that car, and she faced them all alone.If only Michael had been around he would have demanded a refund. It rained in, it was noisy, the windows rattled constantly and it was in the garage seventeen times in the first twelve months. Life in the North East wasn't very good either as Glenda and Tom had unfortunately got divorced. They had been married for well over twenty-five years, but their relationship had become stale. It was sad in a way as Tom was lonely and it didn't help when Glenda set up home with Frank, one of their friends.

Glenda asked Kate and Katherine if they would like to go up to the North East for a weekend; she said it would do both of them good to get away from four walls. Despite the car causing so much trouble since it had been bought, it drove like a dream and Kate was proud to have driven so far, one hundred and twenty miles in total which she thought she could never do without Michael at her side. Katherine was a comfort though and they arrived there safely and as she was driving along the roads she felt Michael's presence with her all the way. The weekend was a nice break and Glenda said how well Kate looked although she knew she was far from okay. It broke her heart to see her little sister so distraught. Early on the Sunday afternoon Kate said she needed to get home to the boys. In truth, it was too painful to be with them both, seeing how in love they were and quite rightly so as they had both been through a pretty rough time in recent months. The second anniversary of Michael's death was fast approaching, the summer and autumn long gone. One Saturday evening Kate had had enough, enough of being lonely, enough of watching the television and enough of her sad, sad life. Richard had gone to Wrexham to see Amanda, his girlfriend, and Ian was out with his friends. Katherine was asking if Kate could take her and her friend down town to the cinema and after Kate had dropped them off, she made up her mind to go out by herself.

She went home and got showered and changed, made herself look lovely and went up to the pub in Ribchester where Michael used to take her on the odd occasion they went out together. At first, she sat on the car park and tried to gather herself together. Should she turn and run or be brave and go inside? After about five minutes deliberating, she locked the car door and went around to the front of the pub and next thing she knew she was in the front door. Slowly she made her way to the bar. The barman saw her out of the corner of his eye and came over to serve her. 'Yes, please what can I get you?'

'A Britvic orange please,' she said.

'Do you want some ice in it?'

'Yes, just a little thanks.'

'Nice evening isn't it?' he said.

'Yes it's not too cold,' she replied. She took the glass of orange, thanked him and paid for it and she looked around for somewhere to sit. In the other room adjoining the bar was a television talking to itself and she slowly ventured inside. No one was in there, whew, what a stroke of luck; everyone in the bar had been with someone eating a bar snack and mainly male and female together, but in here she was all alone.

She sat down and started to watch the television, hoping and praying that no one would come in and start to talk to her. Slowly she drank the orange juice and started to relax. She was so pleased with herself, firstly for being brave enough to get dressed up and go out on her own, and secondly for sitting down long enough to drink it. Suddenly, she glanced up at the television screen and, shock and horror, whatever film was on, the lady was undoing her suspenders and taking off her stockings. Kate knew she could not sit watching the film, whatever it was, any longer. She quickly finished her drink, and leaving her glass on the table, she reluctantly walked out of the pub door.

Well Kate, you old bugger, she said to herself, you did something you never thought you could do in a month of Sundays and more to the point you survived it, girl! She went back to her car. The car park was quiet and lonely and she felt very vulnerable on her own. She climbed in quickly and started the engine, steering the car gently onto the road and headed down the lane towards the village of Ribchester, then on towards Blackburn and home. She knew that Michael would have been so proud of her for her spirit and of that she was very sure. When Katherine rang to ask if she would go back to the cinema and pick them up she told her where she had been. 'Mum,' she cried, 'how could you go out on your own? What would people think of you if they knew you were a widow? Did you not feel uncomfortable by yourself?'

'No, I just needed to have some normality again, Katherine, and have some me time, some grown-up time and I was so proud of myself. It's made me feel like a lady again. I'm on my way now to pick you up sweetheart, I won't be long, love.'

On the Monday, Kate told the girls at work where she had been on Saturday evening. Some were shocked, some said, 'good on you, girl,' and the others kept their thoughts to themselves, but Kate didn't need their approval. She only knew that if any one of them had been in her position not one of them could have said they would, or they wouldn't have done it too. Kate spoke to her friend Fran about it when they went back on the evening shift and she said she was proud of her but to be very careful when she went out alone.

NINETEEN

On November 11th, 1995 Kate was at a loss again. It was to be another lonely Saturday night and with the second anniversary of Michael's death looming, she decided to go out to another pub. This time she went to the Rock Inn at Tockholes near Darwen. She pulled up onto the car park and went inside. This time the pub was heaving, it was a popular place especially on a weekend and she should have known it would be, but nevertheless she went into the bar and ordered her usual Britvic orange juice. The barman was an elderly gentleman who was helping his son and daughter-in-law, with it being a busy Saturday night. There were many couples sat close together chatting away and at first Kate felt that she was coping quite well. She had only drunk a quarter way down the glass when the friendly old gentleman came across to her whilst collecting the glasses from the next table. He gently lent across the table and said to Kate, 'Has he stood you up tonight, love?' Suddenly she started to cry, tears pouring down her cheeks and she wanted to say to him, 'No, no he's not stood me up, he's laid dead in a coffin in the cemetery.' She quickly flew towards the bar and slid her half-full glass of orange juice along the counter. She didn't wait to see where it landed and with tears blinding her eyes, she ran towards the door and to her car, where she flicked the remote and, flashing the hazard warning lights, let herself into the driver's door.

Kate could not remember the journey home. She sobbed so hard all the way shaking and crying uncontrollably. She flung open the porch door then the lounge door to a totally startled Katherine and Ian.

'Mum, whatever is the matter?' they cried. 'Come in and take off your coat.'

'Oh my God, do you know what this man said to me in the Rock at Tockholes?'

'No,' Katherine said. 'Oh, Mum, please sit down. Do you want a cup of tea?'

'No thank you. I am so sorry, I didn't mean to come home in such a state, but he asked me,' she stuttered, 'if, if my date had stood me up. I couldn't get out fast enough and I wanted to say to him, you don't understand; he's dead and he's laid in the cemetery. He would have come to the pub if only he could.'

'Mum, you mustn't go out again on your own. I know you are trying to get back to normal,' Ian said. 'This just isn't working for you.'

'I know,' Kate said, 'it was okay last time, but I can't put myself through it again, I just can't.'

'Come on, Mum, we will watch the television together. Tomorrow is another day,' Katherine said. She was so afraid for her mum going out alone especially now with the freezing cold nights; anything could happen to her and that was a terrifying thought in itself.

Kate stayed with them for a while and then she went up to bed. 'Oh, Michael, she cried to the empty room. When will this nightmare ever end? I am so lonely without you and even though I have our lovely children for comfort I need you so very much.' Long and hard she cried into the night, muffling the sound of her sobs with his pillow, the pillow he would never lay his head on again. The bed seemed bigger than ever and when she woke up on the Sunday morning she felt worn out and terribly anxious. In the afternoon, it became sunny, so she got in the car and drove up Revidge Road, stopping near a path that led to an old disused water tank. She got out of the car and walked up the steep path to the top of the hill, climbed up the steps onto the tank itself where there was a public look-out point. The view was spectacular; Blackpool lay on the west coast, and farther along the water's edge lay Morecambe and the Lake District and then on to Barrow-in-Furness with Cumbria following that. Kate stood and looked at the view; there was actually a 360-degree view as behind her were the towns of Blackburn and Darwen with Winter Hill in the far distance with its tall television masts sitting proud on the top of the hill sending signals to the hundreds of people in their houses around town, each of them enjoying watching their own chosen channel.

The sun was now shining high in the sky, shimmering on the sea in the far distance. After about quarter of an hour she had had enough of her own company and decided to head back down the path for home. As she approached the main road to get into her car, she saw to her right a white van speeding down the road towards her. She suddenly thought, if I step out now in front of this van, I can be with him, be back in his arms forever and everything will be all right again. That's all its going to take, just one small step. The van was getting nearer and nearer, her heart was racing, and her thoughts were only of him, it would be that easy. As she walked into the road to get into her car she realised that she had actually let the van go past her. She got into the driver's seat, turned on the engine and headed for home. She felt ashamed of herself for being so selfish. She had so wanted to be with her darling Michael again that she had temporarily clouded her vision, but what about the children, what on earth would become of them? There was no grandma or grandad to look after them, and their nanna, Michael's mum, had little or no time for kids at all. Whatever had she been thinking of, had they not suffered enough with the loss of their beloved dad, whose premature death was a tragedy in itself and also unavoidable, without losing their beloved mum too, when her death could have been avoided? Kate opened the door and saw their faces. 'Hi Mum, did you have a nice walk? Where did you go?' said Ian. 'Just up to the tank and back. Yes thanks, it was lovely up there. The sun was shining, and the birds were singing, but I am so glad to be home with you two guys.'

The winter months were already upon them and the anniversary date of Michael's death was fast approaching. Kate could not believe it was nearly two years since he had gone away. She prayed for him every day without fail, never left the house without saying goodbye to him and still thought of him constantly. Days at work were better for her; she threw herself into her job and kept as cheerful as she could. Her friends at the health centre however could see right through her. They knew she was really no nearer getting through her bereavement than she had been months before. It was a heartache none of them wanted to experience, but all of them knew that one day they would. One day Kate decided to take the advice of the bereavement counsellor. He had told her to write a letter to Michael, to put down on paper all her feelings and all she would have said to him had he lived. How she felt without him and basically anything and everything she wanted to talk to him about but now couldn't.

Here is the letter she wrote: - 12/10/95

My Darling Michael,

I know that you will never read this letter unless you are sat on my shoulder whilst I am writing it. I really hope you are, sweetheart. I miss you so much. I feel I can't stand any more of this grief without you to share it with. I want to see you, to touch you, to feel you in my arms and I know I never shall again. How can I explain to anyone except you how I feel? We shared every joy and sorrow for twenty-four years. I feel I have been cut in half, every day I feel like I am slowly dying without you. I wake up and it starts all over again; each day is the same, the pain goes on and on. Without you by my side I don't want to live. Nothing makes me feel happy any more. A lovely day means nothing, and my life is so empty it's hard to put into words. I want to walk in the fields, but only if you are by my side. I want to see the sea again down by the crabbing bridge, to see the Needles but only with you, and I know I never will again. I know you would never have left me if you could have helped it, and worst of all we never said goodbye. All my life I shall never forget your lovely face on the landing, when I stroked your cheek saying, 'Wake up, sweetheart, please wake up,' but you had already gone from my life and you could not come back. I don't know where to start to pick up the pieces of my broken dreams, I don't know how to live without you, Michael. How do you live in Heaven without me? Do you cry for me like I cry for you? Do you miss me every waking minute and be glad to go to sleep to shut out the world for just a few hours? Is Heaven like Hell without me? I was not prepared for losing you, sweetheart. I never would have been, even with time, but so quickly, so quietly, you had gone forever, and, in my heart, I know you did not suffer for very long. It had to be like this, for you were too special to have suffered long. God must have thought so too. It's Christmas in a few weeks, another Christmas without you. I can't see another hour in front of me let alone another Christmas. How many more Christmases before we can be together forever? I went to Ribchester today, then up past Sale Wheel Woods. Do you remember when we went there just the two of us on August Bank Holiday Monday 1993? Everywhere I go, I only have lovely memories of you, of times we spent together. We will never have times together again, sweetheart, not on this earth. Thank you for all your love to me, for all the millions of times you have been there for me when I have needed you, and for our three lovely children who remind me of you, each in their own special way. Ian, he looks so much like you, he thinks like you and talks like you, his knowledge is widespread, and he remembers things like you. Richard, he is as tall as you, he is the only person in this world who puts his arms around me, and Katherine, how she cares for me and would make things better if only she could. All their ways are part of you and so much more.

Michael, my love for you is beyond words; it is for all eternity. I shall keep you in my heart forever until the day I am in your arms again.

Wait for me, sweetheart
Your Darling Wife
Kate.xxxxxxxxxxxxxxxxxxxxxxxxxxxxxxxxxxxxxxxxxxxxxxxxxxxxx
Twelve days later Kate wrote to him again - 22/10/95

My Darling Michael,
I need to talk to you, like so many times in my life I've needed you to help me. I can't stop crying. If it is not openly, it is inside. I want to tell you how I feel. I feel totally alone in this grief. It's so easy for people to say how well I look, if only they knew what was going on inside they would never say it. I am glad they don't see the real me inside. I am not a pretty sight to say the least. I am lost, desperately lonely, confused, empty, sometimes bitter, and always seeking for an answer. My books

help but I know the answer is only in ME. I hate the way I feel, but it is out of my control at the moment. Life really has taken its toll on me. I am frightened without you. You have always been there for me. I need you so much, I always have done, and I know I can't have the impossible, yesterday and you. It's days like today that I am glad you are buried. I need to come and talk to you and to know your body is still here on this earth with me. Your grave is one of many, I am one of many, all feeling the same emptiness that comes with losing someone you have built your world around. You are still my world, Michael, I think of only you, I can't get you out of my mind. I don't want to do, but neither can I go on punishing myself like this. I don't want to, and I won't go back on my tablets although I know I really should do, but I will come back to this again and I must go through it now. I can't delay these feelings any longer. I see couples walking together and my first check is, are they holding hands? I want to go up to them and say please hold his hand because one day you may not be able to; do it whilst you have time. I can't make the world as I'd like it to be, not everyone is like we were, nor do they want to be. I hope you are happy, at least happy enough for now. I worry where you are, who you are with. It's awful not really knowing but having to believe anyway. I have slept most of this afternoon; I am either silent, sleeping or shouting, not much of a mum eh? I must find some purpose in being here, but I seem to have lost the will. It's easier to do nothing and think of you than go out in the car without you by my side. These days Katherine and I ride in silence; she is reading her book and I am deep in thought. I pause to make a drink and wonder, what you would say to me if I was talking to you instead of writing it all down. Taking me in your arms would say it all but that cannot be, and I still have to find some answers, sweetheart.

I Love You
Kate xxxxxxxxxxxxxxxxxxxxxxxxxxxxxxxxxxxxxxxxx

Kate went to bed that night and her sleep was restless. The words she had written to Michael were swimming in her head, but she knew she was right to put her feelings down on paper. To some people the very thought of writing to someone who was dead was just plain stupid and a total waste of time. They would never know what had been said, but they were not to Kate, and they were not going through this hell called grief, like her, so she dismissed these thoughts and concentrated on following the advice Dave had given to her, for what was the point of asking for help if she were not to at least try his strategy?

23/10/95

My Darling Michael,

Thank you for coming into my dream last night, when that lady in the square said to me, 'Are you all right now?' it was lovely to say, 'Yes I am'. I was by your side holding your hand and all the world was right again. It is twenty-three months today since you died, one more month to go before I can say it's been two years without you. The fear of the next month looms in front of me because I know when I have faced that day I shall start all over again into year three. I don't know how I survived year one and two, but I did, just. I wish there were no more years to face without you. What I would do or give to be with you now is nobody's business. They were talking at work about booking next year's holidays, where they were going and how they would travel. I wished I could have gone for an early lunch, so I did not need to listen to them, but life goes on, Michael, for everyone and mine has stood still. Wherever I go, I carry you with me in my heart and deep in my soul because you are still so much a part of me and you always will be, sweetheart. I'd like to stop the world and get off.

Wait for me, Michael
I love you
Kate xxxxxxxxxxxxxxxxxxxxxxxxxxxxxx

01/11/95

My Darling Michael,
Just a few lines today. It has been a better week for me. Although I think of you all the time, sweetheart, I know you are not coming home, and I have been thinking about sorting out your clothes, only thinking, but it is a step nearer. I am now counting the days down to the 23rd, it will soon be here; the months fly by and carry me with them. It feels strange to feel a bit better and I don't really know why I do. I suppose I know deep down, I can't just curl up and die, although I have wanted to do so many times these past twenty-three months. Some small part of me wants to live again as life is so short and I need to have something to go on for, for me, not just the children. Maybe this is called moving on I don't know, or maybe tomorrow I could be back in the depth of it all, but it gives me a little hope of a future and I still feel like I am walking into fog and then seeing clearer bit by bit. Stay by me, although I can't see you, I want you to stay always by my side and you know you will be forever in my heart until we meet again. I miss you so much, Michael, every minute of the day. Please be on my shoulder today and every day.

All My Love, Sweetheart
Yours
Kate xxxxxxxxxxxxxxxxxxxxxxxxxxxxxxxxxxxx

18/11/95

My Darling Michael,
It is soul destroying being here on my own, I feel like I am going crazy without you. Katherine is at Guide camp this weekend at Waddow and Ian is out with his friends. I don't want to ring anybody, I just want you. I hate the loneliness, the total emptiness of life here. I wish I was with you tonight. Where are you I ask myself over and over again? The road in front of me seems never-ending. I hope I don't live a long life because this is hell on earth. Wait for me, Michael, some day we will be

together. I wish it was now, I've had enough. This pain never goes away. I thought I had come to a turning point but who the hell am I kidding, I can't go forward, not on my own. Why did this happen to us? Can't he pick on somebody else? Life has been one big battle, always fighting to keep going. I don't know why I haven't given up by now. God knows, I'd like to. I need you, we never said goodbye, you just went out of my life so quickly. Why couldn't we have had more time? Why did I not understand what was happening to you? I am sorry, sweetheart, I really let you down that night, but I didn't know you were going to die. Why did you die and leave me? Why did you not take me with you? You've never left me before. I miss you. I wish with all my heart you could come home again. Why can't you just make some contact? I won't be scared please, please, show me you are still here with me tonight. I don't like being on my own; I'm not scared, I'm just lonely and lost and broken. Please be there in the chair or anywhere so I can see you.

I Love You, Sweetheart
Kate xxxxxxxxxxxxxxx

29/11/95

My Darling Michael,

Two years ago, at this time we laid you to rest, a bitter cold day and such a long, long time ago. This heart of mine is broken; my spirit is broken without you. Why, why, why? I shall never stop asking God why? He must be sick of me, but I won't let up on Him. I thought I was coming around a few weeks ago; I got to a point of feeling nothing, just emptiness and now here I am as bad as ever and at war with the world. I know I am hard to be with, it's just that I can't be bothered with anything any more. I feel like a match that has been spent and is no more. Can't face tomorrow, let alone Christmas and a New Year to follow. Why is everyone telling me I must go on for the kids? I know that, I don't need to keep being reminded that I have been left here for a purpose. I wish I could have come with you, I hate being here on my own. Why has God been so cruel to us? I always defended Him to other people, said there is always a reason for famine and hurt and death, but now I can't defend Him any more because this time He has crushed me. I can't come to terms with why. What have I and the children done wrong to be punished yet again, more so what have you done, my sweetheart, to deserve such an early death? You were such a perfect husband and dad to us, it is no wonder my heart won't mend, how could it without you? Despite all these letters I really have tried to get over this grief, but I can't help how I feel. You were so much a part of me, sweetheart, and I guess you always will be. Time won't heal this pain, this total void that losing you, has left me with. My whole being is broken nothing feels normal any more. I am a different person than I was, and I can't ever see me feeling normal again, not in this world without you. Other people seem to get over their losses, did they love like us? I don't think so! I need you so much, I miss you so much, please stay forever by my side although I know I can't see you, please keep your promise to be on my shoulder.

My Love, Today, Tomorrow and Forever
Your Heartbroken
Kate xxxxxxxxxxxxxxxxxxxxxxxxxxx

TWENTY

At times, although she needed help from her friends and relations she also had to think for herself and follow her own heart. She knew every single person was routing for her in their own caring way and some of her closest family and friends wanted her to find someone else. They could see her slowly being destroyed by all this pain. She had lost a tremendous amount of weight although she was eating enough. The weight was being kept off by her constant fretting for Michael, but only Kate knew when, if ever, she would be able to let go and move on to a new relationship and at the moment that was, and as far as she was concerned, light years away. When she was at work or at home, or even when she was out with other people, which was seldom, she hid her feelings very well. The last thing that she needed was for people to get fed up of listening to her, or feeling that she was being miserable all the time and she truly did have some good times, especially with Chrisanna her best friend in the whole wide world. They laughed and told jokes to each other like the old days when they had worked together with Michael in the pricing department at Walpamur Ltd. It was good for her to be with friends who cheered her up and made life a little more normal again. Even when she was with the children it was not all doom and gloom; they laughed together, reminisced endlessly about Michael and the times they had enjoyed, especially the times they had shared in the caravan playing games. They talked of when they went down to the beach at Highcliffe and of them buying their toys at Gee Gee's shop. They had enjoyed some wonderful holidays together, each July down in Bournemouth. Silly little things that the kids had done or said and had got a good telling-off for and, bless them, they really did not know what to say to her to make her happy again. The situation to them was irreparable without their dad; their mum and dad fitted together like a hand inside a glove. They had seen with their own eyes just how close Michael and Kate had been; little things, like kissing and cuddling together on the settee whilst they were watching the television in an evening. How they would be caught snogging in the kitchen when Kate was cooking the tea, these three children had seen love at its height and now they were seeing how devastating life could be and how raw the pain was on their mum's face now that he had gone. A life snatched away in minutes and a lifetime of loneliness to follow. They had their own lives to lead now and all Kate wanted for each of them was to be happy.

Richard broke off his relationship with his girlfriend and started to see another girl. She had a lovely little girl aged five and they were happy together. Soon he moved out of home and went to live with them both. Kate missed him terribly, but she was happy to see him settled and he still came home for his lunch often and called on her during the day if he was in the area. Ian was out seeing his friends and he went out on his bike quite a lot too. It was hard to know just how they coped with their loss as Kate struggled with it herself, and in later years she felt guilty for not being there for them. But when she mentioned it to them all they said was that she was there, and not to ever feel like that. They knew she loved them unconditionally, and that she was always there to listen to them whenever they needed her. Ian was hell bent on having a motorbike. He had left school now and was learning to be a mechanical engineer. Richard was working for a telecoms company and he was happy in his work. Things were at least working out for the boys and Katherine was doing very well at school. She had not decided yet what to do when she finished at Pleckgate High School, but she knew she wanted to go to Blackburn College for further studies. July 1996, another summer holiday to get through and they did. It was getting to be normal now to have a holiday together at home although Kate could well have afforded to go away, her heart just was not in it.

The caravan had long been sold and Katherine was fifteen now and she went out with her friends when they had returned from their summer holidays with their parents.

On Wednesday the 14th of August 1996, Kate went up to the cemetery to Michael's grave. Today at noon it would have been their Silver Wedding Anniversary. She had asked Michael just before he died if she could have an eternity ring to celebrate their special day and when he had died so suddenly she had found some money that he had been quietly putting to one side to buy one for her. She placed the money inside of an envelope and marked it 'Eternity Ring' and periodically she added some money to it until there was enough to go to the jewellers and buy herself one. It was on one of her days off work that she took the money from the wardrobe where he had kept it and she went to buy herself a beautiful five stone eternity ring, a gift from him from beyond the grave. It was something she had wanted for so many years and he could not have afforded one without so much notice, hence the three years it would have taken Michael to save up enough money for it. Bless him, she had no idea that he had already started to save some money so soon and it meant a lot to her that he was planning so far ahead. Three years on and their special day had arrived, but how ironic that she should be doing this without him to share it with. She bought some flowers from the florist and put the boxed ring into her handbag and got into her car and drove up to his grave. At precisely twelve, the time that they had been married at St Cuthbert's C of E Church in Darwen twenty-five years ago, she knelt at the side of his grave and looked up at his name on the head stone. She said to him quietly, 'Michael, I have bought this eternity ring with some of the money you left in the top box in your wardrobe. Happy Silver Wedding Anniversary, Darling. I miss you so much and I hope and pray that wherever you are right now that somehow you can see me and share this moment with me. Please God, look after him in your Heaven above and don't ever let him be on his own and please God, most of all, give him All of my Love'. The sun was shining down on the two of them; one knelt praying on the grass, crying, and longing for him and the other at peace in God's Heaven. She tried to remember the bereavement book's words; 'he is in a better place, remember, it's like taking off your coat and leaving it there on the coat stand. The body below is just his coat and he is there no more, he is in Heaven above, and he is safely home.'

One Sunday afternoon towards the end of the summer holidays, Kate and Katherine went up to Michael's grave as they always did at the weekend. They never missed going even if it was pouring with rain and it gave them comfort to know he was still near even though they knew that he could not know they were there. It was a pleasure to keep his grave tidy and to put fresh flowers on the headstone. As they drove along the road to where the cemetery was, they passed a white van where a man was busy washing it. Kate recognised the man as one of the engineers who came to her electrical appliances whenever they needed mending or servicing and she wound down the window. 'Hello, you, come and clean mine after you have finished that one,' she said with a smile.

'Hello Kate,' he said. 'What brings you around here? How are you? Long time no see?'

'Not too good, John, I am afraid,' she replied. 'Could be better I guess.'

'Why, Kate? That's not like you, what's the matter?'

'You don't know do you?' she said. 'Michael died, John, it's coming up for three years in November and I miss him terribly.'

'My God, no I didn't know, I am so sorry Kate. Whatever happened?' 'He had a massive heart attack on November the 23rd 1993,' and she told him briefly what had happened. Poor man, he didn't know what to say to her. He had known Kate for years although obviously, it had been some time since he had been to the house. The other engineers had been in her area at the time something needed mending or servicing and he hadn't heard of anyone saying Michael had died.

'Well,' she said, 'I had better let you get on with cleaning the van, John. Katherine and I are just going up to the grave with some flowers for him. We go up every week. I am surprised we haven't seen you before when we come along your road. It's been nice to see you again, John. Take care bye then.' As they were setting off his wife came to the door and Kate said hello to her. 'Bye,' he said, 'and Kate, I am so very sorry.'

'I know, thanks,' she replied. They set off then along the road and turned through the gates that led into the cemetery. It was a nice sunny day and they laid his flowers with care. As always Katherine left her mum for a few minutes by herself; she knew Kate wanted to talk to her dad. It was something all the children did. They knew they had to leave Kate for a few private moments so she could tell him about her week, how much she missed him and to pray for him to be happy up there in Heaven but most of all to wait for her until she could be with him. She kissed his name on his headstone as she always did and told him how much she loved him and that she always would do. Katherine waited by the car, checked her mum was okay and noted her tears streaming down her face. They drove as usual in silence down through the cemetery gates and back along the road where they had come in. 'Home, Katherine.'

'Yes, Mum, let's go home,' she replied.

The dark nights were soon upon them again with the long hot summer evenings a thing of the past. As the third anniversary of Michael's death was fast approaching, Kate had resigned herself to widowhood. After all, how many widowers did she know of that were anywhere near her age? Well actually there were none and although she missed Michael as much as ever, a tiny part of her wanted to live again instead of just existing. She desperately wanted someone to love her again, to feel someone's arms around her and hold her close, someone who would make love with her. She had had to suppress those feelings for nearly three years and at times the feelings of never making love again was overwhelming, after all she was still only forty-six-years-old but nearly the age that Michael had been when he died. One evening in early December 1996 as Kate was preparing to go back to work to do the evening shift, she noticed a domestic appliance service engineer's van parked across the road at Sandra's house; she was one of Kate's neighbours who had looked after the house during Michael's funeral. She reached for the telephone directory and looked up her phone number. 'Hi, Sandra speaking,' said the voice at the other end.

'Hi, Sandra, it's Kate across the road. Who is the service engineer there with you please?'

'It's John, do you want him?'

'Yes please, can he spare me a minute? I am just going back to work but I need a quick word.'

'John,' Sandra shouted, 'it's Kate across the road. Can you nip across when you have finished here?'

'Course, tell her I will be over in five minutes, can she wait?'

'Yes,' Kate said, she had heard him, 'tell him I have ten minutes before I set off.'

'Will do then. Bye Kate, see you.'

'Bye, thanks again, Sandra.'

About five minutes later there was a knock on the front door. Kate went to open it and there stood John. 'Oh, thanks so much for coming, John, the strip at the bottom of the washer is coming off and nothing will stick it back,' she said. 'Let's have a look at it,' he said, and he promptly grabbed her around the waist in a little shuffle-like dance. It was so nice and so unexpected. She really appreciated his warmth and friendliness. He looked down at the kick strip which was hanging loose near the floor. 'I'll order one for you,' he said, 'it will be about a week or so and I will come back and fix it for you.'

'Thanks, so much, John, will there be a charge?'

'No, it's covered in your service contract.'

'Okay, that's great, I must go now, or I will be late for work. I will make sure you have a cup of tea and a Kit-Kat waiting for you when you come back to fix it.'

'Look forward to it,' he said. 'Don't forget, one sugar and a little milk. Take care, Kate, see you soon.'

TWENTY-ONE

She went to work feeling lighter than she had done for some time. It was good to see John again; he didn't always come to service their washing machine but he had been to their home many times over the years since they had moved there, and Michael had always joked with him about the Kit-Kat and the cup of tea being ready for him on arrival. They usually had a chat if it was a lunchtime when Michael called home for a quick bite, and he always commented on what a nice chap John was. Two weeks later on the 18th of December 1996, John knocked on the door. He had come to fix the kick strip. Kate was poorly in bed at the time and she heard a knock on the door. Wondering who it was she grabbed her dressing gown and ran down the stairs. She opened the door to see this beaming smile and John stood there with his tool box.

'Oh my God, John,' she said. 'Don't I look awful? I have had a tummy bug in the night and I fell back asleep.'

'You look just fine to me,' he replied.

'Now I know you are only trying to be nice, John, and I haven't got your cup of tea and a Kit-Kat ready,' she laughed, 'but I will make it in a minute,' she said and she ran upstairs to clean her teeth and make herself more presentable. She felt so poorly; she had been sick and had the runs and, as she was so terrified of being sick it had been a traumatic experience for her, especially on her own. She didn't want to wake the children and mercifully they had no idea she had been so ill.

Kate came downstairs and made him a cup of tea and reached in the fridge for a Kit-Kat. Michael always joked with her as every time the window cleaner came or any workman came the Kit-Kats and the cups of tea were served and today was no different. 'Well you don't look too bright, Kate,' John said. 'I hope you feel better soon. Have you done all your Christmas shopping?'

'Yes, most of it but right now I couldn't care less about Christmas. What are you doing this year, John?'

'The usual family get-together. I love Christmas I always have,' he said. They got talking about their families and John talked of the loneliness in his life. He had two lovely children, a daughter and a son, and his wife was someone who Kate knew when she was a little girl. When Kate lived at the Spar shop, John's wife had lived next door but one to her. They had never played together as Kate was four years older than her. Had they not bumped into each other in the supermarket many years ago she would never have known who he was married to. From the short conversation, they had shared, Kate, who was sitting down the hall on the floor, so she would not spread her germs, realised that his marriage was far from all right, in fact he was downright miserable in it and she felt so sorry for him.

'You know, how cruel is life? Here I am lonely and without a husband and you are just as lonely even though you have a wife! Your kids keep you going and so do mine.'

'I just live day to day, hoping that things will get better, but I don't see a light at the end of the tunnel and it's a bloody long tunnel too.' He carried on with the kick strip and Kate went into the lounge and sat in the chair. She felt sorry for him and for herself, life is so unpredictable, and we just have to get on with it she thought.

'Do you want another cuppa, John?' she called from the other room. 'Yes, why not please I will,' he said. Kate made another cup of tea for them both and John asked Kate in more detail about Michael's death. 'It sounds the most heart wrenching time for you, Kate, I am lost for words'. She could feel herself starting to cry and quickly pulled herself together.

'I know, I miss him so much,' she said. 'It's like I've lost my right arm. I wouldn't wish this on anyone although each one of us has to face this one day. It's the price you pay for loving someone so much, but nothing prepares you for a sudden death.'

'If he had, had cancer I don't know how I would have coped with it, but God, John, to collapse and die within five minutes of me getting home from work is just so cruel and soul destroying, twenty-two years together and not even a good-bye darling let alone a kiss and to say how much you loved and cherished each other, or that you would wait for each other on the other side. A week is like a month and a month is like a year, but we have to go on, there is no choice in the matter.' John finished his tea and started to put his tools away in the box and with the kick strip fitted, the washer looked like new again.

'All done,' he said, and he stood up and walked along the hallway towards the vestibule door. 'I really hope that you have as best a Christmas as you can, Kate,' he said and gently he placed a kiss on her cheek.

'Thank you so much for mending the strip and it was really good to talk to you,' she said, 'I hope your Christmas is a better one than you think it's going to be.'

'We can only wait and see,' he replied.

'See you again, bye for now.'

'Bye and thanks again, John, hey you forgot to say I hope you soon feel better,' she shouted. 'Sorry yes, I really hope you are ok soon' and they both laughed.

Kate didn't go back to work until the New Year. She had felt drained over Christmas and she did not go out until Christmas Eve to do the food shopping. The tummy bug had really floored her, and it took her all her time to get through the festivities. She realised she had got so run down over the past few months and her body was telling her to take it easy. By the New Year of 1997 she felt a bit brighter and booked herself her usual dental check-up. It was on a Tuesday morning, January the 7th and Kate's day off. Ian had gone off to work and Katherine was upstairs getting ready for school.

'Come on, honey bunch,' Kate shouted to her, 'you are going to be late this morning.'

'Coming, Mum, won't be a minute,' came the reply. Down the stairs she came, looking so lovely as usual. She had grown into a fine young lady and she had matured so much over these past few years, her dad would have been so proud of the children he had left behind. She so much enjoyed going to Pleckgate High School each day. There was never a time when she said she didn't want to go. Kate kissed her goodbye and waved to her from the lounge window as she always did each day. Seconds later someone knocked on the door. Thinking Katherine had forgotten something, Kate went to answer it. Standing at the door was John with a big grin on his face.

'Hi,' he said, 'any chance of a cup of tea this beautiful winter's morning?'

'Yes, but it will have to be a quick one,' she replied, 'I am just going to the dentist.'

'Nothing serious I hope.'

'No just a check-up. I'll put the kettle on. How are you?' she said. 'I am okay thanks, I just thought that as I was over this side of town, that I would pop in and see how you were and have a quick chat. Are you better by the way? And how is the kick strip?'

'Yes, I am better thanks, but it really knocked me sideways that bug.' 'Are you next door but one fixing an appliance for Barbara?'

'No, I came to see you. I waited until your daughter had gone to school before I got out of the van.'

'Well, that's really thoughtful and nice of you thanks. How did your Christmas go after our heart to heart?'

'It was okay. I had a nice time with the family, but things are no better at home, doubt they ever will be judging by the lack of attention given to me and the lack of lovemaking.' Kate didn't know what to say except she was sorry to hear that. He wasn't the type to go for the sympathy vote and although she didn't see John very often, she knew he was a kind man, a good husband and a devoted father to his children. 'Don't you both sit down and discuss things together?' Kate ventured to ask.

'It's impossible to discuss anything with her and over the years I have given up. She turns over in bed and I am left wondering why I am not being shown any affection. It's been going downhill in that department for a long time,' he added. Kate went into the kitchen to make a drink of tea for them both.

143

It was nothing to do with her what problems they were going through and as much as she liked the man she wasn't getting involved in any marital problems; she had enough to cope with herself at the moment, but she was willing to listen to him and not to judge. Kate took herself off to the dentist and John went on his way to do his day's work. She pondered about the things he had said and felt sorry that after more than twenty years of marriage it had come to this. Worst of all, their children knew nothing was wrong between their parents as there had been no arguments in front of them and according to John, the problems between them lay behind the bedroom door. John started to telephone Kate during the day when he knew she would be alone and sometimes he would be waiting for her on her way to work. He knew what route she took. She was always a creature of habit. She was on a certain road at a certain time each Monday, Wednesday and Friday and she stopped to chat to him often. They giggled like two young teenagers. Life had suddenly picked up for Kate and John seemed happier too. He was cheating on his wife by seeing and ringing Kate, but this was still a very, very new friendship. Kate never thought any further ahead than the telephone calls or the quick meetings they had. They never saw each other in the evenings and Kate said nothing at all to the children, there was nothing to tell at the moment; they were doing nothing wrong except meeting each other on a road and talking. To the world they were just good friends, but it was plain to see that they were getting ever closer to each other. One day, whilst she was at work a beautiful bouquet of flowers arrived for her. The card simply said: Love from Marty xxx. The girls were very inquisitive,

'who sent those,' they asked her.

'No one you know,' she replied. But one girl, her friend Liz, got it out of her and she swore her to secrecy. 'He is just an engineer who I know. He sometimes comes to mend my washing machine, and don't read anything into it. We are just good friends, and besides he IS married.'

'Why Marty?' Liz said.

Kate laughed, 'it just so happens that he likes the group Wet, Wet, Wet.' John rang her the next morning, careful to wait until she was on her own.

'Thanks so much for the flowers, it was a really nice thought,' she said. 'How are you today? Have you time for a cup of tea?'

'I'll have to see later on as I am busy this morning, but I may be able to spare you five minutes this afternoon.'

'Okay see you later then.'

By the 20th of February 1997 he was calling on her as and when he could do. That day he knocked on her door in the morning and she let him in. He came into the kitchen where she had gone to put the kettle on and they talked for a few minutes. Kate was standing in front of him and suddenly he took her in his arms and kissed her tenderly. It was so unexpected. She had never been kissed for three and a quarter years and his kiss was so passionate that it took her breath away. She looked up at him with loving eyes and she knew there and then that they had both found something very special between them. There was no thought of jumping in the sack or of making love there and then on the kitchen floor. It was all about getting to know each other and building on the friendship they had found, being comfortable in one another's company before they were to take the next step where, if they did, there would be no turning back. That afternoon she went out shopping with her friend. She told no one of her new-found love as they were both in no position at the moment to do anything about it. He was married and as far as Kate knew he had no plans to end it soon, but he wasn't happy at home with his wife, of that she was absolutely sure; if he had been he wouldn't have been snogging her in the kitchen. She started marking her diary with a letter K and circling it when she had seen him, and they talked endlessly on the phone if time would allow it especially on a Saturday morning, when he could ring her as his wife was working in town and when she could talk. Katherine was working in the local bakery shop on a Saturday until one p.m., so the house was generally empty, and Ian went into town with his friends.

They discovered so many things that they had in common, little things, like they both had a crown on their front tooth on the left-hand side. They had cut their chins in the same spot when they were teenagers and neither of them had a brother but both of them had a sister; in Kate's case she had two. They both liked the same music, did not do well at school and both of them had been bullied by one person or another in their school days.

There was so much to learn about each other and they crammed in as much as they could in the times they were alone. It was lovely and heady all at the same time. They had so much fun. John was so witty, and Kate had tears of joy streaming down her face whenever they were together. He was so good to be with and when they had to say good-bye, she couldn't wait to see him again. Her birthday was on the 28th of February and they decided to meet. John had taken the day off work and they met in the cemetery near to the grave where her darling Michael was buried. Kate had just put some flowers on for him and walked back to her car parked on the road nearby. It seemed strange to be meeting there but as John lived near to the cemetery it was the most sensible and private place to see each other.

They sat together in Kate's car and John leaned over and gave her a kiss and a birthday card. It read: **Love from a friend xxxxx** She said she would have loved to have been able to give him a birthday card for his birthday which was the next day, but it was not possible. It was ironic that they had even been born one day apart although he was four years younger than her. Tomorrow he would be forty-three-years-old and Kate was forty-seven today. The coincidences just kept on happening. 'I really wish you a happy birthday, John, for tomorrow,' she said and kissed him gently on his lips. They continued to see each other daily, mainly en route from wherever John was working and when Kate was on her way home from work. They never spent more than a few minutes together as he had a heavy work load and she didn't want to jeopardise his job or their relationship. He took time out on his half-day Fridays which were only once a month to be with her if that was at all possible. Between them they made time to see each other if only for a short time every day. They both soon realised that this was not just a fling; he was looking for happiness and a permanent relationship and so was she. They both had been lonely for much too long and they knew through John's father dying at forty-seven-years-old and Michael dying at the same age, that life was for the living and they were grabbing the chance of happiness together. John saw her if he was going to his karate class and he was increasingly taking chances to see Kate as much as possible. In fact they both were, but love has no boundaries and he was just as lonely and lost in his marriage as Kate was in widowhood.

Kate did eventually tell the children she was seeing John, but they never realised to what extent the two of them were feeling for each other. They had very little time on their own and when John called on her unexpectedly one morning (he knew she would be alone that day), he had brought her a surprise. She answered the door and there he was grinning from ear to ear. 'Go and put the kettle on, sweetheart,' he said. 'Can I borrow your stereo a minute?'

'Course help yourself,' she said. She went into the kitchen and came back into the lounge with two steaming cups of tea and a couple of Kit-Kats. 'Here we are,' she said, and John came over and kissed her longingly. The stereo suddenly started to play his favourite song 'Love Is All Around' by Wet Wet Wet and he started to sing to her. 'I feel it in my fingers I feel it in my toes,' the song carried on and so did he. Kate was so overwhelmed by his thoughtfulness and they kissed each other long and hard. He held her in his arms and she felt so much love for him as the music played on.

They made love that day for the very first time in the privacy of her home. He took her hand and led her upstairs towards her bedroom. To stop the gossip from her neighbours should the curtains be drawn unexpectedly, they decided to kiss each other on the landing. She wasn't a brazen or brash type of girl. If she had been she would not have been so lonely for so long, but if and when she was ready to give herself to another man it had to be with the right one and not just a one-night stand. She was a very attractive woman who needed someone who would love her tenderly and John was the one that she wanted. Tiptoeing carefully, she went into the bedroom and took the duvet off her bed and she handed it to John who laid it down onto the landing floor. He waited patiently for her to go and get changed. As she came out of the bathroom towards him his face lit up.

He had never seen her looking so lovely. There she stood before him in a beautiful red silk dressing gown, wearing a pair of white lacy knickers with a matching bra peeping from inside. He took her in his arms and gently peeled off her gown. She lay down beside him and he kissed her passionately. Their lovemaking was tender and he knew how shy she was, but it did not matter at all to him; there was all the time in the world for them to get to know each other, to learn of the newness of their bodies and to reach the heights that were there in front of them. She had thought this day would never come, when she would feel ready to love someone again. They clung to each other as if it was only a dream and soon they would wake up. When she looked up into his eyes his smile told her he would always be there for her. Never again would she be so lonely, for this was their day, a day when they had made a strong commitment to each other and the future was theirs for the taking. Gently and with such tenderness, John had made love with her. There was so much passion between them, they had been starved of love and affection for far too long and they both craved for the love that they had found in each other. John had fulfilled in every way her hopes, her expectations of a pure new love. It had been just over three years since she had been held in anyone's arms and she hoped and prayed that the end of her tears and loneliness were soon going to be behind her.

TWENTY-TWO

They continued to see each other every day even if it was only for a short time. Their love was going from strength to strength and Kate was besotted with John and him with her. She would meet him after work or he would ring her when he had finished his jobs and she would get into her car and find him in a certain street. When John went to his karate lesson she would meet him afterwards and they talked for an hour sometimes or for only ten minutes depending on the circumstances and never once did they fear being caught together. They were only chatting after all and no one knew that they were secretly planning their future together. Kate would tell the children that she was going out to meet John, but even they were blissfully unaware of the plans that they were both making.

By the 28th of March 1997 John had moved out of the marital home and he went to live temporarily with his mother and stepfather. Even they didn't know that his marriage was well and truly over. After twenty-two years together and with two lovely kids to show for it, he had been living each day for a long time with a wife who couldn't or didn't want to make love with him and for John there was no turning back. His wife had unwittingly let him slip into someone else's arms and he had found total happiness within them. He knew that Kate would cherish him always, for she had already shown him so much love and devotion in such a short time together. The hand of fate had intervened and they had both found what they needed in each other without even looking for it. It was a very upsetting time for all his family; his children were distraught without their dad at home and so was his mother who was seeing her beloved grandchildren so heartbroken. Worst still, his wife had no idea he was planning to leave her for good. It came as a terrible shock to them all. His sister, her husband, and his parents could not believe it when he announced that he was actually leaving his family to go and live with Kate and her children.

'How do you know if this relationship will work?' they asked him.

'I don't know,' was his reply, 'I have found someone who loves me with all her heart and she is all that I want and need.'

'You really have no idea how lonely my life has been for a very long time and this is not the first time I have left her as you all know. I only went back last time because of the children and her promise to me to try again. Unfortunately, it has not worked despite ten more years together. This time I have found what I have needed and wanted for so long and Kate loves me so much, I want to be with her.'

'There is no mention of you loving her, John, how do you know it will work out for you both?' his mother asked him. She and his stepfather were clutching at straws right now to keep his family together, but John was adamant.

'I don't know what guarantees any of us have got of staying together forever, but we have been seeing each other over the last three months now, Mum, unbeknown to you, and despite your concerns and objections I want to make a life with her.'

His mother was livid. She liked her daughter-in-law and she adored her grandchildren, but at the end of the day she too was powerless to stop him. Yes, she admitted to herself and to the others that John had not been happy for a while. His holiday photographs had shown him to be forlorn and withdrawn; he had seemed in another world when he was photographed with his wife but bright and smiling when one was taken with him and the children. Kate sent a card with loving words to John whilst he was staying at his parents' house, and she was told by John in no uncertain terms that his mother had said that Kate was not to use their address to send any correspondence to him, and Kate realised that things were going to get ugly.

Kate 'The Other Woman'; she would always feel like they thought of her as just that, and no matter however long they would be together she would always feel that she was the outsider, the one who had broken up a family, made two children heartbroken for the loss of their dad, and a wife who now deeply regretted the lack of love and affection she wished she had shown him, only now, it was too little too late. He had found another woman to share his life, one who would shower him with love unconditionally, love that he needed and deserved and had long been deprived of. John's family were so hostile towards her. His mother rang her at home a few days after John had told them he was going to live with Kate. She told her that John certainly would not stay with her, she said that Kate was far too old for him for starters (she was four years older than John), and that she was just a passing fancy for him. She said he would soon tire of her and find someone else. She told Kate that she was a snob (only because she had a lovely home) and Kate retaliated by saying that she was talking utter rubbish. After enduring a lifetime of twenty-two years in fact with a miserable mother-in-law, Kate vowed to ignore her, for never again would any-one belittle her like Michael's mother had done, and if John's mother did not like her it was of no consequence to her. She would lose no sleep over that conversation or seek her approval or anyone else's for that matter, this was her life and no one had the audacity to intervene in it or tell her what she should and shouldn't do with it. On Wednesday the 9th of April 1997, John took the day off work. He went to his house whilst his wife was out at work and the children were still at school. He bungled all his clothes and some of his belongings into black bin bags, put them in the boot then parked his car on a road nearby. He went back to the house to load up his van and drove up to Kate's house. He went back to his own house later in the afternoon and waited until the children and his wife came home, then he sat down in the living room and told them all that he was moving out. It was like a bomb had been dropped on them, but he stayed calm. He was adamant he wanted to make a fresh start, to live a new life with the lady he had grown so deeply fond of. He told Kate later that evening that the hardest part of all was to leave his kids, but he told both of them that he had to make a fresh start and that meant moving out of the family home. He told them both he loved them deeply and that he would always be there for them except he didn't want to stay in a loveless marriage any longer.

It came as much of a shock at home when Kate announced to Ian and Katherine that John was moving in with them. Ian said, 'Mum, we don't really know him except when the washer needs servicing or mending. He has only called in a few times over these past few months for a cup of tea.' Katherine was very, very quiet. She had been sleeping at the bottom of Kate's bed whilst her bedroom was being decorated and the night John moved into Kate's room, she moved out. She slept on the floor in Ian's room and refused to acknowledge John at all. Kate and John sat down together on the settee, the same settee where they had talked of this night, wondering if it would ever materialise. They talked together until way after midnight and tried to make sense of the children's indifference. Finally, they made their way upstairs to bed. Kate went into the bathroom and had a shower whilst John sorted out his paperwork for the following day. John had a shower after and came back into the bedroom. He was freshly shaven, and he smelt so lovely. Kate had always loved a man smelling of after-shave, but Michael had never been one to wear much of it; he always said that a man's deodorant was enough. The air was filled with the sweet smell of musk, and as she climbed into bed she heard John say to her, 'I can't sleep there, sweetheart. I have never slept at that side of the bed in my life and besides it wouldn't be right, me sleeping where Michael used to sleep. You will have to change sides.'

'I can't' do that,' she replied. 'I too have always slept at this side of the bed for twenty-two years.'

They started to laugh at the absurd situation they had found themselves in and she moved across the bed to the other side. 'I must love you, John,' she said smiling, 'because do you know, I wouldn't change sides for just anyone!' He snuggled in beside her and lovingly put his arms around her. For the first time in three years she was sharing her bed again and it was Heaven. She turned to him and his smile told her all she needed to know. The lonely nights had finally come to an end. He was hers and she was his. Both of them had been so lonely for so long and she couldn't wait to make love with him again. He was tender and loving with her, his kisses told her that her instincts had been right. She had truly found her soulmate and with their arms wrapped around each other tight, they made love over and over again all night until it was nearly dawn. Their lovemaking had been passionate yet gentle and as the dawn finally did break through the bedroom window, they finally kissed each other goodnight. It had been in every sense of the word their honeymoon, a night that they would always remember and as she turned on her pillow to go to sleep, she thanked God for the love that she had found again in John, for she really believed that he had planned this for her. She had not been looking for love but the second chance of happiness had suddenly come her way and she knew that he had delivered. The pleading of an afterlife with Michael had been ignored. The many times she had wanted to die to be with him and the suicidal thoughts were now a thing of the past and she was grateful for his pardon. She felt that God was saying to her, 'Kate, it was not your turn to go.'

The morning sun shone through their window. It was only early April and John stirred in the strange bed.

'Come on, sleepy head, we have to go to work today, he said. 'Are you making the breakfast, or shall I?'

'I will make it,' she said, and they showered and changed then went downstairs together. Ian and Katherine were just getting up, so John and Kate ate their breakfasts first. Ian was the first to arrive in the lounge where the table was set, followed closely by Katherine who was dressed and ready for school. Katherine very rarely ate breakfast, but Ian always did. This morning he ate his cereal in the kitchen alone. Neither of them was rude or argumentative to John but the atmosphere could have been cut with a knife. There was animosity from all sides when Richard called home in the evening the day after John had moved in and he gave Kate a real mouthful.

'You are so full of yourself, Mum,' he screamed at her, 'that you can't see what you are doing.' He reiterated what Ian had said that they hardly knew John and he would not listen to any explanation or reasoning from either of them.

'Don't you speak to me like that,' she retaliated. 'You have no right to criticise me. I love John and we are going to live here together, so you had better get your head around it.'

'Never,' he said, 'and what about the money? It's not yours, it's Dad's and I suppose it's all going to get spent now that you have a new fella in your life!' With that he stormed out of the house and slammed the front door behind him whilst the other two who had chipped in the conversation a little with Richard, went upstairs to their beds.

It had been a long day. John had his van to empty and endless paperwork to do but despite the outburst from her three children, Kate was adamant that no one, not even those who she adored were going to spoil the love she had found. How dare they behave like this, speak to her so disrespectfully. They had seen her so desperately lost and lonely over these past three years, seen her cry more times than she wished to remember and seen her in the depths of despair pining for their father. Had they forgotten so soon how she had lived and why all of a sudden was the money so important that they thought it was their father's and that it didn't belong to Kate at all?

None of them had done without anything since Michael had died and they knew they never would. Kate was really livid, and she apologised to John on their behalf, bless him; all he said was that it was only to be expected.

'We should have at least prepared them for this, love. I am a total stranger to them, they have only seen me when I have called in occasionally for a cup of tea as they said, or to mend the washing machine sometimes when they have been at home for their lunch and here I am moving in with their mum, they think I am a threat and they think I am here to take Michael's place.'

'We need to convince them, Kate, and soon, that this is the last thing on my mind and they need to know that I am here to look after you, to share my life and all I have with you, which as you know is very little. I have no money saved. I have come away from a marriage with only my car and the few clothes I had in the wardrobe, that's all. I am certainly not after your money. I never thought of money, whether you had any or not, so it doesn't matter at all to me, I just want to be their friend not their enemy if they would only will let me. I am not trying to be a stepfather just as much as you are not trying to be a stepmother to my children.'

'I know, John, I am just so sad that they are so against us,' she said. 'It's a time thing, sweetheart, for everyone involved,' he said. 'My parents, my wife, our children, my sister and also don't forget all the friends you have who have only known you with Michael by your side. It's not going to be an easy ride, Kate, for anyone to accept us as a couple and we must realise that by moving in together which has happened so fast that there is bound to be those people who don't agree with it.'

'I don't care who agrees or disagrees with what we are doing. Whose lives are we talking about here? Ours. Her voice was quivering by now and the tears very near.

'Come here,' he said. He held her in his arms and she melted. 'Don't get so upset, Kate, we are in this together. We don't answer to anybody only to ourselves, so let's prove to all those who are sceptical, whoever they are that we know our own minds and that we are not prepared to answer to anyone or ask for their approval.'

TWENTY-THREE

When the girls at work and Kate's bosses found out that John had moved into her home with her and the children they were delighted. They knew that although she had put on a brave face these past three years, slowly inside she was dying of a broken heart. They wished they could have performed a miracle for her and brought him home but even Kate had prayed for that and she knew it could never come true. She thought of all the other widows and widowers who had prayed like her for the very same thing. Her weight had plummeted, and she was now a svelte size ten. She was a different person because of the grief she had endured and now it was wonderful to see the old Kate that they used to know and love so happy again.

News soon got around the offices of the affair Kate was having, and everyone was talking about her. The majority of them wishing her well but there were some however who did not approve of her living with another man, especially one who had left his wife and children to be with her, but it was of no consequence to her and she wished they would just mind their own business. There would always be those who enjoyed a tittle-tattle and she thought that they were small-minded busybodies. Kate knew that some people thought John was a gold digger and she treated them with the contempt they deserved; she knew him better than that and besides, she was no fool. Her children were as important to her as John's children were to him and she would share all she had with them and with John. Money, although much needed, had not brought her happiness. It is something that no man or woman can buy, and she would have lived in a tent or a cardboard box if she could have found happiness again. She had waited, worked through her misery over Michael's death and come out of it at the other end. Life had a strange way of turning around and here it was for her. Suddenly life was worth living again. Her world was sunshine not showers and she was blissfully happy. The smile on her face covered a thousand miles. She had never been a complacent person, but she knew only too well how a life can change in the blinking of an eye, how all your hopes and dreams can suddenly be shattered and broken like a glass bauble which had fallen off a Christmas tree. She knew for certain and without the shadow of a doubt that she was going to take the future she had been given with John and embrace it with all her being.

By the July holidays, things were still delicate between the children and John. When he came home from work he would sort out his stock and put his used items in the shed at the bottom of the garden then go into the bedroom he shared with Kate and wait until she came home from work. She was still working each Monday, Wednesday and Friday evening until seven p.m. and Katherine was still making the evening meals on those days. He chose to wait for his meal until Kate could share it with him, mainly because it was nice to eat together, but also, he knew he would be eating in silence if he ate with Ian and Katherine. She hadn't forgiven him for taking over the new shed her mum had bought and where her rabbit Flopsy had lived. The rabbit was moved into the garden now just underneath the kitchen window and Katherine was worried because it was open to the elements despite Kate telling her that most rabbits lived outside but nevertheless she still was not too pleased. The garage had been emptied to house the things that John had managed to retrieve from his other house. His wife had got rid of a lot of his things in spite, but he soldiered on regardless and was content with the little he had brought with him. His children would not visit him at his new home, but he took them out for the day on a Sunday.

Kate would have loved to have gone with them to share their day and to try to get to know them both. She had only seen photographs of them that John kept on his side of the bedside table, but he insisted they wanted nothing to do with her or her children and despite her insisting she just wanted to be with him, she was told firmly the answer was no. He needed time with them alone. She felt hurt and left out and she thought that John was being unreasonable as each Sunday without fail he would go out early in the morning to pick them up and it would often be six thirty or seven o'clock when he returned home at night. It was like living on her own again on a Sunday and it caused a lot of arguments, but John insisted he did it his way. The children were his priority. He told Kate she was old enough to understand that, surely, and she was told to be mature about it after all it was a time thing for every-one and they had discussed it when he had first moved in.

One evening when they were in the supermarket doing the weekly shopping, Kate saw John talking to a young girl; she looked around sixteen or seventeen with long auburn-coloured hair. She was very attractive and when Kate approached them both the girl stood sideways instead of facing John, and Kate ended up standing in between them. 'This is my daughter Jillian, Kate,' John said, and Kate said 'Hello' to her. The girl politely said hello back and the two of them carried on their conversation. It was so uncomfortable for all of them, but Kate was determined not to flee the situation and she stood in silence until they had both finished talking. After he had kissed her goodbye and Kate had also said goodbye to her, they carried on with their shopping. 'That was uncomfortable,' Kate said. 'Was she with her mum?' 'Yes, she was. But we will just carry on with our shopping too, if we bump into them so be it, if not that's okay too.' It was many weeks before Jillian came to their house. She was eighteen months older than Katherine and Kate found her to be a really nice girl (how could she be anything else with such a lovely dad). She was very polite and a pleasure to be with. She chatted about the things she was doing at college with them both and about her friends. Kate could see how proud her dad was of her and so he should have been. He told her how much he loved her and how he missed her and Luke her brother, but Luke wouldn't come to see where John lived; he was not ready yet to accept the change that had taken place in his life, or to meet the woman who had spoiled it all for him by taking his dad away.

Kate and John had booked their annual leave from work but neither of them felt it was the right time to be going away and leaving the children on their own. Ian was nineteen now and he was working at the same place as Richard. Katherine had just finished school for the long summer holidays; she was going to turn sixteen in October and she was fast turning into a lovely young lady. Out of the blue they had a phone call that week from Kate's niece asking if Katherine was in and could she please speak to her. As it was the beginning of the summer holidays her cousin Sheila invited her to stay at her house in Billingham in the north east of England. She had given birth to a baby boy earlier in the year and she told Katherine she would enjoy her company, and could she go and stay with them both for a week. Katherine was excited and asked Kate to ask John if he would take her in his car, so they could meet Sheila and baby Liam halfway, somewhere near to Harrogate. Kate told John that when Michael was alive they usually met around the Harrogate area, and mostly at a restaurant over Blubberhouses called the Millstone. He said yes, he would be pleased to take her, and he could also meet Sheila and the new baby.

Katherine thoroughly enjoyed the week with Sheila and the little one and the following Sunday the 27th of July they met halfway to pick her up again. It had been a nice week for Kate and John as they too were on annual leave and they spent some quality time together. It was so easy for both of them to get to know each other's little ways and as they were both Pisces it seemed that they had a lot in common.

They shared the same thoughts, the same likes and dislikes; they liked the same food and shared the same taste in music and they both enjoyed the same television programmes except the soaps which bored John silly. They had listened to CDs way into the night for all of that week, then they went upstairs together and shared a lovely warm bath. There was nothing that they couldn't talk about together. He spoke about his wife, how his life had been with her, the good times and the bad and Kate talked about Michael in depth, what had actually happened that day and in the weeks that followed his death. They even went up to Michael's grave together, and after she had laid fresh flowers for him and they were ready to leave, John always left Kate alone to be with Michael in silence. He always patted the top of his headstone and said, 'Michael, I will always love her and look after her for you, I promise.' Kate told John often that she loved him, and it hurt her when he did not reply. She confronted him about it one day and he said that she knew he loved her, and he didn't need to say it. 'But you do,' she insisted. 'I need to hear it from you, all women do.' There was silence and she waited for him to reply but still he did not say it. It took him a while to actually say those words to her. Did he think it was soppy to voice his love to her? She feared he did, but when he finally said, 'I love you, Kate,' it was the most unexpected and wonderful thing in the world for her to actually hear him say it and to know that he truly meant it. It was indeed the icing on the cake.

John's parents kept away from the house; they had no intention of giving their acceptance to this relationship let alone their blessing. He went up to see them both often but he was always met with hostility about Kate, and he didn't seem to get through to them that he was so much happier and content with his new life than he had been for years. Yes, he missed his children dreadfully and he told them both that he loved them every time he phoned them or saw them. Everyone knew that the invitation was always open for them to come up to see where he was living. Luke had never been at all, but the lad was adamant; he didn't want to come up, and John's mother was very upset for her grandchildren because they talked to her about him leaving home and how they both missed him so much. Despite their family and friend's indifferences they continued to get on with their lives. They were totally devoted to each other and if anyone had any doubts about their love for each other they only had to see them together; they were joined at the hip. Kate had vowed three years ago that if ever she was lucky to fall in love again she would never ever be as dependent on him like she had been with Michael. He had done everything for her because she was so bad with her nerves and when he had died so suddenly she had been thrown in at the deep end. Overnight she had become mother and father to the children and she had learnt how to check the car over, the tyre pressure, the water and the oil levels. She had learnt how to use the mower, how to cook the turkey that first Christmas that Michael was not there to cook it, and numerous other tasks that she never thought she could do. Widowhood had certainly made her strong, strong enough to sort out her monthly finances and to run a home, to look after the children which had always been a shared thing between them and she had also learnt most of all to stand up for herself if she needed to, something that she had always let Michael do for her. By October 1997 they had lived together for six months and Kate asked John if he would take her on holiday.

She had never been abroad and her plans with Michael to celebrate their silver wedding anniversary in Cyprus had died along with him. So many plans and dreams had been shattered that day and she never thought the day would come when she would ever get on a plane. After Michael had died she asked Chrisanna if ever God forbid that she was left a widow would she go with Kate abroad and she said that she would. After that conversation Kate felt awful putting her in a spot but Chrisanna did not take offence; she knew what Kate meant and it was left at that.

John said honestly that he had no money to take Kate away. He said he would have done with pleasure had he not got so much debt. His wife was fleecing him for maintenance. She had even shopped Kate to the benefits office via her solicitor, much to Kate's surprise. She had answered the door to find a man from the benefit department asking if he could come in. He showed her his identity card and Kate asked him to take a seat in the lounge. He asked Kate if she had been drawing her widow's pension at the local Post Office and she said yes, she had.

'Do you know you have been withdrawing money illegally?' he replied. 'What do you mean illegally?' she said. 'What is illegal about claiming my widow's pension?'

'Because you are co-habiting with the said John Shorrock, are you not?'

'Well if you put it that way, yes we are living together but he is not giving me any money at all. His wife is taking a great proportion of his wage for herself and the children and the other part is to pay the credit card off which the bitch left him to sort out, even though some of the credit was hers, and what's left after that is for his car loan. There is nothing left for me.'

The man looked sorry for her but he had his job to do so he said as kindly as he could that if Kate paid back the last two weeks of money she had cashed in, then that would be the end of it, but she could not cash any more and so he asked her for the pension book which she got from the drawer in the wall unit and passed it to him. He confiscated it with immediate effect and she wrote out a cheque there and then for the money she had withdrawn, and he gave her a receipt for it. Kate saw him to the door and sat down on the settee dumbfounded. How could the conniving bitch have been so bloody greedy? She waited until John came home and then said to him, 'Guess who came to the door today?' 'I haven't a clue, who?'

'The bloody benefits agent,' she spat at him, 'asking for my pension book and telling me I am not entitled to any of my widow's pension anymore.' He sat there shocked at the way she had spoken to him which he had never heard before.

'Hey, wait a minute, come here,' he said to her. By now she was crying hard and he put his arms around her. 'We will get through this, Kate. I am so sorry, sweetheart. Hell hath no fury as a woman scorned,' he quoted, and she said she was sorry she had spoken to him so sharply.

'Look, John, you have to get this sorted, you have to get some child maintenance for the kids and then we can get on with our lives. If she has her way we will be destitute before we know it, if I can't draw my pension then you will have to give me some money towards the upkeep of the house and the food.'

'I know,' he said, 'I will see the solicitor as soon as I can then we can sort out enough money for both of you. There will be precious left, but I will do my best, you know I will.' Kate knew he had no idea about money or just how much she had and though she was willing to share all she had with him she also had to be sensible and realistic. It seemed a bottomless pit at the moment, but Kate was no fool and she told John so.

'I have never asked you for money,' he said, 'and I never will.'

'I know you won't, but you never refuse my generosity to you. I have bought you loads of clothes since you came here because you had hardly anything to stand up in.' She knew she was being hard on him and it was really directed to the money his wife was bleeding from him. Life was a mess at the moment and until the divorce was through there was no way they could get on with their lives.

It was true to say his wife was out for the kill and Kate hated her more than ever. If she passed Kate on her way to work, she would give Kate a two-finger gesture and it was so humiliating to cross her path. How on earth did she get into this mess? It would have been so much easier if John had already been divorced or if she had met a widower, but she hadn't and if she loved him so much and she did do, she would just have to ride the storm, or alternatively get out of the relationship now.

She had no intention of doing that even with the hostility of his family and the hostility of her own overbearing her. She had found the love of her life in John and they could all go to hell if they wanted to, but no one was going to take her John away from her. She loved him too much for that and he her, so if they had to live in a tent or a cardboard box together then she would do; that was how much she cared for him. He was her life now and no one was going to stand in their way.

TWENTY-FOUR

John and Kate went into the travel agents in Blackburn town centre one Saturday morning in early October to try and book a holiday together. This was to be her first time abroad and she was very apprehensive. The lady was kind and asked Kate if she had a passport; John told her they were about to arrange one after this visit was over. They settled on the Brilliant Apartments in Protaras, Cyprus. They booked an apart hotel, so they would be in an apartment self-catering or they could eat in the hotel if they preferred. They were to fly with Monarch Airlines on Sunday the 19th of October 1997 from Manchester Airport at 5.45 p.m. for one week, and they would arrive back on Monday the 27th at 4.35 a.m. Kate and John were ecstatic. They laughed and joked with each other all the way through town to the post office where Kate had to have her passport photograph taken. They were like two teenagers who had only just met. They finished a few errands afterwards and then went home to tell Ian and Katherine the news of their holiday, only to be met by Ian asking who was going to look after them for the week.

Kate said they would both be okay as it was only for seven days, but Katherine was visibly upset.

'Come on,' Kate said, 'be happy for me. I've never been away since your dad died.'

'Neither have we,' Katherine retorted, 'and who's paying for this, Mum? Probably you!'

'It's nothing to do with you how I spend my money,' Kate snapped.

'It's not yours though, is it, Mum?' Ian added 'its DAD'S!'

'Now look here you two, I have never left you both in nearly four years to go anywhere because I've had no one to go out with. For all your lives I have been here in this house twenty-four hours a day, loving you, looking after you all and Dad, washing, ironing, cooking and cleaning and I have loved every minute of it, so why are you begrudging me a holiday with John for just one week?' Sheepishly, they looked at each other and did the usual, walked out of the lounge and up to their bedrooms. Kate looked at John with tears in her eyes. 'When are they ever going to realise I have a life to live, that doesn't always include them?'

'I don't know, love,' he said, 'but this isn't easy for them.' He always saw the good in everybody, bless him. 'You must realise that they must feel threatened by me, they think I am here to take their dad's place and spend your money for you. Give it time, Kate, they will come around.'

'I know, but they don't realise you have come away from a marriage with nothing but a car and a credit card to pay for, plus child maintenance for your two children. How can you possibly afford to pay for a holiday as well?'

'Yes, but kids never think like that, they think I am only here for the money. We are the adults and we have to make exceptions for them. They love you so much, Kate, they don't really know how much we love each other so they see me as the baddie who's stolen their mum's heart and they think I am also going to fleece you dry into the bargain. Only time will show them I am not a gold digger and I do love you.'

She felt so sorry for him and ashamed that the children had been so cruel in front of him. She hoped and prayed their love for each other was strong enough to ride this storm because if they drove him away from her with their endless insinuations, she knew she could never forgive them and as much as she adored them, that would be the last straw. Yes, John was right; they had to be adult about this and see it from Ian and Katherine's point of view. They were still hurting for their father; they missed him more than Kate could ever know. They kept their feelings close to heart, cried in their beds at night for the lovely dad whom they had so tragically lost. He was everywhere but nowhere and the fact that their mother was besotted with this chap whom they barely knew only added fuel to the flame.

As the holiday approached, Kate and John went out to buy some clothes and a couple of new suitcases. There had been no need for suitcases when they had the caravan; their clothes went straight into the wardrobes and the storage boxes underneath the seating. Every time they bought something for their holiday, Kate was quick to hide it in her wardrobe away from the children; she couldn't face another inquisition of who had bought that and was it a necessity.

When the day finally arrived and their cases were packed and waiting in the hall for the taxi, Kate went upstairs to say goodbye to the children. Ian was very quiet and respectful. She told him she loved him, and the week would soon be over. He was nineteen now, but she felt like he was nine. He looked so forlorn and vulnerable as he told her to have a nice time and she said she would.

'Please be happy for me. I am scared to death of flying; I've never been on an aeroplane before,' she said.

'You'll be fine,' he managed to say, wishing it was him flying in a few hours instead. He loved aircrafts just as much as his father had done. 'Be careful, Mum and I love you,' he added.

'I will do, and I love you too, more than you will ever know. I'll ring you every day I promise, providing I can get through that is.'

'Okay, safe journey, Mum, see you next week,' he said. It was obvious that there was no stopping his mum now; she was going to go to Cyprus with her lover come hell or high water and there was nothing he, Richard or Katherine could do to stop her. Kate walked across the landing into Katherine's room to find her in floods of tears.

'Oh, Mum, please don't go,' she sobbed. 'Please stay here.'

'I can't do that, Katherine, you know I can't,' she said. 'I'll be back before you know it, you'll see, it's only for a week.'

'Mum, if anything happens to you I will have nobody,' she cried. 'Dad's gone and if you die too I'll have no one. Please, please don't go. I don't want the aeroplane to crash.' She was really pleading now. 'It won't crash, darling, oh please don't cry like this, it makes me feel terrible like I am abandoning you. I have never left you before and you are sixteen now. I am only four hours away from you and I will be thinking of you all the time I promise. I'll ring you every day and the money you will need for the week is on the dining room table.' There

166

was no pacifying her. Suddenly John shouted upstairs, 'Kate, the taxi is here. Are you ready, love?'

'I'm coming,' she shouted back to him and she turned to Katherine and said, 'I love you, sweetheart, more than life itself.' She held her arms out and Katherine flew into them. 'It won't be long before I am home again. Be careful and sweetheart, please look after each other whilst I am away. Richard will be calling in daily to make sure you are both okay.'

She turned and walked back along the landing and down the stairs to where John was waiting for her, tears streaming down her cheeks and with a guilt in her heart like she had never felt before. Instead of them both wishing her a lovely time they had unknowingly torn her in two. Ian and Katherine came downstairs to the front door and watched her get into the taxi beside John. They waved to them, both looking so forlorn. She knew they would probably go back into the lounge and sit together comforting each other, or go to their respective rooms and mull over the past half an hour and wonder what had happened to their mum and why on earth she had wanted to leave them and go away with her fancy man. More to the point what would Dad have said had he been here? But Dad wasn't here and they wished again for all the world that he had been. The taxi driver drove like an idiot as they do, trying to cram in as many journeys to the airport as possible in their shift so they could make their money out of people like Kate and John, and scare the living daylights out of them into the bargain before they reached their destination. Why did they drive so fast she thought and why had they had to share the taxi with another couple when all Kate wanted was to discuss with John the conversations she had just had with her children?

They did arrive safely at the airport door and Kate was surprised to find how big it was. John tipped the driver and got their cases onto a trolley and they politely said goodbye to the couple who had shared their car. They proceeded into the check-in area and Kate started to feel sick. How had she let herself believe she could get on an aircraft and fly for four hours with her nerves as they were. John reassured her that she would be fine, and he led the way, holding her tight. She thought that he thought she might do a runner and he was making sure that she didn't.

They joined the queue and he tried to quell the fear he could see written all over her face. His heart melted as he saw how afraid she was becoming, and he told her he would look after her and she wasn't to worry about a thing, not the queues of people or the procedure to follow. He reached for their passports in the bag that they were taking on board the plane and they waited their turn. The check-in desk was fast approaching, and Kate followed John who lifted their cases onto the weighing platform and the lady tied a label around each one. She smiled at them both and asked to see their passports. She gave John their boarding cards and told them to go to passport control. John explained to Kate that once they went through passport control there was no going back to where they had just been. He told her there were plenty of shops through there and she could go to the duty-free shop and treat herself to some luxury perfume or go into the bookshop and choose a book to read on board the plane. The very mention of the plane set her heart racing and she gingerly followed him through to passport control. Never having been in an airport before Kate was totally reliant on John to lead the way, so when he walked towards a large burly man who was sat behind a conveyor belt holding out his hand to her she shook it and said 'Hello'.

'He wants your bag to check it,' John said, adding to the burly guy who thought the whole episode was hilarious, 'she has never been in an airport before,' and the staff of three girls and two security guards all started to laugh. Embarrassed by it all Kate blushed from her head to her feet. Bless her, thought John, who had done this so many times with his ex-wife and children. He gently took her hand and led her to the next set of security guards who had witnessed the whole saga and they took her to one side and frisked her.

Kate took this in her stride as she had seen this so much on the television and she let the man check her. What a fiasco she thought.

'I had no idea it was going to be like this or I would have been more prepared,' she said to John.

'It was so funny to see you shaking his hand,' he replied. 'The staff thought so too. They knew you were nervous as your face says it all. Come on, Kate,' John said, 'let's go and look around the shops. The flight is not for nearly an hour and a half yet, so we have time to browse.' They bought some perfume and aftershave for each other, then went into the bookshop where Kate bought a book to read on the four-and-a-half-hour flight to Larnaca airport. Then they checked the flight details on the many screens around the departure lounge. Kate wished they could just get on board without all the waiting around and John explained that there were so many cases to load onto the plane plus food and pushchairs, that it had to be a two-hour wait for everything to get organised. Finally, the intercom announced their flight was ready for boarding and Kate said she needed the toilet.

'There are toilets on the aircraft,' John said but she said she needed to go before they boarded so off she went to find one. When she came back, John was towards the front of the queue waiting for her. He had a lovely smile on his face. He was so looking forward to their holiday, the first one she had shared with him and where he would have her all to himself.

'What are you smiling at?' she said,

'you,' he said, 'You are like a cat on hot bricks. It will be fine I promise you. I shall look after you all the way there and all the time that we are away, trust me.'

They climbed up the steps and onto the aeroplane and Kate felt herself start to panic, the same racing heart, would it suddenly stop? It was beating so very fast and she was totally out of her depth here. She saw the seats in tidy rows and how near together they were and just how many people there were boarding this plane. If she could have turned around there and then she would have got off, despite so badly wanting to go on holiday with John. There were so many bodies behind her trying to get into their seats. She just followed him as he led her to where she was to sit for the flight. She had particularly asked for a window seat just in case the person who would be sharing their third seat happened to be sick. Yes, here we were again, the same old fear, 'What if?' She tried to block off the fear welling up inside her for if the third person who would be next to John should be air sick she could not run. There was nowhere to run to and she panicked at the very thought of such a ghastly scene, trying desperately not to picture the scenario. John put the hand luggage in the overhead compartment, but Kate tightly held onto her handbag, for inside it was a bottle of antacid for her burning tummy, some ear-phones so if someone was sick she could turn up the music and block out the sound and try to keep calm. 'Please, Lord, look after me, I am so scared,' she prayed. 'Please take us safely there and bring us safely back.' It was too late now, for the pilot was speaking to the passengers over the loud speaker, welcoming them all on board the flight to Larnaca Airport and telling them it was twenty-six degrees centigrade this evening in Cyprus and soon the aeroplane was taxiing down the runway at God knows how many miles per hour. Kate gripped hold of John and dug her nails into his knuckles. 'It's fine,' he soothed. 'We are going to go about one hundred miles an hour down the runway and then we take off.' Heart racing and clinging onto him she tried so hard to be brave. She chastised herself for being such a wet head then consoled herself by thinking how brave she was being, it was such an ordeal.

It was a good hour or more into the flight when the pilot updated them on the progress; they were heading towards some turbulence due to a thunderstorm over the French coast and he told the passengers to fasten their seat belts if the sign above their heads came on. John was sleepy, but Kate was wide awake. She had dreamt of flying and in her dreams, instead of rows upon rows of seats she had dreamt of a dining room suite and a sideboard with a plush carpet to walk on. She knew when she woke up in her bed at home just how her mind was reacting to the thought of the unknown and it made her smile now, for despite the fear inside her and just how absurd the dream had been that an aeroplane could be so luxurious, no, that was only in films or for private jets belonging to celebrities, not on an ordinary aircraft. She had listened to the cabin crew showing everyone what to do in an emergency and she went over it again and tried to remember all the air hostess had shown them. When they had flown for just over two hours the seat belt sign came on and the plane started to judder. Kate grabbed John who was sound asleep by this time and he held her hand.

'It's ok, sweet, it's only turbulence, it will level out when the pilot drops in altitude you see.' He had no idea how frightened she was. How could he, bless him; this was a piece of cake for him he had flown many times, but she had never flown before today. The tears streamed down her cheeks and she prayed to God to let her get off this plane and let the nightmare end and then suddenly she was thinking no, we can't get off as the only way off was to crash and she didn't want that either. She tried to read her book to take her mind off it when suddenly the pilot announced they would be landing in half an hour and she thanked God yet again, firstly for there not being a third person sat next to John throughout the flight although there was a spare seat, (and who might have been the one to be sick) then saying that she was sorry to Him for being such a pain in the arse! The pilot landed the aircraft with pristine accuracy and everyone on board clapped. It was all so new to Kate, and John explained that on most flights the passengers did that as a thank you for a smooth and safe landing.

It was after midnight when they touched down, as Cypriot time was two hours in front of the UK.

TWENTY-FIVE

As the doors were opened and the front passengers started to disembark, John and Kate made their way down the aircraft and as they reached the top of the steps Kate announced that the engines were very hot, and John started to laugh.

'That's not the engines, sweetheart. It's the temperature here in Cyprus it must still be twenty-two degrees, so tomorrow should be a real scorcher.'

'Let's hope so,' she said. 'I can't wait to see Cyprus, 'the jewel of the Mediterranean.' The fear of the flight was behind her now and the coach journey was in front. She was still painfully aware of someone vomiting during the hour and a half journey to their hotel so she sat snuggled up to John and turned her thoughts to tomorrow and what it would be like to sit on the beach with him and to paddle in the warm sea. He had told her of the times he had been abroad and how he loved the feel of the warm sand on his skin. His hands would soon be smooth, and his nails would be clean and white again. John was very particular with aftershave and balm; he looked after himself and loved to be clean shaven at home and also whilst on holiday. They arrived at their aparthotel safely with no mishaps, the coach driver had been excellent; he obviously knew the roads like the back of his hand and Kate and John, although tired from a long journey, collected their luggage from him, thanked him for a safe journey and climbed up the steps and into the reception area.

They were greeted by a friendly team and given the key to their apartment after surrendering their passports to be returned to them on their departure. The apartment was nice and clean. There was a double bed which they had both requested. John had said that abroad there was a lot of single beds and it wasn't always possible to push them together so they had requested a double when they booked the holiday and also a high floor as Kate wanted to have a view of the sea or at least part of it. They unpacked their cases and John took her onto the balcony which had a lovely view of the night lights in the town below. The sky was a beautiful deep navy-blue colour adorning a massive yellow moon which was nestling in-between the glittering stars. It was still warm, and he took her in his arms and kissed her passionately. It was nearly two o'clock in the morning, but it felt like much earlier in the evening. The tiredness they had both felt previously had vanished and been replaced with an overwhelming urgency to make love. Their kisses had aroused the want in each other and as he fondled her breasts in the balmy night air she felt like she was in Heaven. She melted into his arms, the need for each other taking over the need for sleep and as he slowly peeled off her clothes and took her back into their room, he laid her onto the freshly made bed, the cotton sheets enveloping their naked bodies. She whispered just how much she loved him, how much she wanted him and how much her body craved for his. She wanted him so much not only for tonight or for this week but forever and always. They made love way into the night and each time it was better than the one before. Neither of them wanted it to end. They didn't know if it was the Mediterranean night air or the fact that they just couldn't get enough of one another. What they did know was that they had found a wanting in each other that neither of them had ever felt before and as sleep overcame them they lay naked and spent thinking of the week that lay in front of them, and looking forward to many more nights like this before their journey back home.

***

The morning sun woke them up. It was around eight thirty a.m. and children were splashing about happily in the pool below their bedroom window. Kate went out onto the balcony in her cream silk dressing gown and John followed her.

'Lovely, isn't it?' he said. 'Aren't you glad you made the journey now as daunting as it was?'

'Oh John, of course I am. This is a new world for me and it's just so beautiful here,' and turning to him in her sexy outfit she said, 'shall we skip breakfast and carry on where we left off last night?'

'Love to,' he smiled. 'But I can't make love to you on an empty stomach. Let's get some breakfast and then we will come back up eh?'

'Yes of course,' she replied and went back inside to get into the shower. It was lovely and so welcoming. She stood there naked, washing herself when she felt an arm around her waist and suddenly there he was beside her, caressing her body and wanting her again. They enjoyed a lovely breakfast together and talked of what they should do this morning.

'We can go down to the beach and have a swim or in your case a paddle.' she kicked him playfully under the table. They were like two lovesick teenagers and then we can look at the shops later, they close at lunch-time for the siesta and reopen again around five p.m.

'Lovely,' she said. She wasn't hard to please and she was so looking forward to dipping a toe in the much loved Mediterranean Sea, although she had only seen it from the balcony in their apartment. They went back upstairs to get changed but instead of making love again they decided to leave it for later, maybe after lunch when the sun was highest in the sky and they would take a siesta together. There was a rough track which led from the hotel down to the town, across the main road and then another track that lay in between the four-star hotels which then joined straight onto the beautiful white sand and the gorgeous turquoise sea beyond. Kate was awestruck with its beauty. She had seen pictures in holiday brochures and now she was seeing it with her own eyes. They had rung home to Ian and Katherine after breakfast to tell them they had arrived safely in Cyprus and they were both getting ready for work and school. Kate said she would ring again later to see if they had had a good day and to see also how they were coping alone. There was no hostility towards Kate but neither did they sound over-enthusiastic with the news that the place was simply idyllic.

As John and Kate walked down towards the town the clouds suddenly came over which was unusual, and the heavens opened. They took shelter in a taverna where she had a coffee and he had a pint of beer.

It was the craziest of times; one minute she was at home and the next she was sipping coffee in Protaras. The thunderstorm lasted for only a short while and then the sun shone again. If that had been in England it would have gone on for days on end. Soon they were making their way down to the beach at Fig Tree Bay and it was breathtaking. Even though John had been abroad many times he had not been to Cyprus so that made it extra special for them both. Even he was crazy about the place as he stripped off his shorts and tee shirt to reveal a slim body in trunks just waiting to be tanned by the glorious sun. Kate also took off her shorts and as she had a bikini underneath he was soon taking her by the hand and leading her into the warm sea where they kissed and cuddled. She sat on his knee and he felt proud of her body; he wanted her there and then but he knew that he couldn't. It was easy to get aroused with Kate, her breasts were firm in the bikini top and she was very pretty. Soon his body was telling him that he couldn't wait until they were alone when he could make love with her over and over again. They stayed in the sea for most of the morning jumping up and down with the waves and when Kate had had enough she left John to go for a swim on his own. He was a very good swimmer and not frightened in the slightest of the open sea whereas Kate was only happy in it up to her waist.

It went back a long way, the fear of water, when as a child her swimming instructor had made her go in at the deep end in Darwen baths before she was ready and made her swim to the shallow end. She had never forgotten the fear or the support from her school friends for cheering her on and telling her she could do it.

She did do it but, she never forgot the episode or forgave Mrs Scholey for humiliating her in front of the whole class. John felt exhilarated after his swim and they got changed back into their shorts and went to a small café just at the edge of the beach for lunch. Kate could not believe the sheer beauty of Protaras. It was a world away from Bournemouth and the south of England where she had always holidayed with Michael and the children. She felt guilty that she was enjoying herself here in the glorious sunshine in the middle of October with the man she adored whilst he was lying in a lonely grave back at home. In truth she felt like this whenever she was enjoying herself and it could ruin a beautiful day for her. She carried so much guilt for what he was missing and for what she was enjoying. John noticed how quiet she had suddenly become, and he asked her what the matter was. 'I was just thinking of Michael,' she told him honestly, then felt sorry that she had as she didn't want to spoil this time that they were sharing together.

He took her hand in his across the table and said, 'Sweetheart, he would only be pleased for you that you have found someone to share your life with. Don't be so hard on yourself. He wouldn't want it, Kate. He was a kind man and he would only want the very best for you. It would break his heart if he knew what the last three years have done to you, the tears, the loneliness and despair not to mention the weight loss and now it's your turn to be happy again and I am the one who is going to make sure you are.'

'I love you so much that it hurts, and I am so afraid you will be taken from me too,' she replied, tears stinging her eyes.

'I am going nowhere,' he said. 'You can't get rid of me that quick, Mrs Abbotts. We have a life to live and it starts right here and now okay'

'Okay so where to now?' she said and with a twinkle in his eye he said, 'I think it's time for a siesta, madam, don't you?' with that in mind they ran up the rugged path together, their arms wrapped around each other towards their apartment and she looked forward to the lovemaking they were going to share.

After they had been to bed for an hour or so, John suggested they went out to the pool for a swim. It was a world away from anything Kate had ever known; the warmth of a Mediterranean sun shining down on them and she told herself that John was right. Michael would want her to live a good life even though he hadn't had a long life himself. He had always wanted what was best for her, his 'Twinkle Eyes', the girl he had fallen in love with all those years ago and if he could have, he would have given her his blessing. If he could have, he would have laid down his life for her and she for him. Kate and John went to get changed to go out for their evening meal. They had found a little restaurant farther up the road called 'Anastasia's' and they were greeted by a handsome waiter who showed them to their seats. In his hand was a red carnation which he gave to Kate as he pulled out the chair carefully for her to sit down. They ordered their meal and shared some wine. Kate didn't like wine or any alcohol for that matter, but she was determined to try it and after they had finished, they stepped outside to share the warm balmy evening air. It was still so warm for October and John reminded her that this was an all-year-round resort not just a summer retreat. The days were soon over, and the nights were long as it was dark by five p.m., so they went down into the town early in the evenings and called at various tavernas along the way. Shops re-opened for the evening and they spent hours looking for souvenirs for the children and little reminders of their special place to take home to Blackburn.

Cyprus would always have a special place in their hearts; it was their first holiday together where they had shared so many nights and days making love, had shared so much laughter and once some tears when for some reason John had taken something Kate had said the wrong way and she had cried, walking behind him up the rugged path. They had soon made up with each other and snuggled into bed with the beautiful new moon shining down on them from over the sea.

All too soon the week was over, and the coach came to their apartment to take them back to the airport. Kate told herself she was not going to get so worked up on the flight home and John held her close and made sure she had her ear-phones on as she listened to her radio, ever fearful of someone being sick either in front of them or behind them.

It was a night flight and they flew into Manchester at 4.35 a.m. on Monday the 27th of October 1997. The taxi driver was waiting for them at the airport in the arrival department and soon they were on their way home. Katherine and Ian were still fast asleep as they quietly let themselves in the front door and climbed up the stairs to their room. They tumbled into bed and fell instantly asleep. In the morning after their long journey home they had a lie-in and after they'd showered together and eaten breakfast, they unpacked their cases. Katherine and Ian had long gone off to school and work.

TWENTY-SIX

Kate had an appointment with her gynaecologist on the 31st of October. It was a Friday afternoon and she was feeling very nervous. As always in a private hospital there was tea and coffee provided for the patients whilst they waited to see their consultant and she helped herself to a refreshing cup of tea. Soon her name was called, and she was shown into the consultant's room. He was a friendly man who asked her a few questions about her health in general and Kate answered him truthfully. He asked her if he could examine her and after a few minutes said, 'I think you need a hysterectomy, Mrs Abbotts.' 'Oh, I really was not expecting that,' Kate replied.

'Look,' he said. 'It's pointless doing a bladder repair when you have suffered so long with your periods. You are forty-eight-years-old now and the most sensible thing to me would be a full hysterectomy. It is a big operation, but in the long run you will benefit tenfold than just doing a repair. I will of course take out the ovaries and then there can be no worry of ovarian cancer, as all will have been removed.' Kate looked at him and nodded in agreement. What was the point of suffering any more, she thought. John had had a vasectomy, she didn't want any more children anyway, so the most sensible thing was to go ahead and have the operation.

Kate thanked him, and he said he would send for her in the New Year and meanwhile he told her to just get on with her new life with John and most of all not to worry about a thing. Easier said than done she thought and as she walked back to her car she burst into tears. She had never been in hospital before and all the fears of people vomiting came flooding back. She headed down the road to work to do her evening shift and Fran saw her sad face as she walked through the door.

'Oh Kate, how did it go?' she said, as always there to comfort and support her friend. They shared such a special bond that Fran knew as soon as she saw her, that she was upset, and she said go and sit down I'll make us both a brew. When they had finished their tea, Kate told her what the consultant had said and Fran put her arm around her,

'you will be fine, Kate, and don't worry about people vomiting. You will be in your own room with an en suite, your own television, and if you don't want to mix with the other patients you won't need to. It will be like being in a travellodge; you can do what you like, have visitors when you want, and John will be able to stay with you long into the evening. The children will be fine, they are both grown up now and Richard is living with Debbie, so he will visit you often and hopefully you will only be in for a week, then home and a long rest to recuperate for three months.'

Kate hugged her. 'You are always there for me Fran. Thank you so much. I know we are so alike in our ways and our fears. I am sure it is the right thing to do and the consultant was really nice. He has been at the hospital for years and has a very good name.'

When Kate went home and told John and the children she found nothing but support from them all. They told her not to worry about anything and that they would each in their own way be there for her. She thanked God once again for his blessings, three wonderful children and a partner whom she adored. she knew that they really would help her in the coming months. John and Kate shared their first Christmas together and for the first time in years, they went out on Christmas Eve. Although Katherine and Ian were amicable to John it was more than obvious it was going to take a long time to like him, if ever. Katherine felt left out. She had been by Kate's side ever since Michael had died and it was hard for her to share her mum with some-one else. John's children were okay with Kate but there was so much going on with the acrimonious divorce and adjusting to another man's children (Luke came occasionally) coming to the house, but it was far from easy.

Anyone could see that Katherine was wishing it was her dad with her mum and not John. John's children just wanted him home and back with their mother and she was out to fleece him for his betrayal as much as possible. 'Hell hath no fury as a woman scorned.' The relationship between Kate and John would have to be so strong to withstand the enormous pressures coming from both sides, but Kate knew in her heart she had found someone she wanted to spend the rest of her life with, he was her everything. Her heart felt like it would burst with the love she had for him and at times she was blinded by her devotion to him, sometimes not seeing the whole picture of how her children were feeling, seeing her so happy but with another man. It was to take years before they really realised he loved her for herself not for the beautiful house she had or the wealth she owned but for who she was as a person and how much she loved this man, the gift of a second chance for them both.

By the time the New Year of 1998 was upon them Kate had bought new lingerie for her stay in the hospital. She was to be admitted on the morning of Friday the 9th of January for her hysterectomy operation in the afternoon of the same day. John drove her to the hospital and stayed with her until she went down to the theatre. He was told to ring in about four hours to see how Kate was. It was later in the evening when Kate stirred and saw his smiling face looking back at her.

'Is it all over?' she asked him.

'Yes, sweetheart. You were down for three-and-three-quarter-hours and everything went fine according to the consultant, how do you feel?'

'Sore,' she said and instantly fell asleep again. He stayed with her as she drifted in and out of sleep, then kissed her goodnight and went home to the children who were anxious to find out how their mum was. It was a slow recovery; she had to stay in hospital for twelve days and when she came home she was constantly having urine infections, but slowly she began to feel more herself. There had to be no lifting, not even a kettle full of water for at least six weeks; she just had to rest and take things slowly. On the 6th of April, Kate returned to work where the girls were waiting to welcome her back. She thanked them all for the lovely flowers and cards they had sent her, and her working life returned to normal, hectic as usual.

On Tuesday the 12th of May 1998, Kate became a nan to a beautiful baby boy who was born to Richard and Debbie. They named him Corben Ellis. He was born at 4.34 a.m. and Kate was thrilled to bits. That evening John and Kate, Katherine and Ian went up to Queens Park Hospital to see this much-wanted baby grandson and nephew. Kate burst into tears as she bent over his cot. He was perfect in every way. Richard and Debbie were so proud of their new baby son and Joanne was happy to have a new baby brother to love and play with as she was now nine-years-old.

The July holidays were fast approaching, and Kate and John took Katherine with them to Puerto Pollensa in Majorca. They stayed in a studio apartment which Kate had booked without John at the travel agents in Blackburn. It had been a quick decision as the holiday they had already booked in Portugal had been cancelled due to building work nearby. Kate had never booked a holiday before; John could not get time off work, so she and Katherine went to the travel agents in town to change it. They decided to go to Majorca and she prayed they had made the right choice. They flew to Palma on the 26th of July 1998 for two weeks. The apartment was very nice, the furniture was in pine and the only problem was that Katherine had to sleep at the bottom of Kate and John's bed as it was a studio apartment and Kate never realised that that meant one bedroom/dining room. The only thing separating them was a little white wall. John laughed and when Katherine went downstairs to look at the pool. He whispered to Kate, 'No sex then on this holiday, love,' she replied, 'Where there's a will, there's a way ha, ha.'

It was a lovely resort and the weather was perfect. Katherine struggled with the heat and Kate coped a bit better. John loved it so they all lazed on the beach each day. Katherine and John both liked swimming so they booked a day out at the water park near Palma. Kate sunbathed whilst they both swam and went on the water slides. One particularly hot day during the second week Kate said she had a bad headache and she told John and Katherine she was going back to the apartment to get some tablets and to have a lie down. She had only been laid on the bed for about ten minutes, when a knock came to the door. Startled, she went to answer it, only to find John stood there, with a big smile on his face.

'Some excuse you made to come back to the apartment. You don't really have a headache do you, sweetheart?' he said. 'I know you wanted me to follow you, so we could make love on our own, didn't you.'

'Is Katherine still on the beach on her own, John?'

'Yes, she's fine, now come here I want to kiss you all over,' and with that he scooped her onto the bed and they made passionate love. Twenty minutes later, she finally said to him, 'I really had a blazing headache, I wasn't kidding, and it wasn't a come on but boy, I am so glad you thought so, darling,' and they kissed again, happy in the knowledge that Katherine was happy sunbathing down on the beach and oblivious to what they were up to. It was a perfect holiday and Kate felt that Katherine in her own small way was warming a little towards John. He went out of his way to swim with her, to have a joke with her and to make her feel comfortable with him. He told her often that he never wanted to take her father's place, but he would just like to be her friend and if ever she needed anything, anything at all, he would always be there for her no matter what. It was a slow process, but she knew he meant what he said. He never asked to watch any programmes on the television back at home. He always let her and Ian have their choice and by the end of the holiday she smiled more with him than she had ever done before.

TWENTY-SEVEN

In July 1999, John and Kate took Jillian and her friend and Katherine for a fortnight's holiday to the island of Ibiza. They booked an apart hotel where they could eat in or go out self-catering, pleasing themselves which restaurants they went to and the girls enjoyed sharing girly time together. It also gave Kate and John some quality time together. Although they had been lovers for two years now, they were still both in 'honeymoon mode' and it was good for John to share some precious time with his daughter as well. It was good to see them swimming together. Kate knew Jillian and John were very close and one day they swam to an island just across the bay. Kate and Katherine both held their breaths as they watched them from the hotel garden. It was quite a long way to swim but they had talked about doing it for days, trying to decide if it really was too far for them. Eventually they decided to give it a go and what a relief it was as the girls saw them both climb out of the water and on to dry land on the tiny island. Their mission was accomplished and they returned to the water after a short time of exploring. Kate smiled to herself. Was there no end to this man's talents? When they returned to the hotel they were both jubilant and happy to have achieved such a challenging quest. It was a relaxing two weeks but all too soon it was over, and the girls said good-bye to both John and Kate thanking them for a lovely time.

On August, the 28th it was Ian's twenty-first birthday and he only wanted a family party. They went to an Italian restaurant just outside of Blackburn. It pleased Kate so much to see what a fine young man he had grown into. She pondered, wondering what Michael would have thought of him now and how proud she knew he would have been had he only lived to see him reach this milestone in his life. He was happy with his girlfriend Madeline and looking forward to settling down with her. How the years had passed by so quickly. He had only been fifteen on the night when Michael had died so suddenly and even now, after nearly six years without him, she still wondered where did he go although she knew deep in her heart that he had gone to Heaven it still hurt to lose him like that. She made herself return to the celebrations and hoped and prayed that somehow, somewhere Michael was watching them from afar and she hoped he was proud of her for bringing their second-born son up to be such a lovely person; he really was his father's son.

On Monday evening the 20th of September 1999 as Kate went to the chemist next to the health centre where she worked for her prescription, someone crept into the reception area and stole her handbag from her chair. She knew she should have put it back in the cupboard before she left the building but knowing Fran and the other night staff were around, she took a chance. When she returned, she asked the girls where they had put her bag; she thought they had hidden it from her to teach her a lesson. With the look on their faces, she realised that in fact they had not touched it and that someone had taken it. Immediately, she telephoned the police and reported it. The police rang her back within ten minutes to say that the head teacher at the school next door to the health centre, who was waiting in the dark in her office for her husband to come and collect her, had seen someone rummaging in the bushes near to the main gate. On further investigation, the police had found Kate's bag with the contents strewn all over the muddy path. Her bank cards were missing and her cheque book, but worst of all, the thief had taken her diary. She was distraught. Her diary contained so much information; the appointments with her surgeon, the urologist who had prescribed her different antibiotics which were all written down on the days she had attended. Appointments logged when she went in as a day case for an operation and the times when the cystitis had been so bad, she had logged that down for reference and now all that information was lost.

After a few days, her cheque book was returned to her home after being found in bushes in Darwen and in fact the bank had sent it on as someone had handed it in at the counter and the bank just thought it had been dropped by mistake. The new bank cards were ordered and posted to her, but the diary was lost. Worse still it was of no use whatso-ever to the thief, but to Kate it was her bible. It was a lesson to be learnt, what a pity there was no CCTV in the centre at the time but Kate had learnt the hard way and she never left anything on show ever again in reception.

On New Year's Eve, the 31st December 1999, John and Kate went to the Traders Arms in Mellor village, to see in the New Millennium. The pub was packed out, but they enjoyed a few dances together and when the bells of Big Ben chimed, John kissed Kate and wished her a Happy New Year. They were so loved up together and she was so happy with him. John tried to ring his mum and stepfather from his mobile phone to wish them both a Happy New Year, but he could not get a signal inside the pub, so he went outside to see if that would work instead. After about five minutes he came back in and his mood had changed. Suddenly he was at war with the world and Kate tried to soothe his temper by saying that everyone was in the same situation as it was the Millennium; the lines were inevitably blocked. He turned around to her and said, 'Just because your family don't ring each other and stay up at midnight my family do.'

'Look John,' she said, 'don't take it out on me because you can't reach them. Let's go home and we will try from there.'

'No,' he stormed, 'I won't. You go home if you want. I am trying until I do get through.' Kate did not recognise this man; he had hatred in his voice and no matter how much she tried to reason with him it was impossible. There was no sorting this out, so she reached for the car keys in her handbag.

'What are you doing now?' he fumed.

'Going home,' she said. 'Are you coming?'

'Not with you,' he said, and he started to argue with her again. She had had enough of his foul mood, so she walked out of the pub and got into the car.

'John, come on.' she tried once more but he walked up the road and ignored her.

This was a New Year never to be forgotten. John was walking up the road three miles from home on a freezing cold night with just his sports jacket on and Kate pulled up alongside of him.

'Come in the car, will you?' she said but after another mouthful of abuse from him, she carried on along the road and went straight home. As she let herself into the house tears fell down her cheeks. What the hell had got into him she thought. She knew she hadn't said anything wrong to him. Everybody was trying to use their mobile phones or landlines at midnight, but it was just impossible to get through. Weary and hurt, she climbed the stairs and sat on her bed. She just wanted him to come home to her. Suddenly the telephone rang and thinking it was John she rushed to the table by the window,

'Hello,' she said, and John's sister Linda said, 'Happy New Year, Kate. Is John there?'

'No sorry he isn't,' Kate said, 'in fact he is walking home from Mellor as we speak.'

'Why Kate, it's freezing out there?'

Kate could feel the hostility from her and she said, 'We had a row and he wouldn't get in the car. I tried and tried but he was so stubborn, so I came home alone.'

'We will go and pick him up,' Linda said.

'Okay, I will leave you to it,' she said and replaced the receiver. Kate thought of the conversation that they would all be having, his mum and his stepfather, his sister and her husband about their ruined evening and she felt so humiliated by it all and ever so angry. John arrived home shortly after being dropped off by his stepfather and Linda; they had picked him up on the top road and he was freezing cold. Kate was in their bedroom waiting for him but there was no apology. He still blamed her for the row and she blamed it on the drinks that he had consumed over the evening and on the memories and hurt from his son Luke, which ate into him constantly because he had walked out of their house and left them all.

The same hurt that he had buried deep in his soul for the past two and a half years and drink had brought it to the surface. As with any row, they got over it but Kate learned that John always had a payback time. He would disappear into his shed to sort out his stock or go and tidy his drawers upstairs. He was not one to say sorry, in fact he had often said that the word sorry was just a word without meaning and he would always keep her waiting alone for him in the lounge usually for over an hour or more and when they did have words which wasn't very often she was always prepared for the aftermath. She loved him throughout and waited his time until they were all loved up again. Loneliness was not what she wanted but even she had to accept that his ways, although most of the time were very much like Michael's, he was in fact not Michael; he was John and he told her so when he was in a mood, in no uncertain terms.

TWENTY-EIGHT

Richard and Debbie announced that they were going to get married on Friday the 7th of July 2000, at Blackburn Registry Office. Kate bought a beautiful cream suit by Ronald Joyce from a shop in Accrington, she went to Lord Street in Southport for her bronze-coloured shoes and matching handbag and she hired a lovely coffee and cream hat from a shop in Penwortham near Preston. The relationship between Richard, Kate and John was very rocky. At times it seemed that they were getting along fine and then for some unknown reason the money situation would rear its ugly head and once again, Richard would accuse John of only being with his mum for one thing and one thing only. Strangely enough, he never actually confronted John himself; he always said it to Kate. Despite the problems, Kate thought that John would be accepted as his mother's partner at the wedding but eventually John said that he had had enough of the finger being pointed at him and the insinuations thrown at him and although never actually said to his face, were all wrong anyway and he said he would not be attending the wedding at all.

Kate was horrified to hear that he had decided he wasn't going with her. Even on the day he stuck to his guns, but she told him she loved him and that she totally understood his reasons. She went upstairs to get ready and emerged a radiant bridegroom's mother. John said she looked beautiful and for one last time she asked him if he would change his mind. 'I can't, Kate,' he said. 'I am not going anywhere where I am not wanted and I don't want to ruin their wedding day,' and so with tears rolling down her cheeks she left John washing the pots in the kitchen whilst she and Katherine (who looked every inch a lady) drove alone in John's car to Blackburn Registry Office. When she arrived, she was greeted by the photographer asking for a photograph of herself and Richard together. The photographer asked her to smile and she felt humiliated that she had to be told to do so. He of course knew nothing of the rift that was going on in the family and so she obliged. In the waiting room, everyone was gathered together chatting when Kate suddenly saw her little grandson Corben being held by his other grandmother and she felt the tug in her heart for the way that she and John had missed out on so much of his short little life. Kate went to pick him up as he toddled along the floor and she held him close as his mummy and daddy held hands and walked together towards the man who was to join them in matrimony. Kate and Katherine sat on the back row whilst everyone else took their seats and the ceremony began.

After the wedding was over the guests started to make their way to their cars. Kate told Richard she hoped he had a lovely wedding reception but neither she nor Katherine would be going to join them for the meal. She said she was going home to John who she knew would be waiting for them in the lounge when they returned home. John was very sad that she and Katherine had not gone to the wedding breakfast and he told her that she ought to have done, but she said that if he was not with her, then she did not want to go without him. She knew that Richard was only looking out for her, not wanting anyone to take advantage of her as a widow and he more than likely had her wellbeing in mind, but she knew that John was not with her for her money as he had told her so many times before. When she had said she was a widow, her money had never entered his head. It was she who he wanted and she believed him. She knew that other people were sceptical of him because they too were looking out for her but they also had misjudged him and knowing that so deeply in her heart she would prove to them that they too were wrong about John. In fact they were very, very, very wrong.

August the 8th 2000 saw John and Kate head off on their annual holiday. This time they were going to Paphos in Cyprus. After the upset of Richard and Debbie's wedding they were ready to have a good rest and some together time. After a long flight, they arrived by taxi to a beautiful five-star hotel called 'The Azia Beach' on the road to Coral Bay. Nothing was too much trouble, the staff were so welcoming and they all called Kate 'madam' and John 'sir', it made them both feel like royalty.

The hotel was right on the beach although it was quite rocky just there and so they had to walk down a short path at the edge of the hotel to where there was a lovely golden sandy one. The pool was enormous, and the terraces were decked out in rows and rows of beautiful cerise-coloured bougainvilleas. The tables were decked out with pure white linen tablecloths blowing in the warm Mediterranean breeze waiting for their guests to enjoy their evening dinner. It was everything Kate had dreamed of and they settled down to a lovely relaxing time together with plenty of sun, sand and lovemaking. They hired a car for the week and went into Paphos town where there was a quaint old market, then down into Kato Paphos, the old town which was next to the harbour. The hotels in the old town were mostly five star and Kate and John would drive there after their evening meal and go for a drink some nights. Most of them had singers or a group playing so they danced the night away. They were devoted to each other and their love was a joy to witness. Sometimes they went to a karaoke bar and other times they stayed in their hotel where there was excellent entertainment.

The weather was perfect with hours upon hours of sunshine and long lazy days. On the 16th of August, something happened that was to change their whole holiday completely. Kate was lying on their bed whilst John was shaving in the bathroom. They were getting ready to go down to dinner soon and as they chatted Kate was checking her breasts. She did this regularly, especially as her mother had had breast cancer when she was eight. She wasn't paranoid about it, but she did check herself religiously. As she was checking the left breast she gasped, and the conversation went dead.

'Are you asleep, sweetpea?' John said, still shaving himself. 'No, oh my God John, I have found a lump in my breast,' Kate cried. John came out of the bathroom with his towel around his waist.

'No.' he said calmly, 'you must be mistaken.'

'I'm not, it's only tiny but I can feel it,' she said. He sat next to her and she put her hand on his, guiding him to the lump next to her left nipple. 'Yes,' he said. 'There is definitely a lump but it's ever so tiny, sweetheart, let's not think the worst.'

By this time the tears were rolling down Kate's face and John took her in his arms.

'What next,' she said. 'Are we doomed to have no happiness together?'

'Now come on,' he said. 'We don't know what it is yet, so let's not spoil our holiday. We will see the doctor as soon as we get home. It's only a few days away.' He was shocked. Kate could tell he was being brave for her sake and he went back into the bathroom to finish getting shaved. She followed him and slowly said, 'What if I don't live until next year? What if I follow in my mum's footsteps, John?' With tears rolling down both their cheeks they sobbed together. It was a nightmare and she was terrified; he was too but he didn't let on to her. He had to be brave for her sake, but inside he was breaking apart. Cancer, the big C word. His father had died from it and Kate's mother had too. Please God, he prayed, don't let my Sweetpea be the next one. He heard Kate pick up the telephone in the bedroom; she made an appointment to see her doctor on the 23rd of August. They were flying home on the 22nd which was a Tuesday so she asked the receptionist for an early appointment on the morning of the 23rd. Nine a.m. he heard her repeat and he was glad she had at least been positive about it and to get it seen to as soon as they got home. There was nothing more she could do until then and she relayed her conversation to John who was now just getting in the shower.

The following day they headed up into the Troodos mountains where there was the Kykos Monastery. As they pulled up outside they were both asked to wear long trousers. Kate got changed in the back of the Rav 4 into her white cropped pants, and John changed into his chinos. They entered the monastery and it was totally silent; you could have heard a pin drop. There were a lot of tourists taking photographs and there were signs pointing to the rooms where the monks lived. Kate sat down on some steps whilst John took some photographs. All she could do was pray. She prayed like she had never prayed before and she knew she was being thoroughly miserable. All she wanted to do was to go home and see her GP as soon as possible, but for both their sakes, she knew she had to be brave and so she tried to enjoy the rest of her holiday. After all, it might be her last who was to know!

On Sunday, the 19th they went down the path at the end of the hotel. It was in fact 12.45 a.m. and a beautiful, starry, warm evening. They had had a wonderful day together, sunbathing on the lawn, swimming in the pool and Kate had been drinking milkshakes and John drank his beers. They had enjoyed a delicious meal together with a pianist playing love songs to them on the terrace, so to end a perfect evening John told Kate that he was taking her down onto the sands to watch the stars, to walk barefoot along the beach and into the warm night sea. They were all alone, the moon shone down on them and it was a perfect time to reflect on their day. John spoke softly to Kate, telling her how much he loved her and how much she meant to him. He told her he would always be there for her no matter what the future might hold and to remember this night that they were sharing for always. Gently, he laid her down onto a sunbed and made love to her. His kisses were warm on her lips, his breath sweet as he slowly caressed her breasts, his mouth tenderly sucking her erect nipples and she responded to his every move. He slid into her gently and with such ease, their lovemaking reaching its height together. For all the world, she wanted this night to go on forever and they stayed wrapped in each other's arms for well over an hour until their naked bodies had grown cool in the night air and she kissed him tenderly, quietly whispering just how much she loved him and thanking him for all the love and devotion that he had shown to her not just tonight but always. They dressed again in silence and she took his hand. Slowly they walked back along the path and up the steps to their hotel.

They arrived home from Cyprus on the 22nd of August. Kate had an appointment with the doctor the following day to check on the lump she had found. The doctor said she thought it was a little cyst and not anything to worry about but as a precaution she would refer Kate to the breast specialist right away. At two p.m. on Friday the 8th of September she saw the specialist who did an ultrasound scan and he assured Kate that it was in fact a cyst and it was too small to aspirate. He said he would keep a check on her and would send her another appointment in six months' time. Relieved that it was not cancer she thanked him and left the hospital. She rang John right away and told him the news. To her surprise as she walked back to the car he was parked in his van behind her and giving her a beaming smile, she knew how glad he was that it was nothing to worry about and he produced a beautiful bouquet of flowers from the seat beside him. Bless him, she thought. Whatever would she do without him? She loved him more than life itself.

TWENTY-NINE

Katherine was a loner, bless her, and although she was happy enough with her own company, she would stay in her room each evening with Popsy the cat by her side watching television or doing her course work for college. She did have some friends, but she was a quiet and shy girl with no real close friend to share some time with. On Sunday June, the 24th 2001 she decided to go to Cyprus by herself. She had been saving up the money she had earned working evenings and Saturday mornings serving at the bakery at the top of East Park Road. John and Kate took her to Manchester Airport and she flew alone at 4.10 p.m. the four-hour journey to Larnaca in Cyprus. Her coach then took her to her four-star hotel in Limassol. She had only been there for three days when Kate received a tearful phone call from her.

'Oh, please, Mum, can I come home?' she cried. 'I should never have come here on my own.' Kate tried to calm her down telling her of course she could come home and that she would go next door but two to see Jackie, her neighbour's daughter, who worked for a travel firm to see if she could get Katherine an early flight back home.

Apparently through her tears she managed to tell Kate that she had eaten every meal alone, although the waiter had been so kind as to escort her to her table at each sitting and he had looked after her which was nice of him. She had also booked herself on a Jeep safari trip, only to be touched up by the driver whom she had been put next to. Fortunately a kind couple who had witnessed the driver being over-friendly, had asked Katherine. if she would like to exchange seats with the husband so that she could sit next to his wife where she would feel more comfortable. Katherine had accepted his kind offer but the experience had been too much for her and by the time she got back to the hotel she had decided enough was enough and she just wanted to come home to her mum and her own bed. Kate told her she would ring her back at the hotel when she had spoken to Jackie and not to cry as soon she would be home. With that she ended the call.

'What's the matter, Kate?' John called from the lounge where he was watching the television. 'Is Katherine ok?'

'Yes, she is okay, but she wants to come home, John. It's been a real ordeal to say the least and I am just going to Rita's house to speak to Jackie. She will know what to do. I won't be long sweetheart.' 'Okay' he shouted. 'See what you can do, I will make some tea for us.'

Jackie told Kate she would ring the airline in the morning and try to book an early flight home for Katherine and to tell her that she would ring her hotel and arrange everything for her. Kate thanked her and said she was sorry to be a trouble, but it was a lesson to be learnt and she knew that Katherine would never venture on another holiday alone. At two thirty p.m. the following day Katherine arrived at Manchester Airport. She then got a train into Blackburn and Kate picked her up from the station. Tears of joy ran down Katherine's face, she was so relieved to be home and in one piece. She vowed to put the past few days behind her. At the end of September John and Kate were going on holiday back to the Azia Beach Hotel in Paphos Cyprus. This holiday was to be more memorable than the others in one respect, because unbeknown to anyone else they had planned to get engaged sometime during the fortnight and Kate left it to John to decide where and when that would be.

They arrived at the hotel by taxi. It was, as always, a beautiful day. They were shown to their room which was on the second floor this time, a bit disappointing for the height as they usually had a high floor, but they had a full sea view and that compensated for it.

Soon they had unpacked and hung their clothes in the wardrobe and put everything into the drawers. They got changed from the clothes they had travelled in and went down to the pool dressed in shorts and tee shirts, the warmth and beauty of their favourite hotel taking their breath away. John had hidden both engagement rings at the bottom of his camcorder case during the flight from Manchester to Paphos and Kate checked with him that he had transferred them inside the safe which was on the floor of the wardrobe in their room. He assured her he had and then said, 'Don't you go peeping at either of them, Sweetpea, will you?' He had started to call her Sweetpea a lot lately and she liked his term of endearment. 'No, of course I won't, but I can't wait to wear it, sweetheart,' she replied.

They hired a car a few days into the first week and went to Paphos town where there was an old-fashioned market selling fresh fruit and vegetables and there were many stalls selling beautiful handmade lace tablecloths and various sized mats all in the same lace but in different colours. It was a joy to see the talents of these ladies and the locals were all so friendly it was no wonder Kate and John always said it was like going home. Cyprus, the first place they had holidayed together in 1997, it was known as the 'Island of Love', only they knew it as 'Their Island of Love'. There was nowhere else in the whole world where they wanted to affirm their love for each other by giving and receiving rings than on this beautiful isle. The food was delicious at the 'Azia' as always, and each evening they could either dine in the Amphitheatre on the terraces amongst the cerise-coloured bougainvillea or inside in the plush dining room if it was at all chilly. Afterwards, they would go into the spacious bar with the pink and blue upholstered chairs, matching carpet and mahogany polished tables, to watch and listen to the evening's entertainment. There was something different on every night but mostly they were singers and Kate and John would spend the night dancing together before retiring to their room to sit on the balcony in the lovely warm night, watching the ever-present moon. Sunsets and moonlight were like nowhere else on earth to them and it would be in the early hours of the morning before they snuggled in bed where they made love, happy in the knowledge that they were going to be together forever.

During the second week John suggested they went to Protaras the resort they had first gone to back in 1997 and where they had stayed for just a week. He said he wanted to see if it had changed any and Kate said she would love to go and see it again. The beach was of golden sand, the sea turquoise blue and the view from a little church farther up the road than the apartments they had stayed in previously was just simply spectacular. On the morning of the 2nd of October 2001 Kate and John went down to breakfast; they tucked into delicious fried eggs, bacon and tomatoes followed by wholemeal toast and two cups of tea each. They had ordered a packed lunch each which they picked up on their way out of the restaurant. They went back to their room and collected their beachwear, some bottled water and their own beach towels to sit on, on the sand. They were both excited to be going back to their old haunt. Would it be the same as they remembered? They were always talking about it at home, or would it be very different now? They hoped it wouldn't be the latter. The journey along the motorway was as always very enjoyable; they had been on it when they visited the Troodos mountains a few days earlier. Driving on the left-hand side of the road as in Britain was a bonus for John; he drove all day for his work as a Field Service Engineer, so he was happy to not be on tenterhooks.

The sun was shining through the open windows and the warm Cypriot air soothing as they chatted about how they were enjoying every minute of their holiday. The fact that the staff always addressed Kate as ma'am when asking her anything and John was always referred to as sir, made their time there so special. It was just manners on their part, not snobbery, and that was why the hotel was such a success; nothing was too much trouble and everyone should be treated like royalty if only for two weeks in the year. It was just as beautiful now as when they had been to stay there in August 2000. The hotel was family run; it had been in a brochure when Kate and John were looking for a holiday back to Cyprus, but they wanted to go to a different resort from Protaras. The brochure showed pictures of a five-star hotel, it had four floors and two beautiful outdoor swimming pools one with a bridge going across it leading to a poolside bar which was open all day, grassed areas for sunbathing, a small golden sand, man-made beach. It looked idyllic and it immediately appealed to both of them, hence, their second visit.

The signs for Protaras were now showing and they knew they were very nearly there. After about an hour's ride they turned down a familiar road and saw the Brilliant Apartments where they had stayed before. The day was glorious, and John pulled onto the car park near the beach, 'are you hungry, Kate?' John asked.

'Yes, I wouldn't mind our packed lunch soon or shall we have a sit down on the sand? You decide,' she replied.

'Yes, let's just get a breath of Protaras air then we will have something to eat.' They laid out a beach towel on the warm golden sand and drank in the view. What a lovely island Cyprus is, she thought and how lovely it was just the two of them sitting there with no one else to worry about. They had telephoned home the previous evening to wish Katherine a happy birthday; she had turned twenty-years-old on the 1st of October. What a lady she was turning into. She was now more at ease with John. Kate knew it was just a matter of time before she had to resign herself that her mum was leading a different life now than she had been with her dad, and she smiled at the thought that at last there was some peace in the family. They sat for about ten minutes before John went in the boot of the car to get their meals. The hotel had done them proud; there was everything and anything to satisfy two hungry tummies and they had even provided a bottle of water, a small bottle of wine and some Cypriot cake; it was simply delicious. 'Shall we walk through the town and up to the little church, Kate?' John said as he put the empty lunch boxes back in the boot.

'Oh, that would be lovely, then we will have a look in the Brilliant Apartments before we go back to the car shall we,' Kate said. 'Whatever my Sweetpea wants, my Sweetpea shall get,' he said to her and she smiled,

'I love you so much, John Shorrock, do you know that? And I always will.'

They walked along the road, past the shops and most of them were open. The ones which had closed for their siesta would be open again by the time they were coming back to the car which would probably be in a few hours' time and they decided to look at them all then. John wanted to walk to the lovely little church on the hill. It was built with peach and mushroom coloured stones and its beauty was breathtaking. It was up quite a lot of steep steps across the road from the Brilliant Apartments. They had been up there when they had stayed there three years before.

They made their way onto the main road where the familiar Anastasia restaurant still stood. They had had many mouth-watering meals there too and Kate was always given a fresh carnation by the waiter whenever they went there to dine. It was a really nice touch, but then again, she wasn't that special as they gave one to every lady who dined there too. Soon they were making their way towards the path leading up to the church.

So many people visited it and today was no exception. When they reached the top they were amazed at the 360-degree view, not only of Protaras, but of the surrounding countryside spreading for miles and miles which could only be seen from the back of the churchyard. The front looked out to the sea and beyond and all of the shops below where tourists were scouring in and out of each one looking for souvenirs of Cyprus to take home with them, for their family and friends. The little church door was open, but they didn't venture in yet, instead they returned to the back of the churchyard where there was a massive tree. It was planted deep in the ground and around the trunk were a row of cream-coloured coping stones, so people could sit on it and admire the view. Looking up into the branches Kate saw many shreds of material, either in paper, or ribbons, sometimes even tissues tied around the branches blowing gently in the breeze. Suddenly she remembered the last time she had been there and when they had returned to the Brilliant Apartments she had asked one of the staff what was meant by all the different things tied to the big tree up at the church. He told her it was a symbol of something the person tying it on wanted; it represented the need for a prayer answering for a desperately ill person, or a much-wanted child so they would be praying for fertility, a prayer really for anything they wanted in their life or in the lives of someone they loved or knew. 'What a perfect idea,' she had said to him. 'I think that is a lovely way to approach God, and everyone who sees them blowing gently in the wind and there were hundreds, will know that they are not alone in needing their prayers answered too.'

Kate reached into her handbag and pulled out an orange tissue. She climbed onto the stone seating and reached up to a branch, carefully she tied the tissue around a branch when she heard John's voice saying, 'What are you doing that for, sweetheart?'

'I am asking God for us always to be as happy as we are today,' she said.

'Well, your prayer could be answered much sooner than you think. This might add to your happiness even more.' When she turned around he was sat on the seat below her holding her engagement ring in his hand. She felt as if she was dreaming, he must have planned this all the time they had been in Cyprus and although she had wondered when they were going to exchange their rings this was a wonderful surprise. Climbing down she sat beside him. The day was so hot that it took her a minute or two to get her engagement, eternity and wedding rings off her left hand. It looked strange as she held out her hand, now empty of the symbols which she had always treasured. It was thirty-two years since she had been given her engagement ring from Michael and her wedding ring was thirty years old now, but it still looked like new. Kate had been to a jewellers in Blackburn a few weeks before what would have been their silver wedding anniversary. She had paid for her wedding ring to be re-engraved with the same flowers still etched onto it, so when she knelt down by his grave to put on her eternity ring at 12 noon on the 14th of August 1996, the ring would be like new again. It was something she would have done even if he had still been alive; it was pure wear and tear that the pattern had faded as she never did any housework in her engagement ring or the new eternity ring but she would never remove her wedding ring. She had worn it proudly for twenty-five years and every night without fail she carefully put both of them into a little tray in her bedroom until the morning when she would put them on again.

John held the ring. It was still in its black shiny box but open now, glistening in the bright warm sunshine. He waited until she had taken them all off and then he said to her, 'Kate, will you accept this ring and my love forever?'

'Yes, I will and John, please will you Marry Me?' He slipped the beautiful seven-diamond cluster ring onto her finger and in return she slipped his diamond, white and yellow gold ring onto the third finger of his left hand. He had chosen it because it was really different and just perfect for him.

They kissed in the shadow of the tree and were oblivious to anyone around them; they didn't see the people any more, they only had eyes for each other. He took her hand and led her through the old wooden door leading into the tiny church and they sat on a pew together in silence; words were not needed. They each spoke to God privately, both knowing He was receiving their thanks for the love they had found in each other but mostly for the happiness they were now sharing in Cyprus and the promise of their devotion to one another for the rest of their lives. After a look around the church they made their way down the steps and back to the road by the apartments which were now so familiar to both of them. It hadn't changed at all and they made their way through the gardens towards the swimming pool. Instinctively both of them looked up at the balcony which had been theirs for a week four years previously.

The memories came flooding back and Kate said, 'Do you remember the nights we spent sitting on that balcony and looking at the moon and stars before making love in that comfy bed?'

'Yes, shall we ask the manager if we can use it again now for an hour or so?' he whispered. They both laughed and nobody around them noticed the rude gesture that John was making,

'Wish we could do, though don't you?'

'You will have to wait till later for that, Mrs Abbotts,' he said, and she pulled a sad, sulky face at him. They made their way through the gardens down a cinder path which led onto the main street, the smell of Cypriot cooking from nearby houses filling the air. The shops were all now open, but they didn't buy anything; they were happy sauntering along the road arms wrapped around each other and looking forward to getting back to Paphos for their evening meal at the Azia Beach. Soon they were making their way back to the car park and saying a sad, yet happy farewell to Protaras. The journey back was very enjoyable. It was still twenty-five degrees or more and although the motorway was busy, the traffic kept flowing. Kate spent most of the time admiring her new ring. She loved it and couldn't wait to show it to the children, their families and their friends and colleagues when they returned home the following Saturday. Her other rings had been carefully put into her handbag for safe keeping and they both reminisced of the perfect day they had shared.

Back safely at the hotel they showered and changed for dinner. The entertainment that evening was a male singer called 'Anastasia,' he was a great entertainer, changing his jackets to match the songs he was singing which were a mixture of pop and the fifties and sixties. He asked if anyone had a birthday that day and one or two had. John went up to him to tell him of their engagement and the whole room burst into instant applause when Anastasia announced it. They danced until the early hours of the morning then went up to their room. The night was warm and balmy, they sat on their balcony snuggled together on a sun-bed until 1.30 a.m. watching the stars sparkle like the rings on their fingers in a jet-black sky. She was drinking coffee and John was having a beer. About two a.m. they had a bath together and then climbed into the massive double bed. John leant across to take Kate in his arms and he told her how much he had enjoyed their engagement day. She told him it had been the happiest day of her life since 1993. Slowly she slid her hand down the smooth hairs on his chest, down his slim tanned body whilst kissing him passionately on his lips. Feeling his erection was enough to tell her they were going to share a night of passionate lovemaking and as they reached their climax together she smiled up at him and told him she would love and cherish him for always. All the past, the hurt of divorce on his part and the painful death on her part were now to be put behind them. They would never forget their partners for they had given them their wonderful children and not all the times had been bad for John; a lot of his memories were good, but for now they both had to put to rest the past and look towards their future; today was indeed the first day of the rest of their lives.

They flew into Manchester on the evening of the 6th of October 2001 to be greeted by Ian and Katherine waiting to take them home. Kate held out her hand showing her engagement ring to them and they both said, 'Wow, why you didn't tell us about this?'

'Because we wanted it to be a surprise, is that okay?' Kate said. 'Congratulations,' the children said to both of them and in a polite gesture, Ian shook John's hand then they both kissed Kate. Seeing the surprise on their faces could not be described as either happy or sad and Kate quickly changed the subject, asking what had they both been up to this past fortnight and she wished Katherine a belated 'Happy Birthday' again. They were not going to spoil this moment for neither her or John and when they were alone in their bedroom unpacking their suitcases, Kate said she had been disappointed at their reaction. Maybe no amount of happiness would ever take away the reminder that their mother had moved on with her life and as always, she hid from them her hurt.

Richard was as surprised as the other two had been, but she got a wonderful response from her friends and colleagues at work. Knowing how happy she now was, was all they needed to hear. They had been with her through the dark days and now they were sharing in her happiness once again. She was the talk of the health centre from the doctors, staff and patients alike, all delighted to hear her news and wanting to know when the wedding would be.

THIRTY

On the 9th of December 2001 at ten thirty a.m. Kate and John were invited to Corben's christening at St James' Church in Blackburn. It was a lovely service and as he was now just over three and a half years old, behaved like a little gentleman. Kate and John sat together to watch him receive his blessing and then they went back with the party to the local pub for a buffet. Christmas came and went, and John and Kate looked forward to the New Year of 2002 together,. This time as they wished each other a Happy New Year they talked of their future. It was no secret that John and Kate would eventually move out of their current home at some point and buy a home together. John often spoke of feeling like he was living in Michael's shoes and Kate appreciated how he must feel as everything in the house had been chosen by herself and Michael. John had revamped their bedroom in Schreiber furniture and made a beautiful job of it. They had gone to MFI and chosen all the fitted furniture together in pale cream and with the help of the designer, the room was completely different in every way, but he still felt it was the only room in the house where he truly felt comfortable and Kate understood. It was early in 2002 when they decided to go house-hunting. Ian was getting married to Madeline in August and Katherine was happy (sort of) when Kate and John told them both they were going to start looking for another house together. It was a big thing for Katherine; she had been born there as had Ian, but he had a new house being built on the outskirts of Blackburn and was ready to move on with his own life. Katherine was now twenty-one years old so she would be looking for a place of her own in a few years' time, and meanwhile she could stay with John and Kate for as long as she wanted.

They went to a new housing estate being built near the village of Whalley in the Ribble Valley. The show house was available to view, and the garage was being used as an office where designs of the other properties on the estate were on view. Building work was going on all around them. They instantly fell in love with the area; firstly there were views right across the A59 road to Chaigley and Hurst Green, there were fields as far as the eye could see, a real must for Kate. They chose a 'Shelley' type house which was a three-bedroom detached property consisting of a through lounge, a large hall and cloaks and a fitted kitchen downstairs. Upstairs were three bedrooms; a small one and a larger one at the back and a master bedroom on the front with an ensuite. There was a beautiful three-piece bathroom also on the front next to the main bedroom. They could only put their names on the list at that time as they had to sell the house first. They came home elated. Firstly neither Kate nor John had ever been able to afford a brand-new house before in their previous marriages and secondly, Kate knew instantly that she could now leave the family home happily and start her new life with John in the village of Billington. It was something she never would have imagined ever doing before she had met him. How he had changed her whole outlook on life and how she would be forever grateful to God for her finding true love again. She was beyond happy. Yes, it would be strange to leave the house that had stolen her heart when the time came but she loved John and it was now just over nine years since she had lost her beloved Michael and she knew he would have wanted her to be happy again wherever she went to live. More so, he would have approved of Dale View; it was a dream house and both of them couldn't wait for it to be built.

On the 16th of April 2002, the 'For Sale' sign went up in the front garden. At last, the time had truly come for Kate, John, Katherine and Ian to move on. The house held so many lovely memories for them all but poignant ones mainly for Kate; the births of two of her children, her delight at passing her driving test the first time, the lovely years she had spent being a loving and loyal wife to her beloved Michael, twenty-two years of blissful family life before she had lost him so tragically and the trauma she had endured when Kate was in the depth of depression due to the agoraphobia. She still suffered from it now and always would, but thankfully she had learned to live with it. Guilt was still a big part of

Kate's life. She kept her thoughts to herself, but often she would feel deep sorrow for being so happy and she constantly felt sad for the many times that Michael could not share in their family life. The birth of their grandson Corben in 1998, the lives the children were leading now, the three of them not children any more as they had been when Michael last saw them, but adults now and she knew he would have been so very proud of them and how proud he would have been of the way that Kate had carried on the task of bringing them up by herself and how lovely and focused each child had developed in their own way with their achievements either at college or at work. Richard was already happily married to Debbie. He doted on his little boy and his lovely stepdaughter, and Ian was due to be married in August 2002. Michael yet again would not be there to see his second-born son marry the girl he loved, or to witness any of the milestones in all their children's lives which were yet to come, and it cut her to the core. It was soon to be Michael's birthday the 22nd of May 2002. He would have been fifty-six-years-old, and Kate wrote these words in her diary. 'Not a day shall I forget you, in my heart you are always near. As I loved you, so I'll miss you. Happy memories keep you near.'

The previous day a lady had contacted the estate agents and asked if she could view the property. At two p.m. prompt she pulled up outside the house and Kate showed her around. She was delighted with it and immediately said she would like to buy it. There was no quibble on the price; she would happily pay the asking price and Kate said she would contact the estate agents. If the buyer would go down to the office in Blackburn and leave a deposit then the house would be taken off the market and it was hers. John called at the site office in Billington on his way home from work to tell the lady in the office who was selling the Redrow houses of the great news that they had found a buyer for Kate's house. John told Kate later that the look on her face told him the story. Apparently, there had been a problem with the railway behind her office; the land was slipping which was to have had John and Kate's house built on and they were reluctantly coming off site temporarily until the problem could be resolved. The other houses had all been sold and therefore there were no houses available for them. It was a big blow to them both as they had set their hearts on the 'Shelley', but there was nothing they could do except wait and hope and pray the problem could be resolved soon. Kate said she didn't want to look anywhere else until it was a definite no.

On Monday the 27th of May 2002, Kate got a phone call from one of the girls at work.

'Hi Kate,' Jan said. 'I hope you don't mind me calling you at home but I wanted to tell you that the house next door to us has come on the market and it's a 'Shelley'. As you know it's only fifteen months old and our neighbours want to move to another housing estate. It's beautiful, Kate, as everything is new inside. I have just come home from work and the for sale sign is up. It says by appointment only but if you say we work together and that I have just let you know about it I am sure Janet will let you view it, but you need to be quick as it will soon be sold. It's in a lovely position and we would love you to be our neighbours,' she added.

'Oh, Jan, thank you so very much. We will come down as soon as we can and have a look at it. See you tomorrow at work.' John and Kate quickly got ready and set off in the car. As the car pulled up outside number ten, Kate was a bit nervous, after all the sign did say by appointment only, but she couldn't resist ringing the bell. A very attractive lady with black, naturally curly hair opened the door and Kate explained what Jan had told her.

'If you let me just straighten the bedroom you can come in and look around with pleasure,' she said, relieved that they could see it so soon. John winked at Kate and they stepped into the hallway. The lady asked them to remove their shoes which they did, and she disappeared upstairs. After a few minutes, she came down and led them both into the lounge. To see it all decorated and lovely was a sheer delight. It was just as they had imagined their own house would be. The décor was as they had expected; magnolia walls and a cream suite which they had also planned to buy and a beautiful terracotta carpet which went through the lounge and into the hallway, cloakroom, stairs and landing. There was a patio door in the dining area of the lounge leading to the back garden which the lady told them was south facing. In the middle of the lawn they had designed an oval garden making a lovely feature. The laurel bushes were well established and the garden wall full of creepers blowing gently in the breeze. The lady then led them back inside and took them into the kitchen which had maple-coloured units with pewter handles and there were small terracotta tiles halfway up the walls. It was so very tasteful, there was an electric oven and a gas hob, and she said they would be leaving the fridge-freezer and the washing machine all in with the price of the house. Everything was new. There were only the two of them and they apparently liked to move on from each house that they had bought after only a few months.

Kate could not believe their luck; it was now a matter of the price. The lady introduced herself and Kate liked her instantly. Her husband was still at work, but she led the way upstairs to show them the bedrooms and the three-piece bathroom. The master bedroom had fitted units with a space to put a stool underneath the dressing table, double wardrobes at both ends so the whole wall at the bottom of the bed was in a pale pear wood finish. A round mirror was on the wall of the unit and there were matching sets of drawers at each side of the bed and they were also in with the price. There was an en suite with a shower, jade green tiles, a toilet in white and an Ideal Standard washbasin. The carpets in all the bedrooms were a pale mushroom colour and very fluffy. The curtains and rails were being left in all rooms and all light fittings, including wall lights in black in the lounge. The bathroom was lovely with pale terracotta tiles halfway around the walls. The décor was in a pale lemon which complimented the lemon in the tile border. On the white bath was a wooden side panel and the toilet seat matching in pine. The carpet matched the bedrooms. On the landing lay the terracotta carpet leading up from the hall and stairs and with magnolia walls it kept the whole house light and airy. The picture window on the landing looked out towards Chaigley and the countryside beyond. Green turrets of the private school Stonyhurst College, were shining in the distance as the sun was setting behind the hills on the horizon in the west. Kate wondered how anyone could want to sell such a beautiful home. The second bedroom was also painted in magnolia and it was fitted with mirror wardrobes, cream curtains hung at the window and this room would be ideal for Katherine; Kate knew she would love it. The small bedroom had the same matching curtains. It would be an ideal room to iron in or to become a study. The views over the meadow were breathtakingly beautiful and sheep with their lambs could be heard baaing to one another.

They made their way down the stairs to see the last room in the house which was the cloakroom. It was decorated in the same tiling as the bathroom, same walls as the whole house, magnolia and it had a beautiful round, leaded porthole type window. They went into the lounge to discuss the price for this lovely home and Kate asked if she was prepared to drop any. The lady said no as it had only just gone on the market that day and Kate looked at John with pleading eyes. Even though they had got their asking price for the house, John needed to take out a fifteen-year mortgage and the house would not be theirs until the year 2017. It was a big decision and they knew they had to act fast. Kate said to John, 'I think we can manage it, we wouldn't need to buy anything in the bedroom or the kitchen as everything we would have needed to buy were being left. Yes, please we would love to buy your house and we will contact the estate agents first thing in the morning. Please don't let anybody else view it, will you?' she added. The lady promised that she wouldn't do.

The following Sunday, Kate rang Richard and asked if he would like to call up at the house to see if he wanted anything from the loft, but he refused, so Kate, Ian and Katherine went up there to sort it out by themselves. Hurt that he wouldn't come up to the house at least, this was to be his last chance to retrieve anything that was his so Kate silently went through all the boxes. They had to be ruthless now as they were moving home. Both she and Michael had been big time hoarders but by Monday evening everything was packed. The things that needed to be thrown away were being taken to the tip by John and Ian.

THIRTY-ONE

On July 19th, 2002 Ian, Katherine, John and Kate moved to the new house in Billington. The heavens opened and they were soaked to the skin by the time they had finished. It had taken ten trips to the new house before they could finally hand the keys over to the new owner. Kate was so happy to be moving there and she didn't feel the tug at her heartstrings that she thought she would do. John had suggested videoing each room as a permanent reminder of the house she had adored. There was to be no running commentary as John slowly moved from room to room; he told Kate it was not up to him to speak on the tape, just to do it for her as a memory to keep forever if she should ever feel like she wanted to see her beloved home again. A lot of the furniture had been sold; the three-piece suite was going to a man who worked with John and the mahogany dining room suite and the matching nest of tables from the lounge were also sold. Kate was selling her washing machine, fridge and freezer to a girl's daughter at work, so there was not a lot of actual furniture to be moved. Beds and chests of drawers from Ian and Katherine's rooms were coming to the new house as Ian would be staying for a few weeks with them until his wedding and their house was not quite ready, so he and Madeline planned to spend at least two weeks there after they came back from Cyprus where they would be honeymooning.

They were having a new marble and beech dining room suite delivered from Accrington soon and the cream three-piece suite was on order from a shop in Bolton, so they had no choice but to sit on sunbeds until the furniture arrived, but it didn't matter because they were thrilled that finally after five years together they had a house to call their own. Despite Katherine being unsure of the move, when she finally got her new bedroom sorted out, her clothes in the wardrobe and her ornaments on the windowsill, she told Kate that she loved it. The view from her bed across the meadow behind was idyllic, the peace and quietness of their surroundings so tranquil; the only sound to be heard were the birds singing in the trees in the back garden and across the driveway, some sitting chirping on the fence. It made the move a complete success. Ten days after they had moved in, the dining room suite arrived. The sideboard had a cream and mushroom-coloured marble top with beechwood on the doors and drawers, the large dining table had the same marble and was supported by a solid marble cube instead of legs and there were six beech wood chairs which reached down to the floor. The seating was covered in a lovely pale shade of cream and Kate hoped they had been treated with scotchguard due to them being such a delicate colour. They only needed the three-piece suite now which was due to be delivered the following day and the room would be complete. At ten a.m. the furniture van pulled up outside the front door and the two delivery men carried in the lovely Collins and Hayes suite. It was so much bigger than it had looked in the store but as they drove away, and Kate re-arranged the chairs, she stood back and admired her and John's great choice of furniture. The spacious lounge looked beautiful; everything modern and in keeping with their new house. John and Kate took a week's holiday starting on the 5th of August. They went to a furniture store in Southport and ordered a small round glass table to house the stereo system in the dining area. Katherine had an interview the following day at a veterinary practice near Preston, so Kate went along with her and waited in Katherine's car.

Always loving animals, she had a hamster named Robert (a coincidence that it was Kate's father's name) and she especially loved Popsy, Kate's cat that Michael had bought her fifteen years ago. Popsy, now getting an old lady, had settled well at the new house. Kate adored her like Katherine did but John didn't like cats at all. But despite this he grew to love her and was patient fussing over her when she was not well, due to kidney failure. Katherine received a telephone call on the Wednesday morning from the vets to say they were very impressed by her and she was offered the job to train as a veterinary nurse with them. She was delighted.

On the Thursday morning Kate and Katherine went to pick up Kate's hat for Ian and Madeline's wedding which was the following day, Friday the 9th of August 2002. The hat fitted perfectly. She paid the lady then went next door to the florist to pick up John's buttonhole which was a white rose. Kate had ordered a corsage of mixed freesia and as Katherine was to be a bridesmaid, Madeline had chosen her flowers and they were to be delivered on the day. Kate went to the hairdressers on the morning of the wedding for a trim and blow-dry and Katherine and John tidied the house ready for the weekend. Glenda and Frank were coming down from Billingham, and Jean and Peter from Darwen were also attending Ian and Madeline's special day. The heavens opened as Kate came out of the hairdressers and she prayed it would stop if only for the ceremony and photographs to be taken. She got home twenty minutes later, and Kate thanked them both for vacuuming and dusting through the house; it was as always like a new pin. Kate and John went up to their room to get dressed whilst Katherine set off in her car to Madeline's house in the Pleckgate area to meet Cheryl, the other bridesmaid and they would both get dressed there. The time flew by and as Kate and John got into John's car he leaned over and kissed her.

'You look a million dollars,' he said, admiring her long pale lilac dress and matching long jacket. Her hat which was on the back seat was of a deep purple with a lavender trim complimenting the outfit perfectly. She had lilac and lavender two-toned coloured shoes with a matching handbag.

'Thank you kind sir,' she replied. 'I wish it would stop raining though, love,' as by now it was torrential.

'We can't change the elements, Sweetpea, just be glad you've got your brolly,' he joked. Men, she thought, they can always re-brush their hair, shake the rain from their suits, but a lady does not like to look windblown when she is going out, especially today for her son's wedding.

They arrived at St Alban's RC Church near the town centre in Blackburn and John dropped Kate at the door, then he went to park the car. Soon they were being photographed side by side in the lovely church doorway. They made a stunningly lovely couple. John was so handsome in his morning suit and Kate looked gorgeous in her outfit and much, much less than her fifty-two years. It had pleased them both when Ian had insisted John be dressed as he would have had Michael his father dressed, in full morning suit and Kate knew John was secretly pleased by that and very, very proud. They entered the church which was beautiful: the mahogany pews polished for the occasion, the altar was decorated with statues of Jesus and Mary. There were paintings of angels and the cherubs in Heaven. The artist, whoever it was that had painted them so immaculately, was to be commended. Slowly, hand in hand they reached the front of the church and knelt side by side to pray. Kate thanked God for the love Ian and Madeline had found in each other and for the love she was sharing too. She prayed for all her children and the two grandchildren who were sitting just behind her with Richard and Debbie. She prayed for Katherine who looked like an angel in her bridesmaid dress clearly now quite nervous standing at the back of the church waiting for the bride to arrive.

Ian was sat in front of them with Janek, Madeline's brother who was his best man, waiting patiently for his bride and trying not to look too nervous, but Kate who knew him so well, touched his shoulder to reassure him that she knew how he was feeling. They were so alike in their ways; to the outside world confident and strong but inside the nerves were never very far away. He reminded her so much of herself.

The organ began to play the Bridal Chorus by Wagner and the congregation stood to begin the service. As Madeline walked past them linking her father's arm, Kate glanced at how beautiful she looked in her ivory wedding gown with her train and veil flowing behind her and tears welled up in her eyes. The service began with the first hymn, 'Praise My Soul the King of Heaven', and the voices of their many friends and relations who had come to witness their marriage, echoed in the ceiling high above them. Ian and his bride stood side by side waiting to take their vows before God. Katherine and Cheryl (Madeline's best friend) looked lovely in matching lilac dresses. They each had a stole around their shoulders and the little flower girl and page boy behaved impeccably. It was a long service, but everyone enjoyed every minute of it and when the priest pronounced them husband and wife there was a round of applause from everyone.

After the register had been signed and witnessed the last Hymn was announced, 'How Great Thou Art.' It was Ian's favourite and as it was also his father's it had been especially chosen by Kate and the children to be sung at Michael's funeral. How sad it was now at this wedding. He wasn't here with them but Kate felt him near and if he was watching from above she knew he would have approved of the lovely ceremony they had all attended. The Wedding March boomed out from the organ and brought her thoughts back to the present. Slowly she followed her son and new daughter-in-law down the long aisle on the arm of Ted, the bride's father. She glanced behind her to see Kazia (Madeline's mother) linking John's arm. As they reached the doorway the rain had not ceased at all although more than an hour had passed and the photographer suggested that the party had their photographs taken mainly inside the church. If the weather did improve by the time they reached the reception at the Mytton Fold Hotel near Kate and John's house, then some more photographs could be taken, but for now it was back inside.

With the beautiful backdrop of the altar it was a wise compromise and the photographer reeled off photo after photo until he was satisfied he had enough choice to give the married couple for their album. They made their way to the Mytton Fold hotel in Langho for the wedding breakfast. As they arrived the rain suddenly stopped, the sky brightened and now more photographs were being taken in the picturesque grounds of the hotel. After a lovely meal and the speeches were over Kate went over to ask Richard if he would like to come to their new home whilst they changed into their clothes for the evening disco which was to begin at seven-thirty p.m. He refused, and Kate realised the feud between them was far from over. Would he never accept the fact that she was moving on with her life? Upset, she walked away. She was past explanations with him; he would just have to get on with his life and she with hers. Pity, because it could have been so good. She was missing out on his life and of the lives of his children, all because he would not let things go. The new house had all the signs of a lot of money being spent on it and he knew whose money had paid for most of the things there. He also knew that John's wife had taken the lion's share from their divorce, leaving him with a credit card to pay off and his car and precious little else, but what did it matter who paid for what. She was driving around in his brand-new car and she certainly was not also paying for that.

She wondered if it was always going to be like this or would he realise now, that even after five years with John, just how much his father still meant to her and always would do. Did she not still visit his grave every week, laying flowers on his headstone? Of course, she did, and she always would do, Michael might be out of sight but he was never out of mind in her life and Richard had to accept that she had a new love now, not a replacement for his father but a new beginning and if he wanted her happiness and she hoped that he did, he had better get his head around the fact that they were devoted to one another and one day they too were going to be married.

No one knew, but at the bar that very afternoon when the guests were mingling with each other John asked Kate if she would like to be married, stunned, she replied, 'Are you asking me to marry you, Mr Shorrock?' Then she chuckled.

'Yes, but don't go saying anything now, it's Ian and Madeline's day but I know how happy you would be if we did get married.' She found it hard to conceal her happiness but for today she had to. The evening disco was great. They danced until one in the morning and then retired to their room. Along the corridor Ian and Madeline had the bridal suite and a few of their friends were staying over at the hotel too. Madeline's parents went home but Kate and John wanted to share in their first breakfast together as a married couple. It had been a lovely wedding despite the weather and ironically as they opened the curtains on the Saturday morning before going down to breakfast the sun was shining in a cloudless blue sky. After sharing a full English breakfast with their friends and Kate and John, Ian and Madeline left the hotel and went back to her parent's house. Later that day, along with the relations who had arrived for the wedding from Germany and Poland and were staying a few days, Kazia and Ted invited Kate, John and Katherine to their home to watch as the new Mr and Mrs Abbotts opened their wedding gifts. Kazia had laid on a buffet and it was so nice to meet the aunties and uncles with their children who Kate had heard so much about, from Ian. There was of course a language barrier. Shamefully neither Kate nor John could speak German, but Madeline was a good interpreter and as the evening drew to a close they had a small insight into their lives in Europe.

Sunday the 11th of August was a day that Kate and John had planned for the sisters and their husbands and partners to get together. They hadn't had time to chat properly at the wedding, so they arranged to meet at home at eleven o'clock to go out to Sunday lunch at the Stonebridge restaurant in Ribchester village. Over the meal they talked of the wedding, how lovely it had been despite the horrible weather. At least it had been a really warm day. They talked about the bride, how pretty she'd looked and of the men in their smart morning suits. They said what a lovely outfit Kate had worn and how sweet the Polish little flower girl had looked in her white dress and how smart the two page boys had been. Glenda and Frank were travelling home after the meal to Billingham and Jean and Peter were going to Michelle's house for tea in Clitheroe so around two thirty with heavy hearts and fuller tummies, they kissed and said goodbye to one another promising to meet again soon.

Ian and Madeline were going on honeymoon on the Wednesday to Paphos in Cyprus, but they would stay for a couple of nights at Kazia and Ted's house beforehand and the rest at Kate and John's. It would be strange for Kate when he finally left, but they were away for two weeks and their house would not be ready until a few days after they returned. Having an empty bedroom would be strange, as when Richard had gone to live with Debbie, Ian was still in the same bedroom. It was never easy when a child fled the nest; she had missed Richard so much when he had gone and although she was happy for him that he had found someone to share his life with, she missed their chats.

He had always had an arm around her shoulder when she had started to cry, always had time and patience when she needed to talk about the loss and devastation she felt without Michael. He understood how much she needed him for support as he took over the role of man of the house. If they never resolved their differences she would always love him, always be eternally grateful for the support he had given her in the early days after Michael's death, but knowing how close they had always been to each other from the day he had been born, something told her that one day he would be a big part of her life again.

THIRTY-TWO

On Saturday the 18th of August Kate and John went to Scotland to watch the Edinburgh Tattoo. They booked into a travelodge in the port of Leith where the Royal Yacht Britannia was in dock. They made love as soon as they got there as they usually did. The clean sheets were cool against their bare flesh. Time together did not dim their need for sex and today was no exception, but it left them both sleepy afterwards especially after the long journey they had had from Lancashire. Happy but tired they had a quick bath, got changed and went to the pub next door to the hotel for their evening meal. John ordered a taxi afterwards which took them up to Edinburgh Castle where it dropped them just outside the gates. As the Tattoo was not starting for another hour or so they had a walk. Kate had not realised just how busy it was going to be and she started to panic. Joining the crowds heading towards the Castle became like being in a football match crowd; she was being carried along in the crush and she felt she was being swept off her feet. Seeing her face, John tried to steer her away from everyone and towards the edge of the road near the shops, but it was an impossible task, so he gently put his arm around her shoulder forcing the guy next to her to shift a bit further along the street. Kate had an overwhelming urge to run away from it all, her heart pounding as the crowds engulfed her, but there was nowhere to go; she was trapped in the middle of a nightmare and she had no alternative but to stick it out until they reached the entrance. John could see the sheer panic in her eyes and he told her she would be okay soon as it was just the sheer volume of people surging forward all at the same time. They reached the entrance and John handed their tickets to the collector, they made their way up the stairs to their seats and the music began, the sound of bagpipes so beautiful it reminded her of Michael's father George who was born in Leith near to where they were staying and despite the crowds

Kate found herself calming down a little bit and they both really enjoyed the pageant.

John and Kate were so happy in their new house. They knew it would be a long time before they would be mortgage free, but they were prepared to work together to pay the bills and as long as they had each other there was no one more content than the two of them. The road was quiet with only the residents' cars using it and their family and friends. The cul-de-sac was used only by their neighbours so the whole area was a haven of peace and tranquillity. Kate had to pinch herself, it really was so lovely. There was only one problem and that was the journey to and from work. Doing split shifts mornings and evenings were becoming somewhat tiresome. Kate came home in the afternoon after doing her morning shift and soon she was driving back to work for the evening surgery, so when one of the girls on the switchboard was leaving for another job, Kate decided to apply for it. Change was never a big part of Kate's life; she rarely did anything than the norm so when her interview went so well she panicked. Did she really want to change jobs? She had worked for the practice for thirteen years and was happy, but the travelling was getting too much, so when she was offered the position of telephonist receptionist she took it. It was hard to say goodbye to the girls whom she had worked alongside for so long, but she would still be in the same room as them only just around the corner in Community Reception. Switchboard work was in her blood; back at Crown Paints it was all she had ever wanted to do.

John and Kate shared a lovely holiday on the 3rd of September to Tenerife where they both chilled out for two weeks. On Monday morning the 23rd of September she started at her new post. She loved the job, it was a wise move and she only worked mornings, the rest of the day was hers. No more clock watching, it was absolutely ideal.

Ian and Madeline moved into their new house on Friday the 30th of September and it was beautiful. All too soon the year 2002 was quickly coming to an end, there had been so many things happening for the whole family; moving to a new house, a lovely wedding and a brand-new job all within months of each other. Kate was happy, so very, very happy with her life now.

On New Year's Day 2003 Kate decide to ring Richard to wish him a Happy New Year. She knew she had to make a move as months were passing by and she missed him so much. She felt for one more time she wanted to see if he would share her life and if this telephone call did not work then she knew she had done all she could to win him round. He answered the phone and she said, 'Hi Richard, Happy New Year, love, are you okay?'

'Happy New Year, Mum,' he replied warmly, and her heart lurched,

'I thought I would just ring you to see how you all are,' she carried on. 'We are all fine thanks, Mum. Are you and John?' he sounded glad that she had rung him. Even though times had been tough between them she felt that he still wanted to talk to her so she started to tell him just how much she missed him and Debbie and the children. The conversation flowed on from how much she needed him in her life and even if she didn't get his approval for her happiness she could live with that. The thing she couldn't live without was him.

They discussed the things that had hurt him and she told him that he had to accept that John loved her and he was not going to run off and leave her as Richard had implied when the going got tough or the money ran out. They really were together for keeps, she was blissfully happy and next year they hoped to get married. There was a deathly silence between them but it didn't last for long. She could tell he was near to tears and so was she. They had a bond that no one could ever break, her first born son. They had always been so close, even when he was a little boy he seemed to understand her fears, never demanded anything from her or his father. He knew despite everything, she would always be there for him even if it took all her strength. She would take him to school and be waiting by the gate when he came out. All she wanted now was for him to try and forget the past and go forward with her to the future. He was too precious to lose but she had to let him know that if he continued the way he had done then as much as it hurt her he would have to get on with his life, and leave her to get on with hers. She was not backing down and it was tragic, but it would be his loss. Tears flowed from them both as he realised that no matter what he thought or how worried he was that she may get hurt, there was no way he could stop her from being with the man she adored and she was glad she had made the phone call. Now she knew for certain that he was back in her life and this time for good. They would both after all, enjoy and celebrate his thirtieth birthday together on March the 10th 2003.

On July the 5th Kate and John flew into Palma Majorca for their annual holiday. It was destination on arrival and they headed for Sa Coma. The taxi ride was a nightmare as the driver seemed to have a problem with his leg; he could not keep his foot on the accelerator therefore juddering the car constantly. It was the dead of night and they both were glad to get to the hotel safely. He really should not have been driving in that condition and Kate remarked to John that he would never have passed his taxi fitness test if he had lived in England. Despite the ride they enjoyed a peaceful two weeks together sunbathing by the pool during the day, walking along the beach in the warm evening air, then making love on the balcony late into the night under beautiful starry skies.

As with all good times there had to be an end. They had had a lovely holiday, the food was excellent as always in their five-star hotel, they were suntanned and happy and all too soon they were ordering their taxi to take them back to the airport. Thankfully it was another taxi driver who came to pick them up this time for the return journey and for this they were both very grateful.

Madeline and Ian were delighted to learn of a forthcoming event – the birth of their first child. The baby was due in December and after her eighteen-week scan they sailed to Poland by ferry to see Madeline's extended family for a holiday. Both Kate and John were excited to be grandparents again and they looked forward to Christmas Day when they would enjoy sharing a new baby into the family. On the 10th of August 2003, which was a Saturday, Kate and John went back to the Mytton Fold Hotel, this time to book their own wedding. Mrs Hargreaves was a delightful lady and sat with them to ask various questions. The date was decided, May the 8th 2004, just nine months away. It was what Kate had so much longed for. By the time they got married they would have lived together for seven years, one month and six days. They had a look around the rooms and decided on the smaller suite as there would be around sixty people at the actual wedding. The rest would come to the evening reception. John and Kate contacted the vicar later that week when he said he would arrange a day to meet them both to discuss the wedding. It was a dark evening when they arrived at the vicarage but were welcomed by the vicar himself and taken into his study.

The first question the vicar asked was if either of them had been married before and of course John said yes, he had, and that Kate was a widow. He told him he was now divorced. The vicar said they could not get married in church because of John's divorce but he said he would have a word with the bishop to see if there was a way around it. John said he was not prepared to discuss his previous marriage with either the vicar or the bishop. He said in no uncertain terms that he only answered to God as to what went wrong with his relationship and that was that. Kate was proud of him; why should he explain himself to anyone? He had left a loveless marriage and found happiness with another lady, it was as simple as that. The vicar explained that they could have a blessing in the church after a civil ceremony which would be everything a full wedding would have been except there would be no vows as they would have already taken those at the Mytton Fold. They decided to settle for a blessing; it would seal their love for one another before God and their family and friends, there would still be hymns, a reading and the wedding march but not 'here comes the bride' as that music would be played at the civil ceremony. It would be just perfect. They thanked the vicar and he said he would be in touch with them nearer the time to decide on the hymns they wanted playing and to finalise the arrangements.

THIRTY-THREE

December the 4th 2003, baby Anastazia Mia Abbotts was born to Ian and Madeline, weighing 6lb 14oz, she was in the neonatal baby unit at first as she was jaundiced but she was so delicate and very pretty. A first granddaughter and Michael would have been so proud; it was just over ten years now since he had died. Kate and John went to visit them in the hospital to take presents for the baby and flowers for Madeline. Christmas Day was fast approaching, and Kate, John and Katherine invited Richard and the family, along with Ian and his new family for their Christmas dinner. The baby slept soundly in her Moses basket and they all enjoyed a turkey feast. God's blessing of a new child's life was being celebrated by the family on the same day of the birth of His son Jesus Christ. The New Year would bring a new life also for her grandparents, their forthcoming wedding.

Saturday the 14th of February 2004 a Valentine's Day to remember always. Kate and John went to choose their wedding rings; she chose a seven-diamond yellow gold ring with a curve in it to sit comfortably with her engagement ring and he chose a yellow gold wedding band. They were going to their next-door neighbours' evening wedding reception in Lancaster later and Kate wondered how she would be feeling in a few months' time at her own wedding. Her dress had been chosen and on the 6th of March it would be ordered and now they had the rings. She was not having bridesmaids, so they only had to sort out the gentlemen's outfits and the wedding cake which Mrs Joyce was going to make. The colour scheme had been decided for the men and Kate was going to the florists soon to arrange her bouquet and order the gents' buttonholes. It was so exciting she couldn't believe how quickly everything was coming together. To be a bride at fifty-four-years-old was not daunting; it was marvellous, and she was on cloud nine. John saw the sparkle in her blue eyes light up each time she mentioned their wedding day. She asked Richard if he would give her away, but he said he would rather not, so she asked Ian instead and he said he would be delighted to. They went to see the vicar on Thursday the 25th of March to discuss the hymns and the reading. Despite not wanting to give Kate away, Richard agreed to do the reading in church and she was pleased that he would have some input in the ceremony. Strange as it was, she knew he had his own feelings regarding her forthcoming wedding, but the main thing was that he would be there with her.

Saturday the 27th of March was the day of her first fitting for her wedding dress and Katherine went to the bridal shop in Blackburn with her Mum. It was a joy to try it on again and it only needed the straps being sewn on the top of the bodice and taking in a little at the sides. The dress was an ivory crystal satin gown trimmed with bugle beads on the bodice and down the front of the dress. The train which could be detached also had the pattern down the back. It flowed beautifully and was perfect for the older bride. Her crystal tiara and satin shoes were also chosen, and they left the shop happy that after two more fittings they would be collecting it and bringing it home. Anastazia's christening was the day after in the same church where her mummy and daddy had been married and so ended a lovely weekend. On Saturday the 10th of April Kate and Katherine went for the second wedding dress fitting. It was ready at last. The dress fitted perfectly, and the shoes and tiara completed the look. Janice the sales assistant told Kate she looked beautiful and the dress would be stored until nearer the wedding day. Their wedding rings were going to be picked up the following Saturday the 17th of April from the jewellers.

When Kate and John arrived home with them, Katherine said they should go upstairs right away to Katherine's room to see Popsy, Kate's beloved cat. Katherine said she was very poorly, she was seventeen-years-old now and her kidneys were failing. It was inconceivable to think of a life without her, but neither could they stand by and watch her suffer. As Kate stroked her head she turned and winked her eye as if to say, please, Mummy, it's time for me to go. They thought they would give her another day or so but by Monday evening they decided it was time for the vet to be contacted. Katherine worked for them in Fulwood and she apologised for the late hour but asked if it was okay to bring the cat in to be seen urgently. It was after ten-thirty p.m. when they arrived in Preston and by eleven p.m. Popsy was dead. It hit Kate and Katherine hard. She was a little treasure, loved so much by all the family. She had been with them through thick and thin, seen joy and seen tears, snuggled on the bed with them when any of the family had been ill and she was always such a comfort. She purred and meowed every time she was spoken to. She was such a beautiful natured cat.

Kate thanked the vet who had been so gentle with her. It had been over quickly as she was so near to death. They hadn't realised just how little anaesthetic she had needed and now she was at peace. Katherine apologised again for the time, but the vet was on call anyway. They said goodbye and slowly walked back to the car carrying their beloved pet, where John was waiting to drive them home. It was so sad. They drove home in silence. She had lived a good life and for that Kate was thankful, but it didn't ease the pain. She carried the pet carrier upstairs and placed it on the carpet on the landing. Gently she held the lifeless body of her cat and tears rolled down her cheeks. There would never be another Popsy; she was just unique. John wouldn't ever want another cat they both knew that. He had adopted her because she was already living with them when he came to live with them, but Kate knew he wasn't really a cat lover at all, yet he had grown to love her a little bit if he would only admit it. No one could have failed to have loved her, she was just perfect. At three p.m. the following day the 20th of April 2004, Popsy was cremated at the Pet Crematorium and Kate, Ian and Katherine were to collect her ashes later that day. Whilst they were waiting they went to a garden centre next door to buy a tree; it was only a tree of remembrance as Popsy's ashes were to stay in their casket in Kate's bedroom for always.

The final fitting for the wedding dress was fast approaching and as Kate tried it on for the last time before her big day she could not contain her joy. Finally she was to marry her beloved John in front of all their family and friends. The day she knew they would both treasure forever, the day that she had waited for and dreamt about for such a very long time. In fourteen days' time she would become Mrs John Keith Shorrock. Janice, the sales assistant, carefully dressed her and put on her tiara and shoes. Gently she drew back the curtain. She stood there for Katherine to see her mum looking very, very beautiful. Where had all the years gone? It seemed like only yesterday she was trying on her first wedding gown for her own mother in 1971 for her marriage to Michael and now Katherine was watching her mother get ready for the day when she would join John and be his bride. Perfect in every way, the dress and train showed off Kate's figure and both Janice and Katherine had tears in their eyes as she walked slowly to the mirror. She knew that John would love it too. The photographer was coming at six p.m. on the 4th of May to finalise the last details with them both. He wanted a list of close family and any special photos that they also wanted taken. In four days' time it would be their wedding day. The church rehearsal was arranged for the 6th at seven p.m. and everything was coming together beautifully.

Neither Kate nor John were nervous and on Friday the 7th they went to Mrs Joyce's house to pick up their wedding cake which she had so beautifully made for them. It was a three-tier cake in an octagon shape. She had made the flowers and leaves for the decorations all out of icing sugar. They were so real looking, it was hard not to smell them and they matched the buttonhole John was to wear and the flowers in the bridal bouquet for Kate. It was an absolute credit to the lady; her skill was second to none. Carefully, they placed each cake inside three boxes and put them into the boot of the car, Mrs. Joyce wished them all the best for the following day and she kissed Kate with affection. 'Thank you so much from us both,' Kate said. 'We will bring you a piece of it when we bring the pillars back.' Now they were going to the hotel to deliver it and to meet with Mrs Hargreaves to discuss final arrangements for the next day.

John was going to stay with his mum and stepfather that evening and he had arranged to go and visit his sister who lived just down the road from their bungalow. He kissed Kate goodbye and put his morning suit and shoes in the back of Harold's car.

'Don't be late, Sweetpea,' he said and kissed her longingly. 'Soon be tomorrow, my sweet, you won't change your mind, will you?' He winked at her as he climbed inside the car.

'No chance,' she called. 'I will be there on time promise, I can't wait.' She watched as his stepfather drove up the road and he disappeared. tomorrow she would be his wife and all those people who thought or voiced that their love would never last would be eating their words.

THIRTY-FOUR

At eight thirty a.m. the following day Kate drove to the hairdressers for a trim and blow-dry. She took her tiara with her so that Debbie who was doing her hair could show her how it should look as she didn't want to drive home with it on. She carefully removed it as she got into the car. Straight home now, she thought there was no time to lose; the wedding was at 11.15 a.m. and she had been asked to arrive a little earlier as there were some forms to sign before the civil ceremony began. The blessing in St Leonard's Church across the road from the hotel was arranged for twelve thirty p.m. with photographs and greetings inbetween. Katherine was showered when Kate arrived home and she was putting on her make-up in the bathroom, Ian was due at the house about 10.15 a.m. and the flowers were to be delivered shortly, so time was of the essence.

Katherine said, 'Your hair is really lovely, Mum, but where is your tiara?'

'It's on the table,' she said. 'I couldn't drive home wearing it I would have felt silly.'

'Yep you sure would,' she laughed. 'Are you nervous now?'

'No, I am not. Honestly I am really going to enjoy this day. My nerves are put away for the moment because if I get all worked up it will spoil everything.'

'Good for you, come on then chop, chop, let's get you ready, Mum, Ian will be here soon.' Kate put on her make-up and her underclothes. She wanted to put on her wedding dress at the last possible minute so as not to crease it. Ian arrived looking very dapper and Kate wolf-whistled to him down the stairs. The doorbell rang, and the florist handed Ian a box with their flowers in it; John and Harold had had theirs delivered en route. 'Are they nice, Ian,' Kate shouted down to him,

'Yes, Mum, yours looks lovely and ours (Katherine's and his) are lovely too.' Kate asked them the time yet again and for the umpteenth time they both shouted to her, 'time you got into your wedding dress, the car is going to be here in ten minutes.' Katherine came into the bedroom and helped Kate to get into her dress.

'Wow, Mum, you look so lovely,' she said, and Kate gave her a kiss. 'Thank you so much for being a super daughter and for helping me to choose this dress. I hope John likes it,' she added.

'I am sure he will, come on let's go downstairs and I can put on my tiara and get my bouquet.' Katherine looked wonderful and very lady-like. At twenty-two she looked young for her age but ever so stunning. She was dressed in deep plum-coloured trousers and she wore a beautiful dusky pink short jacket and camisole which contrasted perfectly. Her hat matched them both and her long blonde hair flowed like gold onto her shoulders.

Michael would have been so proud of her, his little girl and of his other two sons whom he had equally adored, but especially today as Ian his second-born son was giving his mother away in marriage. He looked a real gentleman in his navy-blue morning suit, a crisp white shirt with the collar upturned where he wore a navy matching cravat. His waistcoat was made of gold brocade and he wore new black shiny shoes to complete his outfit. He was putting his white rose in the buttonhole of his jacket when he glanced sideways as she walked down the stairs to meet him. He looked at her with love in his eyes. He knew how much she wanted this day to come. Her happiness meant everything to him and to his brother and sister. Kate wanted to share this special day with them and with her grandchildren and all the family and friends of both John's and hers who were now waiting for her to arrive. In ten minutes she would be at the Mytton Fold Hotel where she was to marry the man she adored.

The wedding car arrived as she got to the bottom step; it was a 1930 ivory-coloured Beauford with a navy blue open top. George the chauffer said he would leave the top up until they got to the hotel as the rain was only just stopping. There were fresh flowers laid on the back shelf, it looked lovely. Neighbours were gathering to watch the bride emerge from the doorway and they cheered as Kate took the bouquet from Ian's hand and he helped her into the car. Katherine locked the door behind her and took the suitcase containing her mum's and John's clothes for the following day and placed it into the boot of her car. They would be sharing their breakfast with their friends who were staying over in the hotel. She waved and shouted, 'See you up there then,' and she drove ahead of them up the road.

The Mytton Fold Hotel and Golf Complex was only a few hundred yards farther up the road, so it was a very short journey for Kate and Ian. As they arrived through the gates toward the hotel, George stopped the car and put the hood down, they drove along the driveway to be greeted by Stuart the photographer and Jim who was videoing the wedding.

'Give your mum a kiss,' they both shouted in unison and Ian turned to her saying, 'I hope you are very happy, Mum, you look stunning,' and he kissed her on her lips.

'Thank you, I will, and thank you for giving me away today.' They climbed out of the car to more clicks from the cameras and headed up the steps to the little room where the registrar was waiting for Kate to sign some papers before the ceremony began.

'Ready, Mum,' Ian said, 'then let's do it.' She heard the registrar, whom she knew very well ask all the people to stand. The bridal march began and slowly Kate and Ian walked down the red carpet to where John was stood waiting for his bride. Family and friends filled the seats on both sides of the room and for those who had only come to watch the ceremony they stood together at the back. John turned to Kate and whispered how beautiful she looked, and the ceremony began. It felt like a dream as they said their vows to one another and promised to love one another till death us do part. As Harry announced that they were now husband and wife together, the whole room erupted in applause. They signed the register with more photos being taken and turned to walk side by side up the red carpet with beautiful music filling the room. It was official, they really were now husband and wife. All their family and friends were delighted and were waiting to congratulate them as the videographer and the photographer both recorded their happy day. The photographs were taken under a wooden pagoda in the hotel gardens with a multitude of colourful bushes around them and there was a wooden bridge over the little stream which would look lovely on the video, something they would both always treasure and watch in the years to come.

Soon it was time for their blessing at St Leonard's Church across the road. They climbed into the wedding car and everyone else walked through the wooden gates to meet them. The vicar was waiting on the church doorstep as the car drove into the driveway and John handed him the newly signed marriage certificate as proof of their wedding whilst family and friends took their seats inside. Mrs Staziker who had been Kate's form and music teacher at her secondary school was the organist and as she started to play. John and Kate walked slowly down the aisle together hand in hand, her beautiful ivory train gliding behind her with the silver beads glistening in the sun which was shining through the coloured leaded old church windows. Her new tiara was sparkling too and she carried a bouquet of safari and cream roses with freesia. John looked so handsome in his navy-blue morning suit. He had a gold cravat and matching waistcoat his buttonhole had three safari roses the same colour as the flowers that Kate carried. They made a stunning couple and every eye was looking at them, their expressions showing how happy and contented they both looked and how proud they were to be sharing in their wedding day.

The vicar was smiling and waiting for them to reach him at the front of the church, so he could continue with the blessing. He said that all the congregation of St Leonard's were rooting for Kate and John and that they had been in their prayers during the previous Sunday services. He said how likeable John and Kate were and he asked the whole church to pray for them in their marriage, not just that day but in the coming days to follow. The first hymn was 'Lead us Heavenly Father Lead Us' and the congregation rose to sing their hearts out. As the bride and groom followed the vicar to the altar, the second hymn was sung, and they knelt together to pray and to thank God for the second chance of happiness that they had both been given.

Anastazia, bless her, lay asleep in her mother's arms throughout the service. She was only five months old and oblivious to the promises her Nan and Grandad were undertaking. When the vicar had given them his blessing they sang the final hymn which was 'Love Divine All Love's Excelling'. The Wedding March rang out and the church bells rang showing the service was over. They had more photographs taken outside in the churchyard before the wedding car took them back across to the hotel. Soon they were out of the chilly May afternoon and in the warmth of the corridor, greeting their family and friends then sitting down to eat the lovely wedding breakfast that had been prepared for them. They had the speeches and John thanked Katherine for taking her mum for her wedding dress. He thanked Richard for his beautiful reading in the church and thanked Ian for giving his mother away. They stood to cut the wedding cake and smiled to the many cameras flashing in their eyes. All too soon the day had flown by and their evening guests were soon to be arriving. All this was being captured on video and Jim was still hard at work.

Stuart the photographer left after photographing the cutting of the cake, leaving Jim to finish videoing the first dance which Kate and John had chosen to be 'I knew I loved you before I met you' by Savage Garden. The evening buffet was excellent and Mike the DJ had everyone on their feet. The disco was magnificent. What a super day it had been and everyone agreed. It was 1.00 a.m. before everybody left and Kate, John, Ian and Madeline and baby along with a few friends eventually climbed up the stairs, Kate and John to their honeymoon suite and the rest to their own rooms. 'See you for breakfast, Kate, and John, that's if you can make it,' someone shouted.

They sat on the bed talking for ages about the day, how much it had meant to them and how they didn't want it to end. They both said they wanted to do it over and over again and they looked forward to receiving the video tape and DVD from Jim and seeing the photographs that Stuart had taken. They knew both would be very good. It was something to look forward to after they came back from their honeymoon to Paphos in Cyprus. They got undressed and Kate hung her wedding dress on the back of the door, its train trailing onto the carpet. She had loved wearing it, it was sad not to ever wear it again and she said to John that she wanted to keep it forever in the wardrobe in the spare room.

'You looked beautiful today, Kate, I was so proud to be by your side,' he said. 'All the planning was worth every minute and I can't wait to get you into bed, come on,' he laughed and pulled her down on top of him her breasts skimming over the hairs on his bare chest. Their lovemaking was calm and soothing that night as they lay together in the four-poster bed. The heady days when they had first got together when they nearly tore each other's clothes off were replaced now by just as much love and as much passion, but they were comfortable with each other and they both knew it was a nice place to be.

After sharing breakfast with Ian and family and some friends they packed their suitcases and John drove them back home. Katherine was waiting for them and Ian and Madeline and the baby followed in their own car. John got out of the car and came to open the door on Kate's side. He whisked her up into his arms and carried her up the path and over the threshold much to the amazement of her children. They opened some presents and Katherine and Madeline made a cup of tea for everyone. They reminisced of how great a day it had been, and everything had gone without a hitch, no one getting too drunk either. They all agreed how everyone had thoroughly enjoyed both the civil and church ceremonies.

On May the 12th they were off on their honeymoon to the Azia Beach Hotel in Paphos on the beautiful island of Cyprus. They felt like they were going home for two weeks. The hotel had been told that they were on honeymoon by the travel agent in Blackburn where they booked it so when they arrived by taxi transfer courtesy of the hotel, they were given an upgraded room overlooking the tiny chapel in the gorgeous grounds below and with a full sea view.

Wow! It was a stunning room: it had a coffee coloured sofa, a massive king-sized bed, wine and fruit wrapped in cellophane on a beautiful, highly polished yew table by the patio doors. They showered and went down to have a look around the grounds. The pool was still familiar to them as they had stayed there twice before. The staff, as always, were so courteous. It is a family-run hotel and always has had that special touch. Each guest is treated like royalty from the poolside staff to the restaurant staff and the staff on the front desk, still calling Kate 'ma'am' and John 'sir' each time they were asked if they wanted a drink or something to eat. Nothing ever is too much trouble and they so looked forward to two weeks of being pampered. They went back up to their room and made love. It was late in the afternoon when they got up to have a shared bath and they knew that after their evening meal and a dance in the ballroom they would be making love again, John being gentle yet hungry for his lovely new wife and she wanting him more than ever as they had their privacy there and sex was a priority for them both. They hoped they could squeeze a session on a sunbed at midnight on the nearby beach under a beautiful starry sky during their stay. They hired a car and visited their favourite spots like Kato Paphos and the famous Troodos mountains. They went to the hotel next door some evenings called the 'Laura Beach Hotel' which was also a five star and where there was a change of entertainment and some different jewellery shops for Kate to drool over, especially a ring or a bracelet. She knew she couldn't afford either of them without a bank loan! It was a wonderful two-week break and they swam in the lovely warm pool during the day, sipped drinks on the lawn whilst sunbathing in the thirty degree heat lying next to each other on their sunbeds. John quietly camcorded her whilst she slept then showed her herself much to her annoyance, but she laughed at it anyway and told him to delete it before they returned home. He said he would but knowing John's mischief he probably had absolutely no intention of doing so and she knew it.

They went down to the beach at midnight and laid on a large beach towel to make love. Naked and wrapped in each other's arms they kissed and cuddled. It was heaven for them both. The stars lit up the black midnight sky, water was lapping softly on the sand just by their feet and after a little foreplay John gently entered her, his breathing telling her his orgasm was very near. She had never loved him more and at the climax of their union she whispered to him, 'Cyprus the Island of Love' has proved to us yet again that it is also Our Island of Love.'

Whenever they could afford it, they vowed to visit this lovely hotel again; it was such a special place to them both but meanwhile until they returned home from their wonderful honeymoon they would enjoy every moment together sharing their lovemaking and savouring each memory of the sights and the history this idyllic paradise island could offer.

They returned to Manchester Airport thoroughly relaxed and ready to start their new life together. Kate was so happy to be finally married to John and he to her. Their friends and relations saw the glow in their faces whenever they met them. It was more than obvious they were made for each other. To love and be loved had been a blessing from above, she would never forget that or take anything in life for granted for she knew she had been truly blessed with a second chance of happiness and silently she thanked Him once again.

THIRTY-FIVE

A new baby daughter weighing eight pounds was born to Richard and Debbie on Friday the 29th of October 2004 at 11.40 a.m. She was beautiful, and they called her Amelia Grace. Kate and John went to the hospital at visiting time and held her as her doting mummy and daddy, her big sister and brother looked on. Their family was now complete and after a few days rest they both returned home to Lammack. It had been a year of happiness for them all and as Christmas was fast approaching Kate decided to go shopping for a LBD. She found one in a shop in Bolton that had the wow factor as they had been invited to a thirtieth birthday party the following Friday, from a girl who worked with Kate. It was the perfect dress to wear, showing just enough cleavage to be sexy, and with a feather brooch to hide her modesty, black patent high heeled shoes and matching handbag she looked just stunning. She may be fifty-four-years-old now but she certainly didn't look it and by the reaction of the gentlemen in the room that night, she felt a million dollars. December the 4th was Anastazia's first birthday. It was hard to believe it had now been seven months since John and Kate's wedding. They had received the photographs and they were beyond beautiful. They had an album made and had ordered a massive photograph which was hung framed on the wall above the sideboard. Kate admired it every time she sat at the table for her meals; they were a handsome couple and she was so glad they had decided to also have a DVD made of their special day as well as the lovely photographs they treasured.

It was a lovely Christmas and New Year and they hoped 2005 was going to be a great year for all of them. Unfortunately, Kate came down with the flu and sadly missed her god-daughter Hannah's confirmation day on the 16th of January. There was no way she could have attended and sent her apologies to her niece telling her she was in bed and that

John was looking after her. He didn't want to go on his own and so they watched television together in their bedroom. It took its toll on her as she was off work for two weeks. John however was relieved not to have caught it from Kate and was going to work as usual. They must have been run down because in early February they had a tummy bug. Kate was terrified of them both being sick but that in itself took a week to get over and another sick note was taken into work. The new year had to get better, it just had to and by the time of their birthdays, Kate's the 28th of February and John's the 1st of March saw them feeling much better and they took a week's holiday from work. They went into Whalley and to nearby Darwen and mainly chilled out for the week. They were both looking forward to spring being just around the corner. Kate loved January unlike most people who hated it. To her it was the beginning of lighter nights and she knew that around the 25th it would be getting significantly lighter in the evening and hopefully in the mornings too, but now it was early March and the lighter nights were truly upon them. Easter Saturday, March the 26th was a family get-together and John and Kate laid on a lovely buffet. Everyone enjoyed themselves and there was plenty to eat and drink. They loved having all the family at their house; it was a time to catch up with the children and the grandchildren who were growing up fast. Upstairs in the back bedroom was a linen basket full of Richard, Ian and Katherine's toys and the little ones couldn't wait to open the treasure chest and play with the old toys their daddies and Auntie Katherine played with when they were little.

Kate was so glad she had been the hoarder she had become (like her father before her). It was so lovely to watch her grandchildren chat and play; it reminded her of days gone by, happy days nevertheless when Michael was still around. He would always be around in the voices of their children and the laughter of the grandchildren that Kate and John had been blessed with.

They had a long weekend away starting on Friday the 6th of May. In two more days they would be married for one whole year. John took Kate to York for their special celebration and they stayed in a Premier Inn a few miles outside of the city centre. It was lovely to be away again even if it was for only a few days. They made love as soon as they arrived at the hotel, they were always hungry for one another despite the years they had been together and they never imagined it being any other way. They unpacked their clothes and shared a bath before going down to dinner. On the Saturday, the day before their first wedding anniversary John drove them into the city centre, they parked the car on a vast car park before walking through the narrow streets and into the shopping centre. York Minster stood there in all its glory. Kate remembered the first time she had ever seen it when Michael had taken the family there many years ago; she was in awe of it then and she was in awe of it now. Nothing had moved her so much as this beautiful church. It was the most exquisite piece of architecture she had ever seen in her life. Never having been to London to see Buckingham Palace or the Tower of London and the Houses of Parliament (which she hoped she would be able to do one day if she could control the Agoraphobia,) this was the next best thing. They went inside and knelt to pray. They stayed in the Minster for a good hour or more admiring its exquisite beauty and they both lit a candle each, one for Michael and one for John's dad, Luke, as a mark of respect to them both. It was on days like these when they were both so happy together that Kate felt the constant stab of guilt. Guilt for the way Michael had died so suddenly, for what he had missed from their lives. She knew how he would have approved of John. He always said what a nice chap he was when he had seen him mending their washing machine in the kitchen back at the old house. She kept her thoughts to herself so as not to spoil the day but nevertheless they were there niggling in her mind and she remembered again Michael's words to her the day she was scared when going for Christmas lunch with the doctors all those years ago, 'Kate, remember I will always be on your shoulder,' and she did.

As they walked through the narrow streets they came to a beautiful shop selling Lladro ornaments and they decided to go and have a look inside. Both of them were avid admirers of the collection and as they walked up the narrow staircase to where the pieces were kept they saw in a display cabinet the couple; the lady held a cream stole behind her back with her arms outstretched and she was leaning forward to kiss her husband. She wore a dusky pink long gown and her light brown hair flowed gently down her back. The gentleman wore Air -Force blue trousers, a white shirt with a blue dicky bow tie and a beautiful cream jacket. He had his arm around her waist pulling her close to him. The name leaning on their feet on the glass shelf read 'Happy Anniversary', and immediately they both fell in love with it. John asked the shop assistant if they could see it closer and she went to get a key to open the cabinet. It was so beautiful and although John had not intended to spend that kind of money for their anniversary he could not leave it there; he knew just how much it meant to Kate. He pulled out his credit card, keyed in his number and carried the precious box back down the stairs. They walked out of the shop both of them grinning from ear to ear. She leaned over to him and on tiptoe kissed his lips, 'Oh thank you, sweetheart, for buying it, it's the most lovely gift for our anniversary and it will match the one we bought from Porto Cristo in Majorca stood on the hearth at home.'

They had a lovely day, and in the evening, they went back to their hotel to get ready for their evening meal. On the Sunday morning, they went to the Jorvik Viking Centre then they did some window shopping before heading home excited with their ornament and happily celebrating their first wedding anniversary.

On Saturday the 22nd of July, they flew out of Manchester to Corfu in Greece for a fortnight's holiday. They stayed in Aghios Gordios where their hotel was set into the cliff side. The views were magnificent but even John, who had a good head for heights, had not expected to be a little nervous looking over their balcony. The people below looked like flies. It took Kate a while to feel at home there, but they had asked for views and a high floor and the hotel had delivered. It was in the nineties for most of the two weeks and they hired a small car so that they could visit Corfu Town and the surrounding area. It was a lovely holiday but there would be no lovemaking on the balcony this time nor on the beach. They had to make do with their room, but love has no boundaries, they just might try it! Then again, maybe it would be better to wait for their next holiday, a week in Cyprus on the 1st of October.

Amelia Grace Abbotts was christened on the day after they flew back from Cyprus on October the 9th 2005. She was nearly one-year-old now and time had flown by since Kate and John's wedding when Debbie had been pregnant with her. It had been a disappointing hotel this time as they did not go to the Azia Beach; instead they stayed in a self-catering apart hotel and they were surrounded by building work, pneumatic drills waking them early each morning. The constant noise was just across the car park from their apartment. John took a video of the site but then again building work has to commence sometime during the year so they did not complain. The weather had made up for it and they had some brilliant sunbathing days and wonderful sexy nights. They hired a car because they were on the outskirts of Paphos and it was a nice change being able to go for meals instead of the hotel food which quite frankly was rubbish. They vowed that when they came back to Paphos again for a holiday they would only stay in the Azia Beach Hotel where they knew it would be perfect.

It was of no surprise after returning from Cyprus to Kate and John, when Katherine announced that she wanted a place of her own. She was now twenty-four-years-old and although she had been reassured many times by them both that she could stay at home for as long as she liked, she was determined to have her independence. Kate was worried for her, as although she said she would be fine by herself, she wished Katherine had known her boyfriend James a little while longer then Kate would have been happy for him to have moved in with her but as she had only met him in the July it was too soon to know if they were going to stay together. She said she would get a kitten for company, but it was still a worry for Kate; she would always be her baby, they were so close, but she had to respect her wishes. The 29th of October 2005 was baby Amelia's first birthday and that day Kate and John helped Katherine to move to Preston. Katherine was working at the Royal Preston Hospital, so it made sense that she lived in Preston and the apartment she had chosen was newly built and beautiful. It was a first-floor apartment and was reached by her own flight of stairs. The day she moved in was a day that Kate would never forget. They had been busy taking her belongings from home to Preston making a few journeys during the day. Her bed was ready and the lounge was fairly straight so around ten o'clock they decided to finish for the day and return in the morning when John would plumb in her washing machine. The fridge was already in place so at least she could have a drink of tea before she went to bed and for breakfast the following day.

Katherine waved goodbye to her mother and stepfather, she thanked them for all their help and reassured her mum she would be all right on her own. It was heartbreaking to see her standing on the doorstep alone. Being a shy girl she had no best friend and Kate felt devastated leaving her, it was like leaving a child alone and abandoned. They drove out onto the main road and Kate started to cry, 'It's awful leaving her on her own' she said to John,

'It's what she wants, sweetheart,' he said. 'She wants to do her own thing, she wants to be by herself and have some freedom. If things go okay with James then she will let him stay over for the night. It's time darling, she's a woman now and you have to let her go.'

All the way back to Billington she cried silently feeling her heart wrenched; they had never been apart since Michael had died except for holidays. She had always been a loner and even at home it had hurt Kate leaving her waving from the bedroom window when they were going out for a while. Many times, Kate had said, 'Come with us, we are only going for a walk,' but she hadn't wanted to intrude on them. Now she had gone forever, flown the nest, the last of Kate and Michael's children to become independent and yet somehow very vulnerable and lonely but putting on a brave face, so very determined to make her own way in the world. They reached home with Kate still upset, so much so that she went upstairs to their room. She was crying so hard that she was sick with getting herself so worked up. It was a sleepless night and Kate was up early the following morning so that they could go back to Preston and see what sort of a night Katherine had had. A mother's love has no end and she was missing her so much it hurt like crazy. There was no turning back; Katherine had put down a large deposit and signed contracts on the apartment for six months at least. Please let her be okay Kate prayed. It was so strange being without her in the back bedroom which was empty now; all her belongings were gone. She might only be eight miles away but Kate felt like she was eighty miles away and she knew she had to get used to it but it was hard and it would take her time to adjust.

THIRTY-SIX

March the 1st 2006 and Kate went to pick up their new car. They had sold the Vectra to a taxi driver and they had ordered a brand new Vauxhall Astra in Star Silver. It was a beautiful car, but Kate felt nervous driving it for the first time. John was working so he couldn't be there with her and slowly she drove it back home. There was something so magical about it, the smell of a new car, the layout of it and the fact that she was the first to drive it made her feel very proud and grateful that they were at last enjoying the finer things in life. Kate still missed Katherine, but she was happily going out with James still. They seemed to be getting serious with each other now and if Katherine was happy then so was Kate. Her job was going well at the hospital and Kate was still enjoying her telephonist/receptionist job at the health centre. Money was tight but she and John were still so much in love with each other that they learnt to adjust. They couldn't afford to go for meals out as much these days as they had a car loan again, but they were blissfully happy together and Kate never took their lives for granted. She continued to thank God for her wonderful husband and for His blessings of the love of her three children, stepchildren and grandchildren too. On May the 1st 2006, Madeline gave birth to Natalia Anna, and Ian and Anastazia visited mummy and baby at Queens Park Hospital. This was a May Day the whole family would remember forever. Kate, John and Katherine visited in the evening and saw the beautiful new baby who had arrived to complete the Abbotts grandchildren. One grandson and three granddaughters and one step granddaughter, perfect!

Sunday the 18th of June 2006 was Corben's first communion and Kate decided to give him Michael's bible. She had given it to Michael when he was confirmed with Richard at St James' Church in Blackburn. It was a gift that she wanted Corben to have. He was after all, their first grandson and although Michael had not lived to see him being born it was a legacy that Kate wanted him to keep. She stipulated just one thing, that he kept it in a safe place so that the pages would not get torn and she asked him to treasure it as Grandad Michael had also done. It was a lovely service at St Mary's RC Church in Langho, Blackburn and they went to the Black Bull Inn at Old Langho afterwards for lunch.

On the 1st of July, John and Kate flew to Venice in the Venetian Riviera. They were staying at the Principe Palace in Lido de Jesolo a beach resort just outside of Venice itself. They drove past fields of sunflowers with their heads tilted towards the beautiful Italian sun. Kate had wanted to visit Italy for such a long time. It was the year of the World Cup 2006 and there was a frenzy of football supporters in the Piazza Mazzini below their balcony eagerly waiting for the cup final the following Saturday. The golden sandy beach was a sea of umbrellas dancing in the glorious sunshine with the warm blue sea just a tiptoe away. It was only a short walk across the Piazza where there were an abundance of shops just waiting for Kate to explore them. The hotel staff were one of the best they had ever stayed in, the food was excellent, and the rooftop pool was awesome with views of 360 degrees across to the Venetian Riviera. On the Monday, they booked a tour from the rep at the hotel and travelled by coach to the port of Venice. Once at the port they boarded a boat which took them across the lagoon to Venice itself where they did some sightseeing in St Mark's Square. The guide bored them to death with tales of St Mark in the fifth century but there was an orchestra playing Italian love songs behind them and the atmosphere was electric. The tour guide took them along the little winding streets decked with beautiful expensive boutiques, and the aroma of pizzas and fresh coffee was so inviting that they went into a cosy café where they were served lunch.

After an hour or so the guide led them along the lovely ornate bridges which overlooked the many small canals. Suddenly they could see black and gold carved gondolas waiting to be sailed on the Grand Canal. They had lovely cherry-red velvet seating and courting couples were oblivious to anyone around them as they sat kissing and cuddling whilst being serenaded by the oarsman who was dressed in a striped blue and white top and black trousers. The camaraderie between the oarsmen was infectious and they constantly bantered with each other as they passed on the narrow canals. The Bridge of Sighs was beautiful yet haunting at the same time; the guide told them that when the prisoners were released, they walked across the bridge on the inside from their cells and they sighed at the sheer beauty and were delighted to be set free, hence the name The Bridge of Sighs. They had a gondola booked by the tour guide and were taken along the narrow canals. It was lovely to see the many coloured houses although a lot of them were in need of repair. Some of them had terraces built on the flat roofs where the residents sat in the warm July sunshine drinking coffee, chatting and having afternoon tea with their friends and family. Kate imagined the views from up there and wished she could have seen them for herself; it would have been awesome.

After some time together they met again with the party and the guide who had booked the final part of the visit. They were taken on a speed boat on the Grand Canal. They headed towards the Rialto Bridge and the speed was unbelievable. Standing at the rear of the boat where there was just enough seating for four people they stood with their arms leaning on the roof of the boat. The warm evening wind on their faces and the spray from the water wetting their hair could only be described as exhilarating. Kate said to John that she wanted to go again before their holiday was over but alone next time so that they could do their own thing and see the sights which were interesting to themselves. The boat that had brought them took them back across the lagoon and to the waiting coach. They chatted about the day they had so enjoyed together and Kate, although she was frightened of anyone being sick on the boat, was brave enough to go a few days later to see Venice again which they did on the 12th of July. Italy won the World Cup and it was absolutely electrifying. They sat together on their balcony, watching the match on a big screen below and when Italy won, the motorbikes were revving up all night long below them in the Piazza Mazzini. The Italians were shouting and chanting in their own language and it was an honour to celebrate their success with them and even though Kate and John got very little sleep that night, to witness the celebrations of the locals and the way that they conducted themselves was admirable; there was no looting, no violence and the sleep deprivation was well worth it.

The holiday had been wonderful, and the staff of The Principe Palace stood in a line to say goodbye to everyone as they boarded the coach to go back to Venice airport en route to Manchester, with special memories that Kate and John would always treasure. When they arrived back at Manchester Airport they went to collect the Murano Glass China man that they had bought in a lovely shop just a few blocks up the road from their hotel. When John picked it up from the desk he knew immediately that it was broken. They went to report the damaged property and they were told they shouldn't have written on the parcel 'Glass Please Handle with Care.'

'Why ever not?' asked John. 'The glass weighs in at over one stone and we could not take it on board the aircraft. It had to go in the hold.' 'Big mistake,' he said. 'They see the word glass and throw it anyway.' John was furious at the guy's explanation and said, 'Look don't tell me any more we paid two hundred euros for this piece of Murano glass and we have followed all the rules. It was far too heavy to have been taken on board so we labelled it and paid for it to be put in the hold. We will try and claim.'

When they arrived home they carefully opened the parcel. The beautiful black moulded hat and ponytail were in a million pieces, the rest of the body was perfect. Kate and John stared at each other in amazement. 'Don't worry, sweetpea,' he said. 'We will try and claim for the damage and we can get another one sent over from Lido de Jesolo, we have the address of the shop. Let's go to bed, we are both tired and we will sort it out tomorrow.' Disappointed at the outcome, they went to bed and in the morning John rang the travel agents. 'Unfortunately, you can't claim for glass. If you look at the insurance document it states so,' Louise said.

'But we couldn't take it on board; he is one hell of a weight,' John replied.

'Sorry that's how it goes, I really wish there was something I could do for you both. You are good customers and I am so sorry but there isn't.'

'Okay, Louise. It's one of those things. We took all the advice we could, but we have learnt a very expensive lesson never to buy glass abroad again or alternately let the shop arrange delivery through UPS. We will still be your customers,' he added, 'thanks anyway, bye Louise.' Kate stood the China man in the corner of the lounge, next to the sideboard with his broken hat turned towards the wall. Later she put him on the bottom shelf of the hall table where he looks okay from the front, but the back of his head looks a mess, but what the hell she wasn't going to throw him away as he is a lovely work of art, damaged or not.

August the 6th 2006 was Natalia's christening day, another celebration in the family. On the 9th Ian and Madeline celebrated their fourth wedding anniversary, their family now complete. The rest of 2006 flew by. They had a lovely family Christmas together, the grandchildren were growing up fast and John and Kate continued to work. Money was tight as usual but they were happy to be together. It was a blessing that neither of them were always wanting new clothes or things for their home, it would not always be this way but until the mortgage was paid off and the car loan they had no choice but to be as careful with their money as they could. They shared things between them, Kate paying for the direct debits and food and John paying for the mortgage and the car loan. They were a great team, they lived for each other and loved each other more with every passing day. They often said how lucky they were to have found the love they shared, and they never took their happiness for granted.

THIRTY-SEVEN

On April the 9th 2007 Kate and John celebrated ten years of living together. They had decided this year to buy garden furniture for the decking which John had built in the back garden. He had made a lovely job of it and now they were able to view the rolling fields towards Chaigley and the busy A59 road which was a main route through from Lancashire to Yorkshire. Instead of a holiday they spent their money on a hardwood loveseat with a cream parasol going through the middle and a large table and chairs with another matching parasol. Both had matching cream cushions on both pieces of furniture and they had enough money left over to buy a laptop computer. Kate had talked about writing a book years ago. Ever since she had been in the caravan with Michael and the children when they were little, she had dreamt of one day writing her life story. She intended to eventually get it published and now that they had bought a laptop she could hopefully fulfil her dream. The weather was not kind to them however that summer and Kate and John, although they were pleased with their purchases, they were miserable to have not gone away on holiday. John said he would have never been able to have afforded both the furniture and a laptop and a holiday but they both decided to try and go away the following year.

Thursday the 13th of September 2007 saw the first paragraph of Kate's book on the new laptop and then because of an error on Kate's part she lost four A4 pages and had to start again on the 26th. Then on Katherine's birthday October the 1st she started it again for the third time; she was hoping this was third time lucky. It was to be a labour of love. She had so much to tell; her life had been a mixture full of love, loss, despair and tragedy but also of so much joy. She wanted to tell her story but mostly she wanted to help people who would benefit from reading her experiences of life. She wanted to show her readers that despite widowhood she had found happiness again with John, and so much love from having had her three wonderful children with Michael who in turn had then produced her lovely grandchildren. Even though she had lost both her parents when she was young, especially her father when she was just fourteen and her mother at twenty-four, she was eternally grateful for the way in which they had brought her up. She was what she was today because they had taught her to be kind, generous and caring. She knew her life had not been easy but everyone has a burden to bear sometimes and she had come through hers and survived. She hoped and prayed that her story would enrich the lives of those she loved and help the people who are suffering now by showing them that despite the odds there will be a new tomorrow even for them.

Katherine and James had lived together for quite a few months now and they had moved into a rented property newly built in Bamber Bridge, Preston but they were looking for a home to buy together and when they eventually found one in Walton-le-Dale they had two terrible young lads as their neighbours. They got to a point where it was impossible to live there any longer so they started to house hunt again and this time they found a nice garden-fronted terraced house in nearby Lostock Hall, which on the surface looked lovely but had many underlying problems. Both had wanted a project, but what a project it turned out to be. It was going to take years to get it to their liking and James wanted to do the work himself which was not easy given that he was working near Cheshire as a Racing Car Designer every day. By the time he got home from work and ate his meal it was nearly bedtime, so every weekend was spent on doing up the house that the cowboy builders had left in such a mess. Katherine was working long hours, but they planned to keep going until it was finished. Week by week it was looking much nicer and more like a home than a building site.

On Christmas day Kate and John invited his mum and stepfather and his daughter Jillian and her boyfriend Rob for their Christmas meal. Luke and his girlfriend Sarah also came, and Marion and Harold invited John and Kate and the others to a party at their bungalow on the 28th of December to round off the year. Kate and John were happy to see their children all settled now. They had all come a long way to accept each other in the family but eventually Kate and John's relationship had won through and Kate hoped now that Marion would see just how happy her son was. Time was certainly a great healer.

On Friday May the 2nd 2008 Kate started with very bad stomach pains. She ate her meal with John but all evening she could not get comfortable and eventually she told him she was going to bed. John took her up and settled her, then he went downstairs into the lounge to watch the television. When he came up to see how she was she said she was no better and he said he would come to bed and be with her As the night went on the pains were more severe and by 6.30 a.m. John suggested that she ring the on-call doctor for some advice. Knowing something was not right herself Kate dialled the NHS number and spoke to a lady who asked her various questions. At the end of the conversation, with Kate still rolling all over the bed the lady suggested an ambulance to get her into hospital immediately. Kate was terrified. What was wrong with her? She asked John to help her get into another nightdress and to fetch her dressing gown and slippers from the back bedroom. The ambulance was at the house in no time and they came upstairs to examine her.

'It's not your heart,' the ambulance man said, 'but we need to get you up to the hospital and check you out.' John followed the ambulance in the car and Kate was rolling in pain on the gurney. The ambulance man gave her morphine, but the pain was still terrible. At the hospital, she was wheeled into A&E where they were waiting for her. Suddenly she said to the nurse, 'I am going to be sick,'

'that will be the morphine,' the nurse said, 'the doctor won't be long.'

They checked her heart and asked many questions and finally sent her to the medical assessment unit where she would wait for a consultant. Eventually the doctor came in and introduced himself,

'Well, how would you describe your pain on a scale of one to ten?' he asked, 'one being a niggling pain and ten being very bad?'

'Eight,' she replied,

'and how would you describe the pain?'

'It's like very bad wind pain; she said, and he told her she was completely right it was in fact colic. He arranged for numerous tests to be carried out; a CT scan, an ultrasound scan, urine and blood tests. Kate was so relieved to know what it was. 'No operation then doctor?'

'No, my dear, just a time thing,' he replied. Kate stayed in the hospital Saturday night and all day Sunday. Eventually armed with painkillers she was allowed to go home. She couldn't wait as from the moment she went onto that ward a girl high on drugs was vomiting every few minutes. She had blankly refused to take any medicine to stop her being sick and the nurses apologised many times for the terrible noise she was making, and Kate asked John to bring his CD player and some CDs and headphones to help drown out the noise. Kate spent two weeks off work, the pain only easing as the days went by. She thought about poor babies who were diagnosed with colic and felt so sorry for them as the pain was truly excruciating.

On the 4th of July Kate and John flew to Naples in Italy. They were staying in Sorrento at the five-star Belair Hotel. They had booked it the previous year, tired of the weather when they had bought the garden furniture and determined to not have another summer as bad as the last one at home. The hotel was exquisite and looked out over the Bay of Naples, in the far distance was Mount Vesuvius and boats were sailing under their balcony coming and going to the island of Capri.

They settled in and hung up their clothes in the wardrobes; tee-shirts and shorts in the drawers along with their swimwear. John took her in his arms, 'Sweetpea, how long have we waited for this holiday you and I?'

'Forever it seems,' she said, 'but there is only a small beach here and I know we knew that before we came, but will you still go down to the water's edge to snorkel?'

'Yes, we will have a walk later and get our bearings. Meanwhile let's make love now, Kate, I want you,' he said. Their lovemaking was all the more passionate with the surroundings they found themselves in; they had a beautiful room, a massive king-sized bed and as the cruise liners sailed in and out of the harbour sounding their horns, the two of them were oblivious to the world below, naked and wrapped in each other's arms they reached their own heights together. It was a lovely holiday. They went on the train from Sorrento station on a boiling hot day to Pompeii. John enjoyed it more than Kate did as she was not into history and they realised they should have gone around with a guide as they missed some of the sights being pointed out to the others who had paid for the tour. Nevertheless, they were glad they had seen it and they both looked forward to going to the Amalfi Coast later in the week. As the coach went around each bend on the Amalfi Coastal road the views were jaw dropping with the height they found themselves at. People were like spots on the ground and boats were bouncing up and down on the turquoise blue sea like toys. It was spectacular and worth every penny to see the lovely quaint houses all built high in the hills. One lady in front of Kate and John on the coach actually pointed out Sophia Loren's house to them. It was so beautiful, perched on the edge of the cliff and overlooking the bay. Kate could only dream of the interior decor as the exterior was just stunning like the lady who owned it.

They spent the rest of their holiday sunbathing by the pool or in the little café bars in Sorrento town, they explored the side streets with stunning boutiques, dresses to die for if only you were a size six and shops selling coral jewellery which John bought for Kate. She really loved Italy. She had loved Venice and now that she had seen the Bay of Naples it had made her want to come back again and again. John also liked it, but he said he wanted a beach holiday next time they went away. He said that there was nothing nicer than to walk along the edge of the shore and paddle in the sea with Kate by his side and he also wanted to go snorkelling and exploring coves. On Friday the 18th of July, they flew back from Naples to Manchester leaving her beloved Italy once more and memories she and John would treasure forever.

Richard and the family had holidayed in Turkey and Katherine and James had been to their beloved Edinburgh. Ian and Madeline had been to Poland with the children and Madeline's mum and dad had been with them to their summerhouse. Jillian and Rob flew to Florida with Rob's mum Jackie, and his sister and family so everyone had had a lovely break. Soon it would be back to dark nights and Christmas would be just around the corner again. Ian was thirty-years-old on August the 28th 2008. He had a party at the Emporium in Clitheroe and everyone enjoyed being together. It didn't seem that long ago that they were celebrating his twenty-first birthday but time had quickly moved on. Katherine got a place at Manchester University as a trainee nurse but after a few months she found the travelling was getting too much for her. Living in Preston now, she was given placements in the Trafford Hospital and some of them were nearly into Cheshire. She told Kate that it was all bed and work, so she decided to look elsewhere for another job.

Kate and John shared their Christmas meal with Katherine and James at their home. She was still looking for a job nearer to home. They made a delicious vegetarian dinner and then on Boxing Day they went to Richard and Debbie's house and they enjoyed a lovely turkey dinner. It was a lovely time and John played games as usual with the children, whilst Kate caught up with the latest news from her son and his wife.

THIRTY-EIGHT

On the 8th of February 2009, they celebrated Harold's (Keith's stepdad) eightieth birthday party at the spread eagle Hotel in Sawley. It was lovely to share in his special day and enjoy a meal together with his side of the family. It was his actual birthday on the 12th, but the Sunday lunchtime meal was more convenient for everyone to get together. Kate looked around the table at his children; there were stepchildren and grandchildren and she thought how lucky they all were to have a parent and a grandparent at eighty years of age. Her father and mother had missed out on so much with them dying so long ago and poor Michael had missed so much too. How life could be so kind to some people and so cruel to others. Glenda went into hospital for a replacement hip operation on the 10th of February; she was in hospital for a week and picked up quite quickly despite the op. Kate sent some flowers and a get well card to cheer her up. It was only one hundred and twenty miles to where her and Frank lived but it still seemed a long way away. The 21st of February was Kate's friend Liz's sixtieth birthday and Kate had bought her some lovely pearl earrings from a jeweller's in town. She was having caterers in and holding her party for family and friends at her home in Mellor. The views from the patio window across the lawn were breathtaking; they could see right along the west coast, Southport, Blackpool and Morecambe and on a very clear day in the other direction they could see as far as Snowdonia in Wales. Kate loved the views from all the windows which were all on the back of the house. The conservatory was especially lovely with four separate dark cane chairs and a coffee table in the centre. Each chair was covered with a pale cream fabric and she often told Liz she would never get any work done if she had lived there. It would take her all day just to gaze out across the fields and watch the sea glistening on the horizon and at night the street lights were shining everywhere. In a year's time, it would be Kate's sixtieth birthday and she would be a pensioner too. Wow, John would really be a toy boy then at only fifty-six-years-old, fancy having a wife as a pensioner she thought. He really would take the Mickey out of her. She turned her thoughts to the party in hand and anyway there was plenty of time to think of next year on another day.

The rest of the year was quiet, and Kate and John reluctantly decided to spend their main July holiday at home. John said he would like a new television over the fireplace and a blue-ray system on a console table enabling the floor standing silver television to be sold making more space by the radiator. He would decorate the lounge and that would take the two weeks that he had off work. They set off to Bolton and chose a television. When they got it home, they realised it was going to be too small over the fireplace, John drew an outline on the wall and they decided they needed the next size up, a forty-two inch one. The shop exchanged it but there was a penalty for opening the box; they knew it had not been put onto the wall but because they had broken the seal they had to have some money knocked off the price. John was annoyed, but the sales assistant said that rules were rules and they paid the difference and happily brought home the larger television. It took the whole of two weeks to decorate the room and soon they were going back to work. Kate had been a bit fed up as it was a job for John to do and she felt a bit lost although both of them were looking forward to their newly decorated room.

'A holiday next year, John,' she shouted from the kitchen. 'Please don't let us ever do this again.' The lounge looked lovely; the television was perfect on the wall, they were right to get the bigger size and they snuggled on the settee together that night to watch their favourite programmes. Tomorrow it would be the end of their holiday and back to work as usual.

On September 5th, 2009 Kate had her two-year appointment with the breast specialist. He had left the two-year gap as the breast lump that Kate had found whilst they were on holiday in Paphos, Cyprus back in 2000, had turned out to be only a water cyst. The registrar had decided to aspirate it and as the needle was pushed into the lump it disappeared which he explained was just water but because of her mother's history of breast cancer they saw her each year from then on. By September 2007 her specialist said the next appointment could be in two years' time and here she was waiting with John in the outpatients' department at the hospital. There were only two people before her and soon she was getting undressed ready to see her consultant. He was a friendly chap and Kate really liked him. After checking both breasts and finding no more lumps he said she would have her mammogram and if that was okay then he would send for her in another two years' time, if not then he would write to her. He shook Kate's hand and returned to his office. The nurse who was in attendance said to Kate, 'He will write to you anyway, he always does.' Reassured by her remark Kate thanked her and said, 'Where do I go for my mammogram now?'

'Oh, that's not today,' she said, 'you will be sent for that shortly.' Kate said goodbye and returned to the waiting area where she told John what had happened.

'Crazy,' he said, 'what was today for then?'

'Just catching up on his backlog. I got myself all worked up for nothing. I shall just have to wait for my appointment coming through.' When the appointment did come through, Kate enquired at work if it was all right to take some time off and she was told she would have to work the time in. Annoyed by this she rang the hospital to re-arrange an appointment for an afternoon so she needn't take time off and was told that afternoon appointments were not available any more but would a late morning be of any use instead of a nine thirty a.m. slot. Kate said it would be and she was then offered a 12.15 p.m. appointment. Kate thanked the clerk and decided to take a day's leave anyway and also it would be nice to have a long weekend, she would attend the mammogram and then do a bit of shopping in Accrington town centre.

By the 16th of November Kate began to wonder where the promised letter was from her consultant, although, she only had the nurse's word that he would write one. But she knew only too well never to presume that the mammogram was okay she needed to know it was, so she rang her GP's surgery and asked if they had heard.

'No,' the receptionist said, 'try the mammogram department and see if they have received the result.' So she did. 'No, we don't get the result here it goes back to your consultant,' said the receptionist at the hospital. By now she was getting a bit exasperated. Why had no one told her properly what the procedure was? The consultant's secretary gave her some spiel about him being on holiday and that she would type it ASAP. Kate gave her a few days then she rang again. 'Just refresh me, what am I looking for?' So, Kate relayed her the story to jog her memory and she said she would get it in the post and she also said the consultant wanted further tests. This set alarm bells ringing in Kate. 'I will write to you if I need to or send for you in another two years' time,' she remembered his words. So, there is a problem she thought, something is not straightforward because why would he need more tests? By Wednesday the 25th of November with still no sign of the letter, Kate rang his secretary again. 'Good morning,' she said. 'I was just thinking of you, I am sorry, but your letter still has not been done.' With that Kate said to her, 'look you are a colleague of mine and even if you weren't, you have really let me down. You promised days ago to get that letter to me and you still haven't even typed it.'

'Does the consultant know how pulled out you are?' Kate asked,

'I have to prioritise my work,' she replied and, 'I have been told to send for the patients who need operations.'

'Oh, don't talk to me about priorities I have worked at a health centre for nearly twenty-one years and I know all about prioritising. Just get the letter typed,' she fumed,

'I will,' she replied, 'I will stay until eight p.m. tonight to do so.' 'Good, I shall wait to receive it soon then,' Kate said and abruptly put the phone down on her. She burst into tears then. What the hell was going on and when would she have ever found out if there was a problem with her breasts if she hadn't had the knowledge to chase the damn result? She thought of some poor old lady who after nearly six weeks of thinking everything was all right to suddenly wake up one morning and find a letter behind the door telling her everything certainly was not all right at all. Kate went to work the following day and after she had finished she drove straight home. There was a message on the answering machine from the secretary curtly telling her that the letter had been typed and if Kate would care to ring her office she would read it out to her over the phone. After all the messing about Kate was tempted to just wait for the postman to deliver it, but she thought again that with all the trouble that she had been through to find out what was wrong with her, that she would let her read it out loud and the sooner the better.

'Mrs Shorrock speaking,' she said with her posh telephone voice. 'You left a message on my answering machine earlier today.'

'Yes, just let me get it,' was her reply. 'The consultant has found mild irregularities in both breasts and he wants you to have a more invasive mammogram and an ultrasound scan,' she said.

'When will that be?' Kate asked.

'just let me see, yes there is an appointment on the 7th of December at nine thirty a.m., can you make that?'

'Yes thank you,' she said, 'what about the ultrasound scan?'

'You will be getting a letter from the X- ray department within the next couple of days.'

'Right thank you I will wait for that. Good-bye.'

'Goodbye,' she said. She was a lot more human than the last time Kate had spoken to her. The next day a letter arrived asking Kate to ring X-ray and make an appointment for the ultrasound scan, the first available was to be on the 18th of December, one week before Christmas day. This whole sorry episode was turning into a total nightmare.

As it happened Kate and John had taken the day off on the 7th of December to do some Christmas shopping and she was glad that he could go with her. The mammogram was more uncomfortable this time and the radiologist asked if she could do the left breast again which she did. When she put the X-ray on the lit screen she said it had been worth doing it twice and told Kate she could now get dressed. She told Kate to contact the consultant's secretary in two weeks' time if she hadn't heard anything regarding this new result and Kate said she would.

'One down,' Kate said to John on the way out of the hospital, 'one more to go.' They went into Accrington town centre to do some shopping and Kate chose a lovely Sekonda watch from John for Christmas. It seemed like an eternity before the ultrasound scan appointment and Kate asked Ian if he would take her. He said he would as he knew the hospital layout; he went there for his physiotherapy appointments. They arrived ten minutes early and there was a lot of ice on the ground. The snow had been relentless over the past few days and Kate was grateful that she was not driving there herself.

They had a wait of around twenty minutes then the nurse asked Kate to undress to her waist and put on the little cape for privacy. She was shown into the X-ray room and greeted by a lovely foreign doctor. Kate could not make out her name and the doctor asked her what had been going on with her breasts and Kate explained that the first mammogram had shown there were mild irregularities in both breasts and Kate told her she was on HRT patches of 100mg every three to four days.

'You should not be on hormones at your age,' she fumed, 'why are you on them for so long?'

'I had a hysterectomy in 1998 and I have been on them ever since.'

'No, no, no, hormones,' the doctor said in a very dramatic manner. Kate looked at her stern face and felt about an inch high. The doctor proceeded and when she had finished she turned to Kate and said, 'I can see nothing.'

'You can't see anything,' Kate repeated thinking she had heard her wrong.

'No nothing,' the doctor said again, 'you will have to wait for the report being sent back to the consultant now,' the nurse said, 'it is just a case of time.' Kate thanked the doctor and went to get dressed and still not convinced by the outcome, she went back into the open door of the X-ray room and asked the nurse if she had heard the doctor correctly. 'Yes, she said she could not find anything wrong.' Relieved if not confused she went over to where Ian was waiting for her.

'Well, Mum, how did it go?' he asked.

'The doctor said she couldn't see anything wrong,' Kate said. 'I am so confused, what has all this been about then all these months of worrying not to mention the tears and frustration? I can't settle until I know what's going on and I don't think I will know anything till after Christmas now, do you?' His face was etched with worry, bless him, he knew his Granny Walsh had breast cancer at the age of just forty-five years and died of secondary lung cancer at sixty years, and his mum was going to be sixty–years-old in February 2010 and that was only eight weeks away from now, he thought. He drove her home and dropped her at the door,

'are you coming in?' she asked him.

'Yes, Mum, I will do, can I have a biscuit to put me on please?'

'I'll go and get you one,' she said. As she opened the fridge door she thought of Monday when she should be ringing the secretary for the results of the second mammogram; it would be two weeks since John had taken her to the hospital. She ran upstairs to get the secretary's phone number from her bedroom. There might just be a chance of getting this wrapped up before Christmas. The secretary answered immediately, and Kate asked if she had got the report. She said she had but it had not been read yet by the consultant and that he would be in on Monday the 21st December and could she let her know then. Kate said she would be on annual leave that day and she could ring her at home anytime that day. At nine thirty a.m. the telephone rang, and it was the hospital saying they needed the results of the ultrasound scan before the consultant could tell her what the outcome was.

It was agreed that Kate could ring on Christmas Eve morning from work and she would be told of the results. At nine-thirty a.m. Kate went into a private office upstairs where no one could hear her conversation and dialled the direct line. She held her breath as the phone rang at the other end and suddenly the voice said, 'secretary speaking.'

'Hi Mrs Shorrock speaking, you asked me to ring you this morning for my results,' her heart was pounding out of her chest.

'Yes, I asked the consultant this morning what he wanted me to say to you and he said, "Tell her there is nothing to worry about."'

'Oh my god,' Kate said. 'Thank you very much, I know we came to blows the other week, but this has been going on for so long. It will be four months since my consultation with him. What happens now?' 'You will be sent an appointment in the New Year, if you have not received one by the end of the first week in January ring me and I will sort one out for you, but you should hear before the end of that first week.'

'Thank you so much. Have a nice Christmas,' she said and as she replaced the receiver she burst into tears. 'Oh God, thank you for answering my prayers. I have waited for all these weeks to hear her say that I have nothing to worry about. I thought I had breast cancer like my mum.' Kate went out of the office and along the corridor to the stairs and she could not stem the stream of tears running down her face. When they saw her, her friends thought the worst.

'He says that I have nothing to worry about. I can't believe it, I can't believe it,' she cried again, and everyone was hugging her and giving her a kiss saying this is the best Christmas present that you could ever have.

THIRTY-NINE

As Christmas Day 2009 approached life had become a nightmare for John; his mother had been poorly for a year now and she had lost two and a half stone in weight. It was terrible to see how frail she had become and how thin her body was now; she was barely six and a half stone and in an awful lot of pain. On Christmas Eve Kate and John went to the Royal Blackburn Hospital to visit her and she was laid curled up asleep with a sick bowl in her hand. Afraid she might wake up and vomit Kate gave John the shush sign and he acknowledged and crept quietly around her bed. He went to ask a nurse for the update on her condition and as Kate sat there looking at her she stirred.

'Hi, Kate,' she said, 'are you on your own?'

'No, John is with me,' she replied. 'He is finding a nurse to see how you are doing.' Soon, John pulled open the curtain a little and bent down to kiss her.

'How are you, Mum?' he asked, and she told him she could not go on like this for very much longer. 'You have to do,' he told her. 'Everyone is rooting for you, Mum, you have to keep fighting.' It was plain to see that she was losing the battle and who could blame her she had been through so much. The nurse told John that the consultant surgeon and his colleagues were having a meeting on Christmas morning to discuss their next step. Later as they were leaving the hospital he told Kate what the nurse had told him. It was clear that Marion was close to death and something needed to be done for her soon. They went home with heavy hearts and John rang his stepfather and told him the surgeon would be in touch in the morning. Harold thanked him and told John he was grateful for some progress as he also knew how desperately ill she was.

Early on Christmas Day the telephone rang, and Harold asked if he could speak to John; he told him they were taking Marion down to theatre and they were going to operate on her. John and Kate were going to Ian's house for their Christmas meal and Harold said they must still go as he would ring John as soon as there was any news. It was a quiet morning, both of them lost in thought and they prayed the surgeon would get to the bottom of Marion's problem. They set off to Ian's house and called in at the cemetery to put the wreaths on Michael's grave and John was putting one on his father's grave. They called to see Jillian and stayed for a short time. She was tearful for her Nan and John tried to reassure her that it was for the best.

'If she dies, Jillian,' he said, 'at least she will be out of this terrible pain and suffering. It's been going on for months and I know you hate to see her like this as well as grandad and us. How long is it going to be before she can't take anymore?'

'I know,' Jillian said and it broke John's heart to see her so upset. Marion was like a mother to her. They were so close. They rang each other every day to have a chat and when her own mother was being horrible to her which was pretty often, she always turned to her nan for comfort and she told her things about her life that she never would have discussed with anyone else. John's mobile rang shortly after they had finished their Christmas meal and he went into the lounge to take the call. Kate followed him and they sat down on the rug together whilst the surgeon explained to John that he had taken away Marion's bowel after finding a blockage. He went on to say she had been only forty-eight hours away from death and that she was in a critical condition in the intensive care ward.

John thanked him for all he had done, and he told the surgeon that he would pass the message on to his stepfather to save him having to repeat it all again. Harold was so relieved to hear that his wife had at least pulled through the operation. It was a last resort for her and John said they could all visit her on Boxing Day morning, but it would only be for a short time.

Harold informed John that his sister and her husband were on their way up to Blackburn from Suffolk where they lived. John said he was so pleased they were coming as he knew only too well that there was every chance of their mother dying, and he wanted his sister to be at the hospital to see her as soon as possible before or if that should happen. John and Kate returned to the others and Ian said he was so sorry that this had happened on Christmas Day, but John said it was the only thing that could be done for Marion and they all hoped and prayed that she would pull through. On Boxing Day morning John and Kate went in their car to pick Harold up from his and Marion's home and they went up to the hospital together. As they sat in the waiting room John's sister Linda and her husband Keith arrived and they hugged one another in turn, through their tears. The nurse said only two were allowed at the bedside and only for a very short time. Harold and Linda went in to see her first. Harold's children were also waiting to see Marion; she had been their stepmother for nearly thirty years and they were concerned for their father who after all was now eighty-years-old, but as usual he was coping remarkably well under the circumstances and he came back from the intensive care ward with a great big smile on his face, looking very relieved. It was John and Peter, his stepbrother's turn next and Kate said she would go in afterwards with Jillian. Kate was scared in case anyone was vomiting in the ward but to her relief no one was. Bravely she followed Jillian to Marion's bedside. They both knew now why the others had been so cheerful, there was Marion, sat up in her bed and looking tired but much better than everyone had been expecting. Kate gave her a kiss and they stayed a short time. Jillian didn't want to leave her nan so Kate left them together and returned to the waiting room. The others were chatting about how well she looked and John reminded them that the surgeon had said she would be all right one day and then the next she could be back poorly again. It was very early days and she had been so very near to death.

Marion stayed in the hospital for two more weeks and then she was asked to go to a rehabilitation centre in Burnley, but Marion was having none of it. She was determined to go home soon and despite all the family telling her otherwise, she did do in the middle of January 2010. The district nurses came to the house daily and helped her with her stoma, but she continued to be very weak. She didn't get dressed any more as she was only comfortable in her nightdress and dressing gown. One night around twelve thirty, Harold telephoned John and said she was in terrible pain and that he had sent for the ambulance. Apparently, her hip had come out of its socket due to the amount of weight she had lost. It was pitiful to see her struggle to move or even to turn over in her hospital bed and a belt was designed to keep the hip in place but to no avail; she was too poorly to be bothered with anyone trying it on her. John visited her in the hospital every day and Kate went up every few days. Periodically she came home but it was clear to them all that Marion was very, very poorly. Sadly, on Saturday March the 13th 2010, the day before Mothering Sunday, she died in the hospital and John was by her side holding her hand. Harold had just gone to speak to his daughter in the next room and when he came back to Marion's bed she was gone. John told him as she died a tear had rolled down her cheek but no words were spoken. The diagnosis was lung cancer so after the operation for the bowel blockage she must have already had advanced cancer of the lung from which there was no way back.

John came home from the hospital in the early hours of Saturday morning after first taking Harold back to the bungalow he and his mother had shared for thirty years and Kate felt his pain. He knew, in fact they all knew, she was free from all her terrible suffering now, but their loss was still hard to bear.

Quietly as tears rolled down his cheeks he whispered, 'I am an orphan now; I have no mum and I have no dad either.'

'I know darling,' Kate said, 'but she is in a better place now with your dad and there will be no more pain for her.' Slowly and with a heavy heart she led the way upstairs and back to their bed where they snuggled up to each other and eventually fell asleep. After the funeral at Sacred Heart Church in Blackburn on March 19th, 2010 they went to a lovely pub near the cemetery where they shared a buffet with family and friends, and everyone reminisced of their times with Marion.

As the afternoon came to an end they said their goodbyes to each other, promising to keep in touch and all of them went back to their respected homes, quietly remembering the sad day they had shared. Why is it, Kate thought on the way home, that at funerals people say nice things about the person in the coffin but now they could never hear it? We should all tell one another just how much we love them, every day or more than once a day if possible and at least as often as we can, because to heap praise and love for the person who is dead is so pointless. They can't hear it now and for so many who would have loved to have heard those special words of admiration it's too little too late. Always remember this when you next see the one you love, for today is the first day of the rest of your life and theirs.

FORTY

The year was to see many unforeseen things that were going to happen in Kate's life and things would never be the same again. The day after the funeral John and Kate drove down to Peterborough to collect his new works van. It was a lovely day and they chatted about the funeral they had attended the day before. They shared a packed lunch together in a lay-by before continuing the three- and three-quarter hour drive to the depot. Kate always went with him to collect his new van, it only happened every three years or so depending on the mileage John had done, but they both looked forward to the trip whenever it was. The day was long, but they had no one to answer to and they arrived home safely around eight o'clock that evening. The day after, John sorted out his stock which had been stored in the garage and put it back inside the new van.

June the 1st 2010 was a day which Kate would remember forever. An appointment for a flexible cystoscopy had been arranged for her due to her recurrent bladder problems and the consultant was happy to announce that everything was perfectly normal and unfortunately it was an irritable bladder and something that Kate would have to live with. With mixed feelings at the diagnosis, yet very pleased that there was nothing sinister wrong with her, Kate kissed John goodbye at the hospital, thanked him for going with her and she headed back to work at the health centre. As she keyed in the code on the reception door at work she was almost knocked over by Lindsey her colleague who came out of the door at an astonishing speed, red faced and obviously livid. Instantly Kate knew why. A few months before, Lindsey had been to see their manager unbeknown to Kate, and after wondering where she had gone and a bit cross because she had been missing for a while, she came in the door looking very pleased with herself.

'I shall be finishing at one thirty p.m. next week when I cover for you,' she announced. 'I have just been to see our manager and I told her I want to still go home at one thirty p.m. instead of twelve-forty-five p.m. and she has agreed to it.'

'You can't do that it's not fair. You will get paid overtime or take time off in lieu and why should you when your allocated hours are only four and a half?' Kate said.

'Well I am,' she replied, 'I am sick of coming in early and only doing my hours. I am going to go through until one thirty p.m. as I usually do even though I am covering.'

'Lindsey ,can't you see that it's just not fair, you will either get far more days off or if you take the time as overtime you will be getting a lot more pay, more to the point you don't need to stay when I am on leave as Catherine the afternoon girl will be in at 12.45 p.m. and if she is on leave I shall be in. There is not enough work at lunchtime for three people as it is. You know how quiet it is so you would be getting paid or having time off for doing nothing!'

Kate was furious. She knew that Lindsey wanted more hours and she was hell-bent on getting her own way even at the expense of her two other colleagues. It was more than obvious she had twisted their temporary manager around her little finger and as she was new to the job she had whole-heartedly agreed with the manipulation, but Kate wasn't having it. She would have to discuss this arrangement with head office when she got home and see what they had to say about it. It was a difficult morning and Kate was glad to go home. How dare Lindsey try to gain time or money behind their backs. She had asked the previous managers before if she could do that and she had been refused outright. Now she thought she could get around a new manager but not if Kate had anything to do with it. There were only the three staff in community reception: Kate who worked 8.15 a.m. to 1.15 p.m., five hours; Lindsey who worked nine a.m.to one thirty p.m., four and a half hours because she had two children to get off to school and Catherine who worked 12.45 p.m. until 5.00 p.m., four and a quarter hours.

The switchboard had to be covered all day and Kate hated the cover in an afternoon, but it had to be done. If Catherine was on leave or off sick the two-morning receptionists had to share her shift between them. It wasn't often at all that Catherine did ring in sick but once she rang to say that she had the flu, so Kate offered to stay and do the afternoon shift; she could have overtime for this or time off in lieu. But it was only in an emergency as there really was no spare money in the kitty for overtime, which brought Kate back to the present and she went straight home to make the phone call to her manager. After explaining the situation Kate was reassured that there was no way Lindsey would get the extra hours and that if she had to do any cover then she would open the reception at 8.15 a.m. and she had to leave her post at 12.45 p.m. as she had done for the past seven years she had worked at the health centre. Relieved that she had got the problem off her chest Kate thanked her for sorting it out. Kate carried on with her job in the days ahead as she knew that there was no chance of Lindsey getting anything extra, either in terms of money or time. It had been a good try, but it was never going to happen. Now the day had arrived, the day that Kate had dreaded. Lindsey had finally been told hence, the slamming of the door and her absence for at least half an hour from the office. Kate's manager had been helping out in reception whilst Kate had been to the hospital and as she hung her coat up on the cloak hook, she heard her say, 'I'll leave you to it now.'

'Have you told her about the cover?' Kate asked. She knew by the look she gave her that the deed had been done.

After about half an hour or so the door opened and in walked Lindsey. She was absolutely furious. Kate was answering the switchboard and as she returned to the back desk where the mail was waiting to be sorted, she felt someone come up behind her. Thinking she was going to help her with the post, she turned around to find her face right up to her chest, she was so near her that Kate could feel her breath and she snarled, 'I know what you have done, Kate, you have reported me for asking for more hours when I cover reception.' her face was as red as a beetroot, and Kate was shaking. 'Well, Kate, you had better watch your back,' she snarled again, 'because I will be watching you every step of the way, so remember, I will be right behind you so you had better cover your back.'

'I knew you would take it like this,' Kate said, 'just think about it, it's not fair on any of us. I would like to say I will be in at eleven thirty when Catherine is not in but I can't, we all have our allocated hours and so it's not fair for you to take more.'

'Oh, you always have to be the best, Kate, haven't you,' she snapped, 'always have to have more hours than us, don't you?'

'It's only half an hour difference for God's sake and you have your extra work upstairs every afternoon topping up your wage, so what are you complaining about?' Kate replied.

There was no reasoning with her and she blanked Kate for the rest of the morning. She went out for a cigarette as usual a few times whilst Kate held the fort. She knew this was not going to be solved with a simple explanation. If you crossed her she was venomous, and Kate decided to just get through the morning as best she could. She was still shaking after the confrontation and it was only eleven a.m. It felt like she had been in reception for days not just a couple of hours. The atmosphere could be cut with a knife and Kate knew that the girl who Lindsey went for a smoke with would take her side. She could see them on the CCTV camera in the corner of the room, they were chatting and walking across the car park together giggling and, although the problem was nothing to do with the other girl—she was just another receptionist working for the treatment room in their reception room—it still was going to be uncomfortable working alongside the both of them.

At twelve thirty p.m. their other colleague came in to do her afternoon shift and the mood in reception was frosty to say the least. Kate acted as normal as she could do but as she got her coat on to go home she knew they would be talking about her as soon as she had left the room. Kate went straight home, and she rang John, telling him what had happened.

'You need to ring your manager,' he said. 'That's bullying, Kate, and she needs to know how she has reacted to being told she can't have her own way.'

'I hate confrontation, John, you know that,' Kate said near to tears, 'but I'll tell you this, it's the principle of it all and if my mum and dad have taught me anything in my short life with them, it's principles and I would do it all over again if I had to. She just thought she could pull it off. The stupid thing is, she would not have got away with it, as the lady who does the time sheets would have realised what was going on, but what's done is done?' Kate made a cup of tea, she went into the conservatory, sat on the wicker sofa and thought about what John had said. He was right she knew that, but she didn't want any more hassle. Maybe she should just leave it and hope Lindsey would see reason overnight and apologise to her in the morning. They had always got on so well together despite them being from totally different backgrounds; she had told her she had been expelled from school but Kate didn't hold that against her and they bounced off each other. They laughed each day especially at Kate's wit and she had always said how Kate had taught her all she knew. When she had got the job in reception alongside Kate she had sent a lovely card of thanks that was written from the heart. Kate had told her manager after the interview that she thought she would be okay for the job. Now after this morning's horrible episode it seemed longer than the seven years they had worked side by side every day and she hoped it could be mended between them, but she wasn't holding her breath.

After much deliberating, she decided to ring her manager but she wasn't in so she spoke to her deputy who was horrified to hear that a member of staff had stooped so low as to bully Kate; twenty one years' service against seven years' service it was so sickening. She asked her if she wanted to put an IR1 form in (an incident report) but Kate said no she didn't, thank you. She told her she did not want any more trouble. She was glad it had come out in the open and she told her that she hoped that would be the end of it. It was John who had said, she as their manager ought to know that she had been threatened and that maybe it would be put down on record.

'You were perfectly right to inform me; we do not condone that sort of behaviour, Kate, so leave it to me and don't worry about it any more I will deal with it.' Grateful that she knew the outcome of it all, Kate thanked her and said goodbye. The next day the two girls came into reception and neither of them spoke to Kate. It was obvious that they were the best of mates. It was so uncomfortable, but she had no regrets for yesterday and with her stony face she knew that a night's sleep had not changed a thing; she was still fuming with Kate for interfering. They each did their work. Fortunately the diary was listed each day as to who was doing what; Lindsey was on the franking machine and Kate was on the post. It was great to get out of the office and go up to the post room out of the way. Lindsey answered the switchboard promptly and if Kate moved forward whilst she was seeing to a patient she quickly moved and blocked the way so Kate had to go back to her desk at the back of the room. She felt like an outcast. She was being as awkward as she possibly could be and Kate started to hate her. She knew what she could be like when she had talked of her home life, if she didn't see eye to eye with someone in the family, now Kate was getting the same treatment.

Christmas was soon upon them and it had been a hard few months. Kate knew things would never be the same between them now and then the call came from Catherine; she rang in sick. It was a Friday afternoon, typical of Kate, she immediately offered to cover the afternoon shift. Lindsey thanked her for stepping in as a Christmas meal had been arranged and Kate wasn't going to it anyway. They had to speak sometimes as the CCTV had to be shown to Kate due to an incident and she thought that was a breakthrough at least, but then things reverted to her not speaking to her again and they were back to square one.

On Monday the 6th of December 2010, Kate also came down with the flu and this meant the switchboard would have to be covered all day as now two staff were off sick with it. Kate always had an agreement to ring Lindsey at seven a.m. if ever she was unable to go to work then there was time for her to get ready and be at work to open the switchboard for 8.15 a.m. When she eventually went back to work things seemed a little better, they chatted a bit more during the morning and it seemed the break away from each other had done them both a world of good and as the morning progressed she told Kate that Catherine was also better from her bout of flu but that she wanted some time off for a holiday now with her husband; they weren't going away just doing some Christmas shopping together. The afternoon shifts needed to be covered by them both. She told Kate that she would need to cover two out of the three days as she had done more cover when the two of them had been off with the flu. Kate retaliated by saying she could not help being ill and that overtime had been paid for her trouble. It wasn't fair that she had to do more cover just because of that. It turned out that Kate did end up doing the two days cover and Lindsey did just the one. She thought what the hell, by now she was sick to death of the awkwardness between them. She knew now that she was going to make Kate's life as miserable as she could do. She was a total bitch to be with and it certainly was payback time on her part; Kate would certainly have to watch her back as she had already been threatened with back in June.

It was obvious that they could not get past this episode and Kate made up her mind that when the staff moved into the new health centre which was being built just up the road, she would not be going to work there. Enough was enough. Kate voiced it that she didn't think she would go there when they talked animatedly on odd days, but as it was only December and they would still be at the old health centre for at least another eleven or so months it would give Kate time to save up some money; she was already getting her pension and so she could plan well ahead. It was sad to think that they had been so close, bounced off each other every day and were known to their colleagues as a great team. Their mornings had flown by because they had enjoyed each other's company and got the post and the results from the hospital out to each department in record time, answered the switchboard promptly and efficiently. It was a lovely job and Kate couldn't bear the change which had arisen between them both. She was distraught to realise what a swine she had turned out to be. She had taught her all she knew and although she didn't have a good telephone voice like Kate had, she answered the calls in a friendly manner and everyone thought she was a really lovely person. Yes, she was, until you crossed her and then she would chew you up and spit you out.

FORTY-ONE

Christmas 2010 passed by and John knew how unhappy Kate was at work. Gone were the smiles as she kissed him goodbye in the morning as they went their separate ways to work. They talked to each other every day after Kate had finished at 1.15 p.m.; she always rang him on her way back to the car park. He had no words of condolence for her and he hoped and prayed that Kate would have the strength to stand up for herself and not let her be forced to quit the job she loved, but it was not to be. On Wednesday the 26th of January 2011 and after another morning of the computer being logged off should Kate get near it to answer the switchboard and another trip to the car park for yet another cigarette with her smoking buddy (it was the third time they had gone out that day already leaving Kate to hold the fort) she looked around the office sad and disillusioned. Her working life of twenty-two years that she had devoted to her job in reception which she really loved with all her heart was quickly becoming a place where she dreaded to be. Working with someone she was beginning to hate was an alien feeling to Kate and she so wanted things to be all right again between them, but it wasn't. She saw them both walking back across the car park on the CCTV screen towards the main door of the health centre. They were giggling as usual together and sharing something even Kate couldn't be bothered knowing about. As they keyed in the code of the office door Kate heard the ping of an e-mail on her computer. She dutifully went and sat at the back of the room and opened it.

It was from the deputy building manager asking Kate to go on a course on February the 23rd 2011 at a venue at the other side of town. She stared at it and read it over and over again. Was this woman completely stupid? Had she not remembered that the previous year Kate had asked for a meeting with her to explain that she could not go on courses? She only just managed to sit in a fire lecture every six months without bolting for the door, due to the debilitating agoraphobia. Kate had been mortified when she was told that she would have to go and see an occupational health physician to explain herself (she was told it was to cover the both of them). Obviously, her word was not enough. Her previous manager had accepted her word but in all fairness, she had witnessed how upset Kate had become when she had sent her on a course and Kate hadn't slept all weekend knowing she would be in a room with a lot of people for hours on end. It was true to say that the only people who feared fear were those who had experienced it and so Kate wrote a reply. 'Sorry, but I shall not be attending the course on the 23rd of February 2011. Regards, Kate.' Ping here it comes again!

'Hi Kate, can I ask you why you do not want to attend? I may have to refer this issue to HR who said training had to be undertaken.' Regards. 'Hi yes, the reason why I will not be attending is because of the issues discussed with Occupational Health when I attended last year.' Thanks Kate.

'Kate,' not 'Hi' or 'Dear just Kate,' 'I need to discuss this with our manager.'

Wow, you know when something inside you just snaps? Well something just snapped in Kate and she got up from her chair and went into the other reception room. She was definitely not going on any course. The physician had been very understanding and he had sent a copy of the letter to Kate as well as to her manager saying:

Thank you for referring this lady to Company Health. I saw her on the 26th of August 2010. In answer to your specific questions:

1. She continues to be fit for work.

2. She does have an underlying medical condition. As you mention she suffers from agoraphobia, however, she has done well to cope with this and this does not affect her ability to be in work or her attendance at work.

3. However, in terms of adjustments I would advise that she should be restricted from attending training that she feels uncomfortable attending, which is usually larger groups.

She would be fit to attend one-to-one training.

Yours sincerely

(Dictated but not signed) and his name and letters behind his name followed.

Kate was crying inside, and she was on the verge of walking out the door. Instead, she went to the ladies' room. I am not staying here another day she heard a voice inside her head, I hate it and I hate who I work with. It's not going to get any better and I am making myself miserable with these morons, enough is enough, her decision was made. After a few minutes, she composed herself. She was giving nothing away to anyone and she returned to the office, keyed in the code and went straight to her folder in the top drawer of the cabinet marked 'reception'. She started to check through her personal file as to what was hers and what was important and what was just work stuff. She picked up her diary and in the back of it was a few postcards that she had sent to the girls in reception over the last few years; one was from their honeymoon in Cyprus and one was when John and Kate had been on holiday to Corfu in Greece. Bending down inside the cupboard underneath the counter she found her cup and her spoon, and she put them inside her bag which was by her computer near the door. It was lunchtime then and one of the girls offered to go and make a cup of tea. Kate gave her another cup which was also hers and said she would like a tea please. Looking around and unbeknown to anyone Kate was checking if there was anything else she needed to take with her. Satisfied that there was not she turned her attention to the patients at the window and answered the incoming calls. The girls were flitting in and out of reception and Joan who worked for one of the doctors in the other room asked Kate, 'Are you okay? You look in deep thought?' 'Yes, thanks I am fine, Joan, sorry I was miles away,' she lied.

They ate lunch, and as time passed by Kate went to the ladies' room again, she washed her cup and glanced at herself in the mirror. She vowed that she would never use that toilet or wash her hands in there ever again. She looked in the concourse as she walked through it back to reception. Patients were gathering for their appointments in the treatment room and she realised that she felt nothing, such was her determination to get the hell out of the place and never to return. She placed the second cup inside her bag. She was now satisfied that everything she wanted or was hers was comfortably tucked away inside it. She quickly printed off the e-mail that had been sent to her only a few hours before, the straw that had broken the donkey's back. All she needed to do now was to get out of the door, at 1.15 p.m. then she would be free. Unbelievably and after all the trauma she had been through, no tears were near and she felt strong and determined. She knew that after the last e-mail she had received that morning, that there was now no turning back; she was leaving her beloved job and the many treasured friends she had made for twenty-two years, friends who had been with her through thick and thin, in the dark days of her bereavement when Michael had died so suddenly.

The same friends who had also shared in her happiness when she had married her beloved John. In another five minutes she would be out of the door with no one knowing of her plans for the future not even herself. She glanced at the clock, only two minutes to go now and she reached for her coat.

'What are you doing this afternoon, Kate?' Catherine asked her.

'I am meeting Liz my friend. We are going into Whalley for a coffee,' she replied.

'Well you enjoy your afternoon,' she said.

'I will do thank you.' Kate had to walk through an open doorway into the main reception area in order to say goodbye to her other friends as she always did. Liz, a friend who she had known from way back turned to say goodbye and she said, 'Kate, I won't be in tomorrow or Friday, so I will see you on Monday.'

'Oh, you have a lovely long weekend, love, see you Monday.' (Oh no you won't a little voice inside of her head said).

She continued through reception and the girls shouted goodbye to her. She opened the final door and walked out onto the corridor and around the corner towards the automatic doors at the entrance to the health centre. She walked forward as they parted company for her, stepped outside and gulped in the fresh air. She walked towards her car which was parked in its usual place in the corner of the car park. Cigarette stubs were all over the soil belonging to the person who was responsible for her taking this action today, along with others who had the same filthy habit. Kate opened the car door with her fob and sat behind the wheel, she got out her mobile phone from her handbag, the first person she always spoke to was John and this day was no exception.

'Hi darling,' she said to him and he said, 'Hello chick boo.' She loved his pet names for her that he used whenever they spoke to each other. 'Where are you off to, Sweetpea?'

'I need to talk to you, where are you?' she said, trying but failing to sound normal.

'Just off Whalley Road. What's wrong? Are you ok love?' he said. 'Not really, John, I'll tell you when I see you. where are you parked?' He told her which street he was parked on and with one last look at the health centre she started the engine and drove out of the car park for the very last time.

Kate saw John's van at the bottom of the street where he said he would be, and she pulled up just in front of it, he came out of the customer's door and beamed his loving smile at her.

'I've walked out, John, and I'm never going back there, not ever,' she blurted out to him.

'Why, what on earth has happened?' he said. She got the copy of the e-mail out of her handbag and gave it him to read.

'What!'

'I know,' she said in reply, 'I went to Occy Health last year to explain myself and I am not going on a course. It has been so awkward again this morning with Lindsey. I said we could just work together now things are so quiet in reception instead of having days when one of us does the post and the other one does the franking machine. The rota isn't really necessary any more now, but she said no, she wanted to keep things as they are despite both of us twiddling our thumbs for much of the morning. The managers won't let us help with the podiatry list any more and sometimes the mornings are so long.'

'She is just being awkward, John, and I can't hack it any more. I am going up to see Les and Liz to see if he can help me to put a letter of resignation together, I can't go back there.'

Tears were spilling down her cheeks now, not because she regretted what she had done. It was the sheer frustration of months and months of trying to hold it together. John took her in his arms and told her that whatever she decided upon he would go along with it. He knew she was making herself ill at that place, the joy had gone from her through the fall-out and all he wanted was for her to be settled and happy again no matter whatever it took.

'You go and see Les and Liz, we will talk when I come home and Kate, you know that I love you so much, we will work it out together. Don't worry, sweetheart, and be careful driving. I will see you tonight.' 'Thank you. I am so sorry, darling, but there is no going back. I hate it now and I am not making myself ill over her.' Kate climbed back into the car and John got into his van in front of her. He started the engine and put on his hazard warning lights to say goodbye. I am so god damn lucky to have you she whispered to the fresh air, her thoughts speaking out loud. John, you are my rock and you always will be, she vowed to tell him that tonight in person when he got home.

He had always been there for her ever since they had met. He had wanted her before she ever knew it and despite a messy divorce he had been her soulmate and she his. He was totally reliable, and she knew that he was only a phone call away whenever she needed him. Kate rang Les and he answered the phone immediately. She thought he must be in his office at the time. She asked him how long he would be at home for as she thought he had just called in for his lunch. He said he would be in all afternoon as he was busy with some paperwork and she asked him to tell Liz when she arrived home from her son's house to wait there with him whilst Kate drove up to their house. She told him that she wanted to see both of them urgently and she asked him to ask Liz not to set off for Whalley where they were supposed to be meeting for coffee and a chat. She arrived at their house a short while later and Liz opened the door.

'Are you all right, Kate?' she asked, a worried look on her face.

'No, I need to talk to you both. I've just walked out of my job.'

'Come and sit down in the lounge. I will just make us all a cup of tea,' she said and Les came down the stairs from his office into their lovely lounge. The sun was blazing in through the patio windows and the breathtaking view was as spectacular as ever. He bent down to where Kate was sitting and gave her a kiss,

'Hi Kate, what's the matter'? he said, and she began to tell him the whole sorry story. He sat back on the other sofa facing her. After a minute Liz came in with three cups of tea.

'You do know, Kate, that if you go ahead with this there is no going back.' Liz heard him say.

'I know,' she said quietly, 'I can't hack that place any more.' She told them both of all the problems she had been putting up with, how Lindsey was taking half of the royal mail to the front counter so as not to have to be standing next to Kate to sort them out, she was taking the blood and urine results forms also over to the same counter where patients who were queuing at the treatment room reception desk had every chance of seeing the hospital results of other patients. 'If she had been caught she would have been disciplined for exposing patients' confidentiality.' Kate continued, 'but I don't give a damn about that. She should be caught, and she is just an awkward swine to be working with. It's payback time for me. I told over her for trying to get more hours behind my back. It was the sneaky way in which she did it with a new temporary member of the management staff who didn't know any better. Anyway, she hasn't got her own way after all, but now I am the one who is suffering for it, but you know what, I would do it all again because she is jealous of the extra half an hour I have each day. Stupid really, because she has been given an afternoon job upstairs and she is happy with that for the time being. When the new health centre is built, she is hoping for a full-time position so there are only a few months to wait.'

They both listened to her as she explained the way her life had been for the past seven months, and then Les said that it wouldn't be a bad idea if Kate went off sick for the next two days; it was Wednesday the 26th of January 2011 and it would give her and John time to talk it over for the four days including the weekend.

He looked at Kate and she said, 'but I have only just been off sick over Christmas with the flu.'

'So what?' he said, 'if you aren't going back it won't matter and if you are, then it buys you some time.' He sat back and leant on the sofa, his usual calm self and as she looked across at him, he turned to her and said, 'I am wasting my time aren't I? Your mind is made up, Kate, isn't it?'

'Yes, you are right, I don't want to work there any longer. I can't get past this and as I have no intentions any more of going with them to the new build in November then I might as well finish now.'

'We are not prying,' Liz said gently, 'but can you manage for money?' 'Yes, it won't be easy and there will be nothing to spare, hell, we have the mortgage for another six years, but I am not making myself ill and I know that Lindsey knows what she is being like with me. If I need to ask her anything and it will happen, she won't help me. I don't trust her now, if she can get her own back in any which way, she will do, so I am finishing. I just hope she gets brought to justice for bullying. I should have put an IR1 form in when I was asked if I wanted to.'

'I should have made a complaint against her when she snarled at me, she was two inches from my face. I was trembling at her vicious tongue, her eyes were evil, and she told me she would be watching me every step of the way and that I had better watch my back. I stupidly thought that she would say she was sorry to me as she knew she was wrong for trying to get more free time or hours but when she was told she couldn't do she turned nasty. She was only out for herself. It didn't work, and I should have known that the bosses would have squashed her idea because her time sheets must be authorised. It's too late now and I know that I will be okay. John is a tower of strength, I am not on my own and I shall survive. Money will be tight, but I shall be happy given time to get used to being retired, the very word is alien. I was supposed to be working until I am sixty-five and here I am not even sixty-one and I am walking out. Glenda always says to me 'GOD is good' and I believe He is. I shall survive as Gloria Gaynor sings. Ha, Ha.'

Kate asked Les then to help her to put a letter of resignation together:

27.1.2011

Please accept this letter of my intention to resign from my employment with immediate effect. Under the circumstances I would like you to waiver the requirement for me to work during my notice period.

Yours Sincerely

PS Please send me a self-certification form to cover for Thursday and Friday.

'Thank you for helping me, for caring and understanding me,' Kate said to them both. 'Liz, we will have some lovely times together now as we are both retired. Let's look towards the future and plenty of coffees. She kissed them and got into her car and headed down the road home.

FORTY-TWO

Kate pulled into the driveway, shattered at the events of the day. John came home from work around six p.m. and he could not believe that Kate had taken such a devastating decision to walk out of the job he knew she loved and also, she had left her friends behind who were oblivious to all the trouble that had been going on. At the same time, he totally understood why she had done it. He knew she could not have carried on working any longer under those circumstances. He realised also that their lives were never going to be the same again, not for a few years at least until he retired and received a pension. Money was a big issue. The mortgage had six years left to be paid and their plans for a new kitchen and an easier lifestyle for them both with two wages coming in were suddenly blown out of the window, but her happiness and their love for each other were so much more important to him and he vowed to support her in any way he could do for as long as he lived. There was nothing more important to him than Kate his precious Sweetpea.

The switchboard had to be opened the following morning and so John rang Lindsey's house and he asked her daughter if she would bring her mother to the phone. When her husband answered, John asked him if he would tell her to open the switchboard the following day and the day after that too as Kate would not be in work. He asked what the problem was, and John replied, 'it's complicated'. Satisfied that John was going no further by way of an explanation he said he would pass on the message to his wife when she returned home. Kate and John talked until it was late and with heavy hearts they went to bed. She had a very sleepless night, she lay beside John listening to him softly breathing and she constantly went over the days that had led up to her decision to leave the health centre. As the early hours approached she fell into a fitful sleep, tossing and turning until dawn, and as morning appeared she got up, showered and dressed and they shared breakfast together. Today was the first day of the rest of her life, and although she knew there was no going back, somewhere deep inside she wondered if she would ever get an apology. She rang her immediate manager's direct line to avoid going through the switchboard as her voice would have been recognised. She explained that she would not be in that day or Friday the day after and she asked her not to ask any questions. She told her she was not ill and would she please respect her privacy. Kate finished by telling her she would be sending a letter of explanation to her manager via John as to why she was absent from work.

Kate was in turmoil after John went off to work. Sadness replaced the anger she felt at what had been done to her, the fact that through no fault of her own she had walked out of the job she loved but more so, that she had left the friends she loved behind and worse still they knew nothing about any of her heartache. She was loyal and didn't air her dirty washing. She wasn't a gossip, and she had kept it all to herself; only Fran her best friend at work would be told as to why she would no longer be sat at her desk any more, her friend, of twenty-two years would never be sat answering the switchboard again. At nine o'clock she rang the HR department; she wondered why one of them had not got back to her that week with a query. When eventually she got the answer to her question, which was that she was not eligible for a redundancy scheme, she told the lady that it didn't matter anymore as she had walked out of her job the previous day. The lady asked Kate to explain herself which she did, and she also asked if her manager knew about the trouble that had been going on for so many months too. Kate replied no, only her deputy knew. The lady said she wanted to speak on Kate's behalf and that she would ring her back shortly.

After about ten minutes, the phone rang, and it was her manager. She was absolutely devastated as she had just received a phone call from HR, more so she had got the letter of resignation from Kate that John had just handed in at the main reception desk. She was very concerned and asked Kate why it was that she knew nothing about this problem, in fact her first reaction on reading it was that Kate must have just decided she no longer needed to work and that was the end of it. Now it was becoming clear that Kate felt she had no other choice but to resign. She explained that she had spoken about the problem to her deputy and said she had been asked if she wanted to put in a formal complaint to which she had replied no, because it would have made life at the health centre much, much worse for her. Suddenly the tears flooded out and Kate found it difficult to talk. The person she had spoken to at HR was worried about her and something needed to be sorted out. Her manager told Kate she also felt that she needed time to think about a decision as serious as this and she said she would also have to talk to Lindsey which Kate said was fine by her; after all, it was she who had been bullied and her manager said she was not having that in her workplace. She reassured Kate, that she had sorted out far bigger problems during her role as a manager.

It was more than clear that Kate was distraught by these past few months, leading her to take such a drastic step and she told her to sit down with a cup of tea and then to make an appointment to see her GP with the view to getting a sick note for four to six weeks giving her time to decide if she truly wanted to finish or if as was suggested, they could sit down together and work things out. Kate agreed and thanked her for her kindness. She said goodbye and went to make herself a cup of tea before ringing the doctor's surgery and making an appointment for Monday morning. When John rang to see if she was okay, she told him of the phone calls between HR and her manager and he seemed pleased that at least she was getting some support and more so, it gave her the breathing space she desperately needed to decide if this was what she really wanted to do, or if her job could be saved and he wanted whatever was best for Kate. He also had been pondering whilst driving to his jobs the effect it would have on her being alone at home every day whilst he went to work, knowing her nerves were her biggest problem and knowing how much she loved going to work and seeing her friends every day what sort of an impact this would have on her and it worried him greatly. When he came home and pulled in on the driveway she was waiting for him by the back door. How sorry he felt for her as he watched from his van. She stood in the doorway smiling at him, he knew from her face that she had been crying for most of the day.

'Come here, Sweetpea,' he beckoned and he took her in his arms. He knew she was strong in some ways as she had shown in her strength in walking out twenty-four hours before, but he also knew of her weaknesses and how lonely her life was going to be now if it didn't get sorted. She would have some adjusting to do both mentally and financially and he wondered if she could cope with it all.

On Friday morning, she rang Fran and explained to her all that had happened since her leaving work on Wednesday afternoon. Fran listened and said how everyone at work was worried about her. They had been told nothing except that she would not be in work for the next two days. Kate told her of the doctor's appointment on Monday and Fran said she must take as much time as she needed to completely decide on what she wanted to do; there was no rush, the decision was hers and hers alone. On Monday morning the 31st of January 2011 Kate went to see her doctor. She explained in brief what had happened, and the doctor as always was kind. She told her she wanted to give her a sick note for eight weeks because she thought Kate needed that much time to sort out her life. She put on the reason for absence as work-related stress. She also told Kate that if she needed to see her again before the sick note ran out then she only had to make an appointment and they would talk it through.

Kate thanked her. She had always liked her doctor and she was grateful for her compassion. She left the surgery and went straight home. After a cup of tea, she rang her manager and told her the doctor had given her an eight-week sick note and she was told to use the time given to go for a walk and do her shopping as she would have normally done. She wasn't to hibernate indoors for eight weeks but to take time to recharge her batteries before finally ringing her to tell of her final decision. It became difficult after a couple of weeks as cards saying 'get well soon' were arriving and Kate said to John that she didn't want people at work to think she was ill, or that anyone in the family were ill, or worse still, that there were problems in their marriage causing her to be off work for two months. And because of the nature of the problem she had to keep quiet because she had been given a lifeline. Her manager had promised to sort things out and if for any reason Kate did eventually go back to work then she would have had to think of a reason for being off for so long and why. Even Lindsey who had caused this mess didn't know at first why Kate was at home because she had left a message on the answering machine saying, 'Hi Kate, pick up the phone cock, what's wrong? Ring me I am at home, hope you are okay.'

It didn't move Kate one little bit; the sound of her voice only reiterated the feelings of bitterness towards her and she felt more determined to stay at home, lonely as it was going to be. She wouldn't be able to go clothes shopping like she had been used to or be able to save a substantial amount of money each month out of her wages for the next five years as was planned towards her retirement. The days moved on and slowly Kate grew more and more used to being at home. She went for a walk some days down to Whalley village but mainly she cleaned the house and kept up with the ironing. Most of all she looked forward to the phone calls from John; he rang her several times each day to see if she was all right, he knew how lonely she was but he had a lot more years to work and he knew it was her decision to finish and hard as it was going to be, she had to make a life for herself now. Determined to never go back to her job she rang her manager on the morning of her sixty-first birthday, the 28th of February 2011. She told her, that despite still having time to decide if she was to return to her job, the fact of the matter was that she felt no different than the day she had walked out, and she would not be going back. Her manager asked her if she was definitely sure and Kate said she was. She thanked her for her patience and said it was no use prolonging the situation any more and that she was officially retiring.

'Please send me another letter of resignation, Kate, I am sorry you felt we could not have sorted this problem out, but you have obviously made up your mind and I wish you all the very best for the future.' 'Thank you very much, goodbye,' Kate replied, and she put the telephone down. There that's done with now she thought, I can get on with my life now and she went into the kitchen and made herself a lovely cup of tea and sat down to open her many birthday cards.

When John came home she told him what she had done, and he was pleased that she had taken the initiative to not let this episode in her life fester any longer. He took her in his arms and told her how proud he was of her and he gave her a beautiful card. The title read:

'Keep Believing in Yourself'

Every goal that has ever been reached began with just one step –and the belief that it could be attained. Dreams really can come true, but they are most often the result of hard work, determination, and persistence. When the end of the journey seems impossible to reach, remember that all you need to do is take one more step. Stay focused on your goal and remember each small step will bring you a little closer. When the road becomes hard to travel, and it feels as if you'll never reach the end, look deep inside your heart and you will find strength you never knew you had. Believe in yourself and remember that I believe in you too.
By Jason Blume

Underneath the last sentence John had written: - Remember, Sweetpea, I am always here for you till the end of time. I Love You, John xxx
Kate dissolved into tears. She could not love him more, he was truly the love of her life and she knew she couldn't live without him. All the support she ever needed was in John. She deeply loved him he would never know just how much. He was her rock, the perfect husband and lover all rolled into one. She was blessed and grateful for the second chance of love and once again she thanked God for giving her another wonderful husband. She had been so very lucky to have had one husband who had adored her, but to have found another was just the perfect gift, it was as if God had taken one away from her and then when He knew she could take no more grief had replaced Michael with John. Money was tight, she knew it would be and days were long, but Kate had absolutely no regrets about leaving her job. She was lonely but free. She looked forward to the end of the day and when she saw John's van

coming down the road. Her heart skipped a beat as she raced to the back door to greet him. She kept the house beautiful; it was like a show house nothing was out of place. Slowly as she had expected, she came to realise that if she wanted to watch a programme on the television in a morning or catch up with a recorded soap then she needn't beat herself up about it. She had worked part time for twenty-two years and as long as she did the shopping, the ironing and kept everything in order at home then her life was her own.

In the summer, they booked a holiday to Madeira. They stayed for ten days at the RIU Palace. It was a beautiful five-star hotel and they swam in the pool, sunbathed and made love. Time had not changed anything between them they were still like they had been when they had met. Sex was perfect between them and they took advantage of the peaceful location, making love in the afternoon when the sun was at its hottest. John looked after Kate; he was always attentive and showed her the sights in Madeira. They went in a cable car which petrified her and he was so proud of how she coped, he knew she hated heights but she overcame her fear as she knew how much it meant to him to go and to see the Botanical Gardens; what they didn't realise was that they had to go up past the gardens on their right and get on another cable car to go down the other side to reach them. Kate was terrified but enjoyed the views and the plants and scenery were just delightful. After a lovely week, together they flew home to Manchester Airport and then after a few days chilling they went to see John's sister and her husband in Suffolk.

FORTY-THREE

John returned to work and Kate missed him. She waited each night for him to come home and she pottered in the garden, she met her friend Liz for coffee and suddenly the summer came to an end. It was time to adjust again to the long winter months, but a surprise was in store for them both that neither had expected. It was Katherine's thirtieth birthday on the 1st of October and it was James her partner's on the 10th of October and to celebrate they went up to Edinburgh for the weekend. Katherine texted Kate to say that they had arrived safely, and they agreed to speak on the Saturday morning when Katherine had opened her cards and presents. It was strange her being so far away especially on a milestone birthday, but Katherine said she didn't want a party and was happy to have a weekend away. On the Saturday morning, the phone rang, and Kate wished her beloved daughter a very Happy Birthday. Katherine thanked Kate for the beautiful nightdress and negligee which she and John had bought. She said the card was lovely and told Kate what James had given her.

'No ring, Mum,' she said disappointedly, 'I really thought he would propose especially with it being my thirtieth.'

'Never mind, sweetheart,' Kate soothed, 'he will do in time, you know he loves you, but you have to wait until he feels ready.'

'I know, Mum, and I shouldn't have expected it, but you know what, I really did.' Kate could hear the disappointment in her voice and her heart went out to her. 'Please be patient sweetheart he will ask you but not just now,' Kate said trying to hide her sadness too. All Kate ever wanted was for her children to be happy. She had had her third child after her thirty-first birthday and she knew that Katherine wanted commitment and a wedding and a family. 'Have a lovely day, love, I wish I was there to share your birthday and just be happy, darling.'

'I will, Mum, I will just have to wait his time.'

They said goodbye and Kate went to find John, so he could say Happy Birthday too. When he had spoken to Katherine she told him there had been no ring and he said the same as Kate; she just had to wait till James was ready. They went shopping as usual in the afternoon and ordered a takeaway for tea. In the evening they sat together as always watching television when the home phone rang. Kate answered it and Katherine's voice was almost hysterical,

'Mum, Mum, James has just proposed to me!'

'Oh my God Katherine, I can't believe what I am hearing that's lovely,' 'John,' she said to him, 'Katherine has just got engaged!' he smiled and said, 'I told you he would do but in his own time.'

'What is your ring like and where are you now?'

'It's a beautiful solitaire with a platinum band. Oh Mum, I am so happy,' she was over the moon and so was Kate and John. Katherine said James had been carrying it in his pocket all day just waiting for the right moment and when the rain had died down and the street they were on was empty he went down on one knee on the wet pavement and asked her to marry him.

'Oh, that's so romantic, Katherine, now go and enjoy the rest of your evening together. Bless you, we are delighted for you both.' Kate and John spoke to James and wished him all the very best. Katherine told Kate a few days later that he had wanted to ask Kate's permission to marry her but was afraid to in case she told Katherine of his plans. He knew just how close they were and Kate said she never would have spoilt it for him but it was okay by her. After all they had been together for six years now and she knew one day he would ask her to marry him. It was a perfect end to her thirtieth birthday and the beginning of a future, planning a wedding which they both deserved so much.

They came home from Edinburgh on the Sunday afternoon and she rang home to ask Kate and John to go across to their house to see her ring. Kate couldn't wait and after tea they set off to see the newly engaged couple.

The ring was beautiful indeed, and their faces showed the love they had for one another. Katherine couldn't stop smiling and Kate and John were happy for them.

When is the wedding then, they asked but nothing had been arranged yet. Kate hoped it would be in 2012 and in her mind, she started to plan a trip to look for a wedding dress and a mother-of the-bride outfit soon. On Monday the 14th of November 2011 Kate woke up and got showered and dressed. She told John she had decided to go to the health centre to see her friends as they were due to leave the premises at the end of the month and go to their new health centre which was just a few blocks up the road. Some of the staff had already gone but the few remaining were the ones that Kate wanted to see. They had breakfast and John said how apprehensive Kate looked,

'It will be fine, sweetheart,' he said. 'They will be so glad to see you, Kate, it's been nine and a half months since you left, and I am certain they will welcome you with open arms, have some faith, Sweetpea.'

'I know, but what if they don't do? What if they say what are you doing here? You never said goodbye so why are you coming in here now?'

'They won't, they love you to pieces, Kate. Go and say goodbye, put the ghost to rest. You need closure, darling. Be brave go and see them.' She smiled at him ever the rock, ever the sensible one and always on her side. She couldn't have got through these last nine and a half months without his constant support and the love he gave her unconditionally,

'Okay, I will' she said. 'I will ring you when I get home.' He kissed her longingly and winked that special wink reserved only for her. 'I love you so much sweetheart,' she said, 'let's make love when you come home, eh,'

'can't wait,' he replied, 'be ready babe!' After she had waved to him from the front lounge window Kate went upstairs to make the bed, she finished touching up her make-up and put on her favourite perfume, grabbed her jacket and stood in front of the mirror in the hall. Yep, the girl looks good she thought, and she set the house alarm, locked the door and went to get into the car.

All the way there she was apprehensive about just walking in the door and seeing all her friends again, but as she parked the car she looked at the building which she had vowed never to enter again and it felt the right thing to do. She was only going back to say goodbye and never again would she go in there after today. The automatic doors opened, and she walked inside, she saw Fran her best friend working on the front desk. There was a queue waiting so she walked on towards the waiting rooms where she saw Joan, another friend and a beaming smile greeted her. The look on Joan's face said it all. Running towards Kate with open arms she called, 'Liz, Liz, it's Kate. She has come to see us.'

'Oh Kate, it's so good to see you,' she said and when Kate looked at them both they had tears in their eyes.

'I just had to come and see you all before you go to the new build. I couldn't let you go without saying goodbye,' she said, a tear slipping down her face. 'Oh, Kate, come on, let's go in reception, the girls will be delighted to see you,' Joan said.

The door opened and their faces were a picture; how could Kate have ever thought that they would have welcomed her otherwise? She knew Lindsey who had bullied her, had gone to the new build and that made it easier. If she had still been in reception then Kate would have stayed on the other side of the counter. There was no way she was going to speak to her ever again, but that didn't happen because she was no longer working there. Catherine was covering the switchboard and Kate hugged her. The rest of them came in line, first Fran, then Ann all wanting to know how she was doing. She told them the truth; she was lonely and lost at home, constantly cleaning up and keeping the house like a show home. She told them how brilliant John had been since she had walked out of her job, how understanding and lovely he was and although she was lost on her own she had absolutely no regrets about leaving. She said she could never have worked with Lindsey again even if she had apologised for her bullying behaviour. She was very naive to have thought otherwise. Kate stayed about an hour and when Joan said she was ready for going home she decided to go out of the door with her.

Joan had been there the first night Kate had gone to work at the health centre and so it was fitting to leave for good with her too.

They all promised to keep in touch. They said they would meet for lunch occasionally and when the weather was nice they would go for a bar snack in the evening. It was strange to say goodbye, but it was the right thing for Kate to do and it had served two purposes; firstly to put the ghost to rest, and secondly to say goodbye properly to the friends whom she had worked alongside for twenty-two years. They had loved and supported her when Michael died and they were supporting her now. She went back home with a much lighter heart. John came home from work and asked her how the morning had gone.

'Oh John, it was so good to see them all. We were in tears. It was the best thing I did today. It's not like we won't see each other again but it was right to say goodbye properly. They are my true friends and I love them dearly.'

'I told you, Sweetpea, now what about that promise I got this morning. Do you remember?'

'Course I do,' she smiled at him and took his hand and led him up the stairs.

Christmas Day they spent at Jillian and Rob's house for a beautiful meal and the same at Katherine's and James' on New Year's Eve. They went to Richard and Debbie's on New Year's Day and Kate enjoyed having their meals made for them; they were all delicious. The year had been hard, but slowly she was adjusting to life without working. The New Year, they knew was going to be special, in fact very special, as Katherine and James announced that there was going to be a lovely wedding on Friday, September the 21st 2012.

FORTY-FOUR

The days were long, it had been over a year since she had retired and as spring arrived Katherine suggested they have a day together to go and look at wedding dresses and a mother-of the-bride outfit for Kate. She was so looking forward to seeing her only daughter in her wedding dress. She wished that Michael had lived to share this moment and Katherine was sad too that he could not be there to share her special day. She was going to ask John if he would give her away to James and Kate was pleased that she wanted him to step in for her father. On Thursday, March the 22nd 2012 they set off to look at bridal dresses. First of all they went to a shop in Accrington but neither of them could see anything special. Kate suggested they went to Blackburn to where she had bought hers in 2004. As they were driving away from Accrington Katherine said they should go to Clitheroe first as that was nearer.

They parked the car and excitedly looked in the window. Katherine had seen a dress a few days before and as they stepped inside they were amazed at the choice; if they didn't find one here they wouldn't find one anywhere. The shop was full, row upon row of any style, colour or length you could imagine. The shop assistant said her name was Kelsey and she came to greet them. She showed Katherine all the gowns on display and she gave her a plastic marker to hang onto the dresses that she would like to try on. Kate left her to look along the rails.

'Would you both like a cup of tea?' the other assistant offered.

'Yes please,' Kate replied, 'one with sugar and one without, thank you very much.' Kate settled herself onto a lovely cream sofa by the shop window whilst Katherine went through the dresses. There were so many to choose from and she mentioned that she had seen one previously in the window, about a week ago. It was an Amanda Wyatt bridal gown, the style was simply called 'Helen'.

Katherine chose about six dresses to try. She was taken into the dressing room to try each one on. It had a massive ornate gold mirror inside and Kate waited in anticipation for her daughter to emerge from behind the curtain. After about five minutes the curtain opened, and she stood in front of her mum a beautiful bride-to-be, Kate felt the lump in her throat and gently the tears rolled down her cheeks; her treasured and only daughter, a woman now, no longer the little girl she had been when Michael had last seen her. Kate still thought of him every day and today especially she could imagine that if he had been alive he would have been at work picturing his lovely daughter trying on her wedding dress with the expert eye of her mum who he knew had an eye for fashion. It had been inherited from Katherine's Granny, Kate's mum. She was always well dressed and loved the fashion world. It had been passed onto Kate who also loved clothes and today was no exception. Today every detail would be scrutinised, her only daughter was going to look stunning, of that there was no doubt. How sad it was that Michael would never see the wedding of his beautiful girl, but somewhere, somehow, Kate hoped he was looking down on them today and he would have been so very proud, proud of the woman that Katherine had become, and proud of the wife he had left behind nearly nineteen years ago and who had been both a mother and a father to his children despite the agoraphobia and the trouble with her nerves, she had really done such a splendid job on her own.

John sprang to mind and she couldn't wait until Katherine asked him to step in for her father and walk her down the aisle. It would be a day when Michael would be remembered. He had never been forgotten and he never would be. He would certainly have approved of John stepping in for him. She knew he would look after his lovely step-daughter on her special day, how blessed she was to have found the man who adored Kate and she him, the wedding was going to be very special for all of them including Michael; he may not be there in person but he would be there in spirit, hopefully watching from afar. Katherine tried on three more dresses and finally for the second time she put on the Amanda Wyatt gown. It was a mermaid/fishtail style of dress with a strapless sweetheart neckline in ivory. The fabric was made of lace with a full-length skirt and a chapel train. On the body from neck to toe it was covered in beautiful diamante with the neckline showing a diamante brooch, making it shimmer as the sun shone in through the shop windows. She was given a matching short veil to try on which also had little diamantes dotted on the netting and she borrowed some high heeled ivory satin shoes. She was an absolute picture of beauty and it was hard to stop the tears which were trickling down Kate's cheeks.

After the appointments had been booked in advance for the fittings, they were told that the dress would be in the shop in about eight weeks' time. They left a deposit and thanked the girls for all their help and for the welcoming cups of tea. Like two little girls they went back to the car. They had been in the shop for over an hour and a half and it was so worth it. They were both beaming from ear to ear. They went back to Kate's house for lunch and Kate mentioned the bridesmaid's dresses. She said they should go in August as the little ones would grow if they went too early. She told Katherine of the fiasco that had happened on her wedding day to her dad. The wedding dress for Kate had been bought from Bride-Be-Lovely in Manchester along with the three little bridesmaids' dresses, by Kate's mother in February 1971 when the wedding wasn't going to be until August. How could three mothers not have realised that little girls were going to grow about three inches in six months? When the girls tried on their dresses a few days before the big day, all three of them had grown so much that they showed their socks and sandals.

'I was distraught. I couldn't believe it,' said Kate, 'but it was too late by then and the wedding went ahead but all the photos were spoilt. That won't happen again. We will go a few weeks before your wedding day to make sure they fit the children properly.'

Katherine had taken two days' leave from her job and she suggested they go to Preston to see if there was a mother-of-the-bride outfit for Kate, so on the Friday they set off for Penwortham where Kate had seen an advertisement for mother-of-the-bride wear. They went into the shop, Kate so excited, she had a good eye for fashion and today was no exception. The special occasion wear was on the first floor and on the rail in front of her she saw her outfit, a beautiful Luis Civit dress and bolero jacket in a cream satin. The dress was a pleated layered grey and white marbled pattern with wide pleated straps and a sweetheart neckline. She fell in love with it as soon as she saw it. The theme of the wedding was grey, damson and ivory so the colours were perfect. She could not believe her eyes. She looked at some more to try on; one was a lovely baby pink and black dress with a matching jacket and it would have been perfect with a black hat, so they took about four outfits downstairs to the dressing room. The sales assistant was ever so nice. She stood back until Kate was dressed and each outfit was lovely in its own way but the first one that Kate had seen was the one she chose. The straps wanted lifting but the lady said she needed to go back a few weeks before the wedding so that if any other alterations were needed it would be done then. Katherine paid for the outfit and looked at some grey shoes, but they were very expensive, so Kate said she would leave it for the time being and they would look elsewhere.

They left the shop happy now that both of them had found their outfits in the last two days. They never expected it to be so quick and easy, but everything had fallen into place. Kate transferred the money for her outfit into Katherine's account so there were still the bridesmaids to sort out now but that wouldn't be until early August. Kate and John went to the Trafford Centre on the 9th of June to look for wedding shoes for both of them. Katherine had been to tea a few days before and when Kate went upstairs to get changed, she had asked John the most important question of her life,

'I would like you to give me away please?' When Kate came into the lounge they were both smiling. 'I have just asked John to give me away, Mum,' she said, 'Oh Katherine, that's lovely, John will look after you, you know that don't you, sweetheart?'

'Of course I do, Mum, but I just want to say something, please can we include my dad in the day, John? I don't want everyone to be upset that he isn't there to walk me down the aisle but I want him to be involved in some way. He must never be forgotten. You do understand, don't you?'

John looked at her with a sad smile, 'Katherine, I have already thought about that and no, he won't be forgotten not on your wedding day or ever. He will always be a part of this family. Your mum talks of him often and it will be my pleasure to give you away, I am honoured to take his place on your arm.'

Kate looked at him with tears in her eyes. Bless him, he was always so understanding, so gentle with his words. He knew too well of the devastation this man had caused to this family by his untimely death. He would look after Kate forever as he had always promised to when they visited his grave and Katherine's wedding day would be no exception. He would include him in his father-of-the-bride speech and make sure her day was filled with love and special memories of her dad. To him it was a duty and he would be so proud to do it.

'Why don't we have a photo of you and dad, the last one taken by the lake in Bournemouth? You can have it on the table as you are married and then we will transfer it to the wedding breakfast table and finally to the table where you will cut the cake so all day through until the end he will be with us all?' Kate said.

'Yes, Mum, that's a lovely idea. I will get a copy and frame it.' John and Kate wandered around the Trafford Centre a few days later and eventually Kate saw some shoes which would match her outfit. They were made by Faith and were a perfect match to her dress. She bought a bag and planned to visit Blackpool soon to buy a hat. On Friday the 13th of July, Katherine went for her first wedding dress fitting. Kate met her at the shop and Kelsey brought her dress out from the dressing room. It was in a cover bag and as she unzipped it Katherine stepped forward to go into the dressing room to try it on. It was all they had hoped for. It fitted her beautifully and it looked so much nicer on Katherine than the previous one had done because this one was now her own size. It needed a hoop to lift it off the floor and she needed to buy her shoes before the next fitting but Kelsey said she was happy for now without any alterations. Two weeks later they would go back again to choose her a veil as the previous one she had worn the shop had lent her. On Sunday the 5th of August Katherine went to Richard and Debbie's house to pick

Amelia up to go to Preston for her bridesmaid's dress. She was meeting Kate, Ian, Madeline, Anastazia and Natalia the other two bridesmaids on Fishergate car park.

There had been a few difficult moments with Ian and his wife regarding the wedding; they both wanted to know the colour scheme and Katherine had refused to tell them as she wanted to keep it a surprise. They were not happy with that. They insisted that they needed to know so they could match his suit and her outfit which was really not appropriate as they were not part of the immediate wedding party. It wasn't as though he was an usher or anything; he was just the bride's brother and she was her sister-in-law.

It had carried on with texts and e-mails saying to Katherine that she needed to bear in mind when buying headdresses that Anastazia had very coarse hair and Ian said he didn't want her to wear anything which would cause a problem. Again he was told he needn't worry as they (Kate and Katherine) would make sure it would fit securely. Then they both said they needed to be with the children when they went for their bridesmaids' dresses as the little one was very fussy! Again, they were told no as the colour of the bridesmaid's dresses was also a surprise and it did not go down well with them both. It seemed to Kate that they would go to any length to be in on the choosing of the whole outfit if they could have. They had had a beautiful wedding themselves in 2002 and Kate had stayed in the background, yet these two were trying their damnedest to spoil this day because they had not got their own way. They arranged to ring Ian when they had sorted out the dresses and had finished lunch with the girls at McDonalds. They were all a delight to be with, they were so well behaved and tried on their dresses, twirling and leaping around the large dressing room which had a lovely full-length mirror.

Katherine chose ivory lace, full-length dresses for them. They were trimmed with tiny diamante pieces dotted on the skirts and they all looked beautiful. They hadn't got Anastazia's size so Katherine and Kate were going the following day to the Trafford Centre to get it from there; the assistant rang through to Manchester and it would be put to one side for them to pick up. Kate suggested they look for some shoes for the girls as they were near the bridesmaids' dresses, but they couldn't find any to fit them, so they decided to leave it until they went to Trafford and see if they had all the sizes including Matilda's who lived in Norway then they would see what Manchester had. Matilda was James niece, and they had been given her measurements from Kathy (James's mum). They took a chance on the dress and hoped and prayed that it would fit her. They met Ian after a noisy lunch. The three cousins were just so excited. As they handed the girls over to their parents Kate asked Madeline what size shoes both of them were in. She did not say that they were going to buy all four pairs the following day but that was the intention. Katherine took Amelia home and arranged to come to collect Kate after work the following day and they would get a bite to eat in Manchester then shop for the bridesmaids' shoes and pick up Anastazia's dress.

It was raining and cold when Katherine picked Kate up but they made good time arriving at the Trafford Centre at just after six o'clock. They went for something to eat and then Katherine said she wanted to buy her lingerie for the wedding and she also wanted to look at bridal shoes. They found some lovely very high-heeled ivory satin and lace ones and Katherine tried them on; they were a perfect fit and matched her wedding dress too, Kate said she would buy them for her. She insisted that she pay for Katherine's wedding dress, veil, shoes and jewellery and all the bridesmaids' outfits including their headdresses. If there was any money left then that would go towards the reception. They picked up the other bridesmaids' dress then headed to the shoe shop for the little ones' shoes. They hadn't got all the sizes in stock so Katherine said she would order them from the internet and they would be delivered to her place of work within two days. All in all everything was coming together nicely. It was only six weeks to the wedding now and they both wanted to be in hand with everything, so very typical of a mum and daughter.

FORTY-FIVE

In early August, the 11th in fact their main holidays were upon them and John and Kate flew to Palma in Majorca for ten days. It was lovely weather out there with temperatures reaching one hundred degrees. The hotel had been newly refurbished and was modern and beautifully decorated. Kate and John always asked for a high floor in every hotel they went to and more importantly a double bed; this was no exception. They were taken up in the lift to the seventh floor. The room was spacious and beautifully decorated, the porter left after showing them around and Kate and John opened the doors to the balcony. 'Wow,' they said in unison. The balcony had a glass front and it was hard to keep your balance. The people beside the pool were so tiny, it was so very high and Kate had to sit down on the sunlounger. It was going to take a bit of getting used to as she wasn't great with heights. John on the other hand had no problem with it, but the views were to die for – it was going to be a lovely ten-day break together.

They unpacked their cases and John pulled her into his arms. They made love on the king-size bed as the sun streamed into their room. It was to be the first of many days of lovemaking. Although they were alone at home, being in a five-star hotel it was far more intimate. They made love every day and sometimes twice a day. John told Kate over and over again just how much he loved her, and she told him she had never been so happy. They visited Palma and went into the cathedral and then they walked around the shops. They had lunch in the sunshine which was idyllic. Back at the hotel they swam together in the pool and sunbathed by day. They enjoyed the entertainment every night, they always dressed up for dinner; it gave Kate a chance to wear her lovely long dresses and show off her figure which she had always tried to maintain. In an evening, they would sometimes have a walk along the beach and on one particular night under the stars they listened to a tribute band playing Bob Marley's reggae music. It was a lovely break and they both felt much better for it but like everything else in life all too soon, their holiday came to an end and they returned to Manchester knowing that in a few weeks' time they would be dressing up again but this time it would be in their wedding clothes. The day after arriving home from Palma, John and Kate went into Blackburn shopping. They were cutting through the cathedral grounds when they heard a pipe band. The pipers were dressed in lovely kilts and the sound was magnificent. They stood and watched as the wedding car arrived through the cathedral gateway. The bride and her father emerged from the vintage car and stood for photographs. Suddenly Kate said to John, 'Oh Katherine and James would love the pipers, they love Edinburgh and the Tattoo. I wonder how much it would cost to have a lone piper at their wedding?'

'Why don't we go online when we get back home? We can only enquire and if it is too much money then we will have to leave it,' he said,

'Yes what a good idea,' Kate replied. 'It would be so lovely and her late grandad was a Scotsman. It would be just perfect,' they made a mental note of the name Accrington Pipe Band, and went into the mall to do their shopping.

On the Monday morning when John had gone to work Kate rang and booked a lone piper to be at the Stirk House for the wedding. He would await the arrival of Katherine and John and play throughout until the wedding breakfast. It was to be Kate's special gift to her daughter and future son-in-law. She wanted to tell everyone what she had arranged but was afraid that someone might let it slip and spoil the surprise so she told no one except John when he came home from work.

Kate had a message on the answering machine when she had arrived home from her holiday to say that her outfit was ready to be picked up. She had taken it before the holiday to get the straps adjusted and now it had been done. She went with John to get it the day after and he said how lovely she looked in it. She had found a lovely silver and feather hatinator in Blackpool so now it was all systems go. She only needed some tights and her outfit would be complete.

Katherine went for her first fitting to the wedding shop back in July and there were to be two more before the final fitting a few days before the wedding. The second fitting was on Friday the 10th of August. She had chosen a short lace veil edged with satin and it had little diamantes dotted all over it and matched her dress perfectly. This time her hoop was ready which lifted the dress from the floor. She took her ivory satin shoes and as she stepped out of the dressing room all ready for her special day, she looked absolutely radiant, a little shy as the seamstress tucked her breast into the bodice and then apologised for the intrusion. Blushing a little Katherine said, 'It's okay.'

The seamstress whispered, 'Bless,' to Kate, who smiled and said, 'She is very shy.'

Saturday the 1st of September was the dress rehearsal for both Katherine and Kate as she was being shown how to pull on the wedding dress and how to lace it up at the back, she was also shown how to bustle it for when they had their first dance. It was a bit daunting and Kelsey told Kate to allow an hour for getting Katherine ready.

'Really, are you serious?' Kate said,

'yes I am. Leave plenty of time to dress her, because if the lacing up at the back goes wrong and one side becomes longer than the other then you will have to start all over again from scratch.'

'Okay thanks we will do,' Kate replied, and she smiled very reassuringly at Katherine who looked a little gobsmacked. When they arrived back home to drop Kate off they found John writing his father-of-the-bride speech. He had looked on the internet for a little inspiration and had found a few tips from previous fathers.

'It will be brilliant, sweetheart,' Kate reassured him and he laughed, 'piece of cake darling,' she laughed back at him and he winked at Katherine who said she was off home now. She was leaving him to it. Kate had always kept a diary since starting work at the health centre; it was necessary especially when there was cover needed for colleagues who were on holiday or rang in sick leaving Kate to cover for them at short notice. She had continued to keep one ever since and as the wedding day approached she had written: -

Friday the 7th of September, *John needs a haircut for the wedding* she knew that if he had it on the actual day of the wedding then it would be too short. She didn't want him looking scalped. He told her where to go in no uncertain terms and then he said, laughing, that his hair was his business and that she should concentrate on her own. She kissed him on his lips and playfully ruffled his crowning glory.

'Please,' she said, 'please will you get it cut soon,' he just winked at her and went into his garage.

Saturday 8th *Sunbed*

Sunday 9th *Preston for John's wedding shoes*

Friday 14th *Colour and foils @ Vanilla*

Week commencing the 17th *Take bag for flowers to be put on for Friday*

Tuesday 18th * Buy perfume and aftershave, eye shadow and blusher*

Wednesday 19th *Pick up wedding dress from Clitheroe at eleven a.m. with Katherine, Kate to drive*

Thursday 20th *Nails with Maria at ten a.m.* * four p.m. take bridesmaids dresses to Amelia's house then onto Anastazia and Natalia* *Katherine to take Matilda's outfit to The Stirk House at seven p.m.* *Katherine to sleep at home*

Friday 21st *Katherine and James' Wedding Day* *Hair at Vanilla for Katherine & Kate seven thirty a.m.*

The day had finally arrived, all the planning had come to fruition. Kate and Katherine came back from the hairdressers at around nine a.m. and found John putting white wedding ribbon on their Ford Mondeo. It would look lovely as Kate was driving herself to the venue Stirk House. They went into the house and straight upstairs passing a box of flowers in the hallway containing Katherine's bouquet and John's buttonhole. Kate's bag was laid on their bed as John had gone to collect it from the florists whilst they were at the hairdressers. The girls had both had a shower before they went to get their hair done and Katherine went into the bathroom to put on her make-up whilst Kate hung her outfit in her bedroom and took her shoes out of their box. She went into the en suite to put on her make-up and changed into her dressing gown. Katherine shouted that she was ready to get into her wedding dress, her make-up was finished and Kate, mindful of them needing an hour to make sure everything was in place went into the study where she was waiting for her. She helped her to step into the underskirt which had the hoop in, then carefully she stepped into the gorgeous lace gown and gently Kate lifted it above her hips and waist and into place. The laced back had to be slowly pulled together but halfway through, Kate said it wasn't even so ever so meticulously she started again. This time it was okay and she tied it off and pushed the knot down inside of the dress so it could not be seen. She checked the neckline and made sure it was level then she told Katherine to face her whilst she put on her tiara and veil. How very beautiful she looked; her hair had been put into ringlets and her ivory veil lay gently on her shoulders, she had a new diamante necklace on that her mum had bought her when they were in Manchester and she had borrowed her mother's pearl earrings, a gift from the NHS management at head office in Blackburn when she had turned sixty.

Katherine slipped on a pale blue ribbon and lace garter and put on her new ivory satin and lace shoes. Now she had something old, a blue and white handkerchief borrowed from her mum, something new, her wedding dress, something borrowed, her mum's earrings and something blue, the lace garter. She was ready to go downstairs now to collect her bouquet from the hallway, then she would wait for John and her mum in the lounge. Kate returned to their bedroom now as it was her turn to get dressed but when she saw John her heart raced at how handsome he looked. He had put on his morning suit, his new white shirt and he was fastening the damson cravat around his neck. By the wardrobe lay his new black shoes. It took her back to May the 8th 2004 when he had looked just as smart at his own wedding. There was something so sexy about him and her thoughts were suddenly not on the job in hand. The wedding car was waiting outside now, he was early, and John told Kate to take her time getting ready as there was no rush. She put on the Luis Civit dress and the ivory satin bolero jacket and slipped her feet into her new satin grey shoes. John fastened her necklace for her which was a mixture of grey and cream pearls and she put on the matching bracelet, sprayed herself with yet more perfume and stood before the mirror.

'Will I do, sir, as mother-of-the-bride?'

'You certainly will, my darling,' he said. They went downstairs to where Katherine was waiting for them both,

'go and see your beautiful stepdaughter and see if you like her dress,' Kate said. He walked towards Katherine and told her she looked stunning. He smiled at Kate and said, 'you have done good, sweetheart, but I didn't doubt for one minute that it would be anything less.' He asked her if she was ready to go and get married and she linked his arm and gave him a peck on his cheek.

Kate kissed them both goodbye and she asked Katherine to put John's buttonhole in his jacket for him. She turned once again at the door and said, 'See you both at the Stirk House.' The car looked spotless and the white ribbon finished it off. Kate was met by her neighbours and they took a photograph of her as she stepped into the car, she put her hatinator and bag on the seat next to her and with her shoes on the mat she set off to the hotel. She wanted to get there as soon as possible so that she could adjust her hair and put on her wedding shoes. She had to juggle with her hatinator in the side mirror and make sure her bag with the flowers on was safely tucked under her arm. As she pulled up into the car park she saw Amelia, her little granddaughter, shouting, 'Nan.' No time to waste, she got her shoes from off the mat and put them on, she climbed out of the car and put on her hatinator, checked it was straight in the mirror then grabbed her bag and locked the car.

'Are you going somewhere special?' someone said behind her. It was Joan her friend with Kevin her husband. They had got married the year before Kate and Michael in 1970 and the girls had been friends since they were seven years old. They walked together across the car park towards the hotel to the beautiful sounds of Andy playing his bagpipes. He was so smart in his kilt and she was so pleased that she had organised him to play at the wedding. She knew that Katherine would be thrilled to hear the sound as the wedding car approached. The little bridesmaids were excited to see their nan and rushed towards her for a kiss and a hug. They all looked lovely in their ivory dresses with matching headdresses, shoes and silk purses. It was going to be the most beautiful wedding and she was proud to be the mother-of-the-bride. The photographer called her by name and she turned to him as he flashed his camera time after time to get the perfect shot. The guests were gathering at the gate to greet one another and as the cream wedding car approached, the bridegroom and his best man were ushered indoors. James and Simon looked very dapper in their morning suits and Kathy, James' mother and Dave his father made their way to their seats.

After a lot of photographs, they were ready to walk down the aisle. Kate went first; she wanted to walk down to her seat by herself. She saw her friends Chrisanna and Liz turn around to admire her outfit. She felt her choice had been perfect. It fitted in with the theme of the wedding. Grey morning suits for the men, ivory for the bridesmaids' dresses and Katherine looking beautiful in her ivory wedding gown with matching lace veil. John looked dashing in his morning suit and he looked so proud to be walking with his stepdaughter as she slowly made her way towards the man she loved. There were two readings, one given by Katherine's nearly tearful eldest brother Richard and the other one read by James' mother; she looked exquisite in a cerise and pale grey long dress with a matching short jacket. She had silver sandals on and a lovely cerise hat. She looked ever so proud of her youngest son as did Dave. They both liked Katherine and it was plain to see just how happy they were. It was a very moving ceremony. Kate would have really liked them to have been married in a church, but she had to admit she was delighted that their civil ceremony was just as meaningful and lovely. On the table in front of the registrar was a beautiful flower arrangement matching the bridal bouquet, fairy lights were inter-woven onto a pure white curtain made from voile which decorated the wall behind them, but in pride of place, right at the front for all the guests to see in a lovely ivory butterfly frame, stood the very last photograph that had ever been taken by Kate of just Katherine and her beloved Dad.

He was towering behind her small frame, she was dressed in a turquoise blue tee shirt and he was leaning onto her shoulders beaming with pride. It was a perfect picture of her father and his twelve-year-old daughter. Little did any of them realise when that photograph was taken, that it was to be the last one of them together. It was in the summer of 1993 just four months before his sudden and tragic death. It was taken by a lake in Bournemouth where Ian and Katherine had been fishing with him. It was a treasured photograph and all the children had a copy of it. He could not be there in person on the most special day of her life, but Kate had said that she was certain he would be with them in spirit. His presence was everywhere and it made the day even more special to have him there. Never ever would he be forgotten and today was no exception. The wedding breakfast was scrumptious and after the speeches were over the guests mingled and introduced themselves to one another. The two families were very much alike and Kate and John and Kathy and Dave all remarked on how lovely a day it had been, the months of planning, the outfits and the lone piper had made it unforgettable and the Stirk House venue had done them proud.

In the evening, they danced to the resident DJ who provided music for everyone's taste and at one a.m. the party began to disperse. The wedding cake had been cut, the videographers had been on hand all day and the photographer had taken more than five hundred photographs. The little bridesmaids who had behaved perfectly all day were sleepy now and it was time to say goodnight to everyone and goodbye to those who were not staying overnight. The following day Kate and John went down for breakfast; there was no sign of the newlyweds yet but they all waited to greet them as they entered the breakfast room. Hurrah they all shouted, and the couple smiled and said good morning to their guests.

They were rounding off the day at the Newdrop Inn near Ribchester for lunch, but first they were going to have coffee or tea at John and Kate's house. Kate proudly showed them through the house, well the ladies really, as the men were too busy catching up with each other. Some lived quite a long way from each other and James' brother and family had come from Norway, his auntie and uncle were from Australia so there was much to catch up on. The lunch was perfect as always. It was Kate's favourite place to eat. They had driven the scenic route in convoy from

Billington to show James' family the beautiful Ribble Valley where Kate and John lived. After much chattering at the table and endless cups of tea and coffee they kissed and hugged each other on the car park. Some of James' family were in a touring caravan in the lakes so they went on their way and John and Kate led the way through the villages towards the M6 motorway. They waved their goodbyes as each car still in convoy joined the slip road and onto the M6 motorway heading south. It was sad to see them go. It felt like they had known one another for years not just forty-eight hours and as John drove their car around the roundabout and headed home Kate felt a lump in her throat.

It had been a perfectly magical wedding. It had gone so smoothly with everyone looking lovely and enjoying themselves. Even the little ones were running around happily playing together and some of them didn't even know each other. The photographs were going to be stunning. Roger had taken so many. They were pleased that the weather had not dampened the day, although the following day when they had gone out for lunch it was just glorious. They all remarked how it was typical of the English weather. On the wedding day it was cloudy with outbreaks of light rain, yet the following day it was hot and sunny. The photographs of James and Katherine with their white umbrellas in the air would prove the rain had just added to the day.

They were going on their honeymoon to Cornwall in two days' time and Kate and John said they would look after Smokey and Pumpkin, (Katherine's two beloved cats). They needed time together now, there had been a lot of planning over nine months but it had all been so worth it.

FORTY SIX

After the wedding Kate started to plan ahead; she wanted to make amends with the grandchildren and to try and overcome her fear of people being sick and with John's help she thought if they got a sofa bed then the kiddies could come for a sleepover. He said he would look after them if they were ill and that it would be nice for them to come and stay for the night at their nan and grandad's house. The sofa bed was to be delivered on Friday the 19th of October 2012 between seven a.m. and nine a.m.. There was so much going on at Dale View;besides the new sofa bed they were also having a new carpet in the kitchen. John had picked it up and they were waiting to have it laid. It was rolled up in the hallway until that could be arranged. The sofa bed arrived at eight thirty a.m. and the men tried to get it up the winding staircase but it was proving to be a great task as it was hellishly heavy. Kate pushed the carpet into the kitchen giving the men more room in the hallway and she sat in the lounge out of the way. Eventually after they had had a welcoming cup of tea in the study one of the men shouted to Kate to go and have a look to see if she was happy where they had put it. She clean forgot about the roll of carpet in the kitchen and went head over heels over it and flat on the floor. Embarrassed she quickly got up and hobbled up the stairs. One of the men said, 'Are you ok, love?'

'Yes, it's fine,' she said. 'I just forgot I'd moved the carpet into the kitchen.'

'Go and put some frozen peas on it and put your feet up.' he said.

'It will be okay I am sure,' she lied. She knew it didn't feel right but she smiled, thanked them for all their hard work and tipped them a ten pound note each and showed them the door.

As the van drew away, she went back in the lounge she pulled herself over to the phone and dialled John's works mobile.

'Hi sweet, have they been with the sofa bed?' John said.

'I think I have broken my ankle,' she replied.

'Oh God, Kate, what the hell have you done?' he said. She told him how it had been a nightmare getting the sofa bed upstairs and that she had tripped over the damn carpet.

'I am with a customer at the moment, but I will be home as soon as I can,' he said.

'I am shaking like a leaf, John, please be quick.'

'Ring Katherine,' he said, 'see if she can get to you before me.'

'Okay I will but come home soon. I think we need to go to A&E'.' Katherine arrived shortly after Kate rang her and immediately said, 'I think it's broken, Mum. John will be home as soon as he can,' as she spoke John's van pulled up on the drive. He came in and saw his Sweetpea shaking and crying. He gave her a kiss and thanked Katherine for coming to her mum so quickly.

'You get off back to work, love,' he said to her, 'and I will take your mum up to casualty.' John helped Kate into the car and they went to the hospital. The X-ray showed a clean break and Kate saw the consultant who said they would get it put in plaster. It would be six weeks before it would be mended. When John brought Kate home he made her comfortable and then went back to work. Kate said she was okay she could get to the toilet which was off the hallway and the hospital had given her a Zimmer frame to use. It was a long six weeks as John would bring up her breakfast and her lunch then go to work. She was safer in their bedroom as she could use their en suite and she had the television to watch. Kate hired a wheelchair, so she could at least get out at the weekend with John and she was glad that the broken ankle had happened after the wedding rather than before it. On November the 26th the plaster was removed. It had been quite an eventful few weeks but, hey ho, she was walking again by Christmas and her 2012 present from John was going to be the best surprise ever.

Jillian, Rob, Katherine and James came to share the Christmas meal with John and Kate and they opened all their presents together. John had been very secretive about Kate's present and he told her she must not go into the study under any circumstance. Kate wondered what he was up to on Christmas Eve and so after they had all had their meal and the presents were now opened it came as a shock for John to tell Kate to go upstairs and look in the study for her final present. She said she had got everything, but he was adamant she go up and look. Gingerly as her ankle was tender she climbed the stairs and opened the study door.

'Oh my God,' they heard her cry. 'Oh I can't believe it,' Kate was saying and crying at the same time. The tag said 'To my Sweetpea something you always wanted but could never have.' All my love always John. Xxxxx'

The lovely gold ribbon and Christmas wrapping paper lay strewn on the floor and there stood the most beautiful Silver Cross pink and white doll's pram standing before her. In the middle was a gorgeous distinctive porcelain plaque of a pink daisy with a tiny white daisy above it. Kate could not believe her eyes; she had had the old grey pram that was Jean's cast-off and she had begged Rob and Mary for one of her own, but they had always refused her. Now fifty-three years on she finally had her own doll's pram for her dolly Carol who was now sixty-years-old today. Kate got her when she was just two years old and her Teddy was fifty-six-years-old. They could finally be sat together in this lovely pram. It would have pride of place in the lounge for all to see then later be next to her side of the bed in their bedroom. Katherine and Jillian were coming upstairs to see what the crying and commotion was all about, and John was behind them. Kate flew into his arms,

'Oh thank you darling, thank you so much what a lovely thought. I will treasure this Christmas Day forever. You are the best husband in all the world.'

'I was putting it together in the study last night,' he said. 'I smuggled it in a few weeks ago when you were on the phone to Glenda then I put it in the loft, so you would never know.'

'Well I love it so much. When did you get it?'

'Do you remember when we went to look at that pram shop in Barrowford a few weeks ago and you said, 'See that lovely Silver Cross doll's pram over there? Well Joan my friend had a green one when we were little and I would have given the world for one like that but mum and dad wouldn't buy one for me. That's when I thought I am going to get her one for Christmas. I ordered the navy and white one that you pointed to. And I paid the deposit on it. When I got out of the shop I looked in the brochure the lady gave me and saw the pink and white one, so I rang her and asked if she would swap it, so she did.' The pram stood pride of place in the lounge on Boxing Day and Kate showed it to all who came. She thought they would think it was crackers to have it on show but she didn't care, she was over the moon with it. John had done her proud yet again.

In January 2013 it had been two years since she had walked out of her job at the health centre. Her life was lonely and she missed seeing John during the day as she always caught up with him if he was in the area en route home. She had lunch with Liz sometimes or an afternoon coffee but other than that she was on her own. The days were long and she still had six years before John's retirement.

They flew to Portugal on the 1st of September and stayed at the Riu Palace. It was a lovely holiday and they made love often as well as some sunbathing and a lot of walks along the cliffs which were a stunning terracotta colour. Wow, it was hot, and the food was delightful too.

Not much else happened that year and they went for their Christmas meal to Jillian's and Rob's house which was lovely. New Year's Day 2014 they went to the Newdrop near Ribchester for their lunch. They had been going for a few years now and would make it an annual occasion, a real treat for them. They also celebrated John's sixtieth birthday there too on the 1st of March.

Katherine and James asked Kate and John for tea on June 8th, 2014. Kate thought Katherine looked peaky but thought it was just tiredness. After tea they went into the lounge where Katherine announced she was expecting a baby to be born in February 2015. Kate and John were over the moon to say the least and they chatted about where the baby would be born and were they going to find out the sex of the child to which they said yes. They wanted to know so they could choose the colour of the nursery. Kate said she wanted to buy the pram if that was okay with them and they started to make plans for the new arrival in the early spring. The morning sickness was something Katherine had to contend with but apart from that the pregnancy progressed nicely.

On the 13th of August they flew to Paphos for ten days to another hotel near Kato Paphos. They were looking forward to being grandparents again and looking forward to having another baby in the family. Corben was sixteen-years-old now Amelia ten years and Anastazia was going to be eleven years in December and Natalia eight years so it was going to be lovely having a new baby in the family.

Katherine referred to the baby as Peanut. She was sixteen-weeks pregnant now and Kate and John went shopping in Limassol for a sleeping bag. It was beautiful white satin with baby teddies on it. It wasn't cheap but well worth it. The twenty-week scan showed they were having a little boy, oh how lovely for them. On the 28th of November they moved into a lovely detached house in Clayton-le-Woods there was still 10 weeks to the birth and Kate and John helped them to move in. They would be able to decorate the nursery in plenty of time. They shared their Christmas meal with Jillian and Rob and their New Year's Day 2015 again at the Newdrop. The baby was due on the 7th of February, but the day came and went leaving Katherine a little disappointed but still positive. It had been lovely for Kate as she had seen a lot of Katherine since she had left her job for maternity leave so on Monday the 9th of February as there was still no sign of the new baby she went to see the nursery, monkeys hung from trees on the wall and a cot mobile hung over the cot, the bedroom furniture was all ready for baby Allison to arrive. The wardrobe was full of his clothes, it really was lovely.

After a long labour and a caesarean section, baby Thomas Joseph Ian arrived safely at 7.56 a.m. on Monday the 16th of February. Kate and John, armed with a blue teddy and an arrangement of flowers in a lovely blue pottery clown set off for the hospital to see their precious baby grandson and he was all they had hoped for. He was wrapped up in a cream shawl with a little white hat on and his Babygro was baby blue too. They took lots of photos of the new baby with his mummy and daddy and some with his grandad and nan. Katherine was in hospital for a few days and Kate and John left them to settle down with the new baby as James had a couple of weeks off.

John needed an operation on his knee. He saw the consultant on the 20th of March and he had his operation on the 25th of June. It was a day case and he was home by lunchtime but had to have physio on it.

He went back to work on the 11th of August as good as new.

FORTY-SEVEN

Holidays next Camp-de-Mar in Majorca; they were so looking forward to it. They had had a busy year and although they could only afford a week they were ready to chill. It was a good flight on Monday the 17th of August but when they reached Majorca Airport the heavens opened. The mini-bus driver said they had had a few bad days so hopefully it would soon clear. They arrived safely at their hotel only for it to rain harder than ever so they decided to go down for lunch and unpack later. The restaurant was packed out as the swimming pool was nearly overflowing with the deluge of rain. They sat facing each other when all of a sudden John shouted, 'Oh my God' thinking he had seen someone from home that he knew, Kate looked in the direction he was looking only to see his sister and her husband sitting having lunch four tables behind them. What on earth were they doing here? They had only just returned home from Ibiza a few days previously Kate thought, already fuming. It all came tumbling down for her; the one week holiday that they had planned had been gatecrashed. She could not hide her disappointment. She remembered the conversation when his sister had telephoned to say they were home from their holiday and she had asked several questions to John as to which hotel they were going to and what time their flight was. It had all been planned and they had never ever thought that they would follow them, in fact they had been there since the Saturday and now it was only Monday. They would be with them for another five days. Kate could have cried; in fact she nearly did, instead she had to smile and pretend she was okay with it. Never in a million years would she have done that to somebody, but John parent's had done that to them and as daughter and mother a few years ago that was okay they loved it, but not for us Kate thought. The week was fraught to say the least and they knew Kate wasn't happy. She really was blazing mad. By the time it came to

Saturday and they were going home the atmosphere was icy. They hugged as quick a hug as possible and climbed into their mini-cab. That left Sunday for Kate and John and Monday they were going home too. She vowed that never again would she ever tell anyone which hotel they were going to, or their flight details. She would just say the destination, so nobody would spoil their holiday again.

On the 2nd of September baby Thomas and Mummy and Nan were going to the baby clinic; he weighed 16lb 3oz. They went on to a lovely garden centre and had lunch. He was giggling now and a delight to be with. Kate was so happy he was the loveliest baby. Katherine went back to work in November and Kate looked after Thomas whilst she was at work. He was crawling now, and Kate's days were filled she took him for a walk each day, sometimes to Whalley or up to Foxfield's and life was busy again. He was a very good baby and she thoroughly enjoyed him. Katherine had gone back to work part-time so she came to pick him up or Kate took him home.

On Sunday the 6th of December 2015 Jillian announced that she was pregnant but on Tuesday February 2nd 2016 she went for a scan only to find the baby had no heartbeat. It was heartbreaking, and Kate and John were lost for words of how to comfort them both. John was so looking forward to having a grandchild of his own, but it was not to be. They were determined to try again but they needed time before that to get over their loss.

Tuesday 16th of February 2016 was Thomas's first birthday. Nan and Grandad bought him a Thomas The Tank Engine ride on and he loved it. It sang songs and played tunes too. He was growing fast and was a lovely happy baby. Kate adored him and lived for the days she looked after him.

Monday 1st August John took Kate to Ibiza. They stayed at the Panorama Hotel in Es-Cana. It was a beautiful week. They were so loved up. The years were passing quickly but their lovemaking grew stronger and more intense with time and they made love every day. Kate could not have loved him more if she tried. He meant the world to her, always had and always will. She looked forward to three more years when he would be retiring and they could spend more time together.

Jillian was now pregnant for the third time. It was unbelievable that her second baby had had no heartbeat like the first, but thankfully this baby was alive and on the 7th of September 2016 she had her first scan. They were scanning her every two weeks and now on the 21st of September she now eight weeks pregnant. Everyone was praying for them that this baby would survive and, touch wood, the scan was okay too. On the 5th of October baby was moving and Jillian was now ten weeks. By Christmas everything was going well. John and Kate invited the family round for a Christmas Day buffet; there was Richard and Debbie, Corben and Amelia and Jillian and Rob happily showing a bump now. The baby was due in April and John was counting down the weeks. There was far too much food as Kate insisted they have enough! Enough, are you kidding? There was so much food the table didn't look like any had been eaten by the end of the day and a lot got thrown away too.

2017, where had all the years gone? John and Kate met Jillian and Rob for a 4D baby scan. They were invited into the scan room to see the baby; it was going to be a little boy and they were thrilled to bits and quite emotional too. How far technology had gone since Kate had her children; they didn't even have scans then never mind being able to find out the sex and now they could even see his little face and body. How sweet was that?

Thomas was two on the 16th of February. Time had flown by. John and Kate bought him a children's Henry vacuum cleaner and a Thomas The Tank engine scooter. He was so happy; he had wanted a Henry for ages despite him being afraid of his nan's vacuum. Kids are so funny but lovely too. After a lot of thought Katherine and James decided it was time for Thomas to go to a childminder. It would save James bringing him every day although he didn't mind that and also it was time for Thomas to mix with little ones of his own age. They stressed that Kate had done nothing wrong which she knew she hadn't but it was an awful wrench for her. At first it was only for two days but it made sense for it to be from Monday to Friday and Kate would look after him when the childminder was on holiday. It hit her hard; she had devoted her days to him and she missed him terribly. Katherine felt bad and said she didn't mean to upset her, but Thomas was the priority and Kate said she understood. He loved being with his little friends and he was taken to playgroups to see other kiddies play. He really enjoyed it and Kate couldn't have competed with that.

Kate and John had been together for twenty years on the 9th of April 2017. It had been the best years of her life; she never forgot Michael not for a minute, but she was blissfully happy. She thanked God often for the life she had now and John took her out for a meal to their favourite place, The Newdrop to celebrate the lovely years that they had shared together.

On the 18th of April Jillian went into hospital to have her baby. It was a long labour for her and baby George Luke was born on the 20th at 6.59 a.m. weighing 7lb 14oz. It was late in the evening when she brought the baby home and John had called en route whilst he was working in the area, so he could see his new baby grandson, so Kate said she would go up the following day to see baby George.

Rob and Jillian were delighted to have become parents at last and they settled down looking forward to the summer ahead.

Richard received a recognition award in Birmingham on the 25th April then on to London to the BT Tower to meet the bosses and share a meal. He deserved the award; he works long and hard for his company and has worked his way up the ladder from an engineer to a planner. Katherine would bring Thomas in an afternoon after she had finished work and Kate went to see them on another day at their house. It worked well, and Thomas was happy.

The holiday for Kate and John was booked; they were going to Cala Bona in Majorca from the 1st to the 8th of August 2017. It was as usual a lovely hotel and as Kate always asked for a high floor, she hadn't bargained for the highest in the hotel. The people in the pool below looked so small and she had to tiptoe onto the balcony and find a chair. She dared not look over unless she was sat down. The view as you can imagine was spectacular. They danced in the evening together, made love often and swam in the pool. All too soon they were back in Manchester. They vowed that when John retired in 2019 they would either go twice a year if possible or go for two weeks together.

It was Katherine and James' turn to entertain them at Christmas this year at their house. They invited Kate and John to share their day with Kathy and Dave, James' parents and they all had a lovely time together. Thomas loved his presents from Father Christmas including a sit-on-excavator from Nan and Grandad. He was obsessed with diggers, dumper trucks, fork lift trucks and anything in the house-building line. Katherine took him daily to see diggers on their way home from the childminder's and he knew the machinery of each one.

The year had ended well, and they looked forward to 2018; what would that year bring for the family? Kate was apprehensive as always, but they had their New Year's Day meal on the 1st of January at The Newdrop at one p.m. which was lovely, and they went home to enjoy the rest of the day together.

FORTY-EIGHT

There wasn't much happening in the first three months of the year. Thomas was enjoying being at his childminders from Monday to Friday and Kate looked after him if she was on holiday and they went looking for diggers and tractors together. He loved days with Kate; she treated him to toys and really spoilt him, they shared their lunches together, watched children's programmes. Grandad rang him each lunchtime and made sure he had some grapes cut up for after he had eaten his first course.

George was christened at St Francis Church at noon on the 8th of April 2018. It was a difficult day for Kate as John's ex-wife and her husband were there too and they ended up sat on the same table as them. Kate looked out of the window for much of the afternoon fortunately Katherine, James and Thomas were invited and that took some of the pressure off, but it was still an uncomfortable day. George was one-year-old on the 20th of April. The year had flown by.

On May the 8th it was John and Kate's fourteenth wedding anniversary. He sent her a beautiful box of flowers telling her how much he loved her and they made love that night celebrating the time they had been together. It had been twenty-one years on the 9th of April and it had flown by. They were devoted to each other and she cherished him and he her. So many people had been sceptical when they moved in together all those years ago; his mother and stepfather, his sister, some of her friends and now here they were into 2018 and loving each other now more than ever.

Katherine, James and Thomas were going on holiday to Cornwall; they had been for several years to various parts and they loved it. They stayed on a smallholding where there were horses and the owner let James and Thomas have a ride in his tractor which fulfilled Thomas's dream. The cats Smokey, Pumpkin and Casper were in the cattery this year, so Kate and John had only the fish to feed twice in the week. The weather had been glorious for them and they didn't want to come home.

On Tuesday the 24th of July Katherine came to see Kate and John before they went on holiday to Crete; they were flying from Manchester on Sunday the 29$^{th.}$ The conversation came around to James who was putting in a bid to build electric cars with two more pals of his. She mentioned that if the bid fell through there was another job he had been offered in Warwickshire. Without thinking that he wouldn't get the job with his pals Kate said, 'Oh that would be okay as John will be retiring in March and we can come and see you.' After they had gone home she relayed the conversation to John and a sudden mist fell before her eyes. Why had she been so dismissive of the other offer? It wasn't a forgone conclusion that the bid would be his and she suddenly thought of the consequences if they were to move so far away. She spoke to Katherine about it and Katherine said she thought Kate had been very blasé and was taken aback by it too. Kate said, 'I am so sorry, love, I have sat down and thought about this and I hope he gets the other job with his pals.

'He won't know for a few weeks so don't go worrying. It probably won't come off in Warwickshire, I shouldn't have said anything to you but I thought you should know that he has been recommended by his previous boss, who refused the offer himself, and was asked if he knew of anyone who would be interested in the job and he put James' name forward. I don't want you spoiling your holiday,' she said.

'It's okay, love, you were right to tell me just let me know when you know something,' Kate said.

It was difficult to think of anything else and when Katherine rang to say that a telephone interview was pending reality set in. The telephone interview went well, and they were going to go and see the bosses in Warwickshire on the 3rd of August at two thirty p.m. 'I can't look after Thomas,' Kate said to her. 'We will still be in Crete.'

'It's okay, Mum, we will take him with us and then after the interview we will go up to Kathy and Dave's and have tea.'

They flew out of Manchester and arrived safely in Crete. They had arranged for a taxi transfer to take them to Rethymnon where they were staying. On arrival they were shown to their room; it was disappointing as there was only a side sea view, so John rang down to reception to ask if there was another room spare. They were really efficient and within ten minutes they were shown to a much nicer room with a full sea view. The balcony was much nicer as the other balcony was made of concrete and they said it was lovely and accepted it. The porter then transferred their luggage.

They went down to the pool bar to get some lunch,

'that was delightful,' Kate said, and John agreed. They had a little walk around then went to their room to unpack. It really was a lovely hotel and they chilled for the rest of the day. They spent a little time in bed before showering and changed for dinner. The hotel was so spread out they were given a map to show them around. There were three pools; one for children and the other two for adults. Kate and John knew there were going to be children at the hotel, but they hadn't bargained for just how many there would be; it was full of kiddies screaming a lot of the time and certainly not for those who wanted some peace and quiet which the two of them did. They enjoyed the night entertainment and they took a taxi into Rethymnon town midweek where John bought himself a knife. He had bought a knife in almost every resort they had stayed in over the years and it was his hobby to keep collecting them. They went on to the private beach. Mostly w there were no kiddies, the sea was quite rough, and the red flag was flying for a few days although it was very hot; you couldn't stand on the sand for more than a second as it burnt your feet. The two of them made love every day. It was so special; they felt as though they were back on honeymoon and Kate slept as always in John's arms. He told her how much he loved her and not to worry about the interview which was to take place on Friday for James. Katherine had promised to keep in touch and Kate sent Thomas his Night Night text every night from Nan and Grandad.

Friday came, and Kate quietly thought about the day's events; she knew they were travelling down to Warwickshire that morning and that

Katherine was dropping James off at the office where he was to have his interview at two thirty p.m. They laid sunbathing on the beach and Kate heard her phone bleep, she reached into her handbag, and read the text: Hi Mum the interview went well he should know if he has got the job by Tuesday next week, love you and Thomas sends kisses. He has been a really good boy today. Xxx Her heart froze; it was happening and she knew there and then that James would get the Managerial job as he was specialised as a motor car racing lecturer at university and he knew the racing car designs like the back of his hand. He was excellent at his job and he would be a wonderful asset to the company if they gave him the position. There was nothing she could do as she lay there in the lovely sunshine in Greece but pray to God for the strength to help her through the next few days as she prepared herself for a broken heart.

All too soon the taxi was arriving to take them back to Heraklion Airport; it arrived on time on Sunday the 5th of August at 1.30 p.m. local time. They had paid the bill and thanked the hotel staff for a lovely holiday and the driver put their luggage in the mini cab. They had a ninety minute drive back to the airport where they were told there was going to be a four-hour flight delay. That was all they needed; the plane had a technical fault back in Manchester and they would have to wait for a replacement plane to fly out to Greece to pick them up. They were given tokens to get some food and a drink and they just had to sit and wait. It turned out to be a delay of five hours not four hours as they were originally told. Tired and a little weary they arrived back safely in Manchester where their taxi driver was waiting to take them home.

James got the news on the Tuesday to say he had been successful; the job was his and they started to plan their future. Kate was devastated Katherine and little Thomas would be going to live three hours away. She lay in bed just thinking of the life she was going to miss out on; she wouldn't be able to pick him up from school next year when he started in the infants class and she couldn't get in the car and drive half an hour for a chat and a cup of tea in the afternoons any more and she could not hold back the tears. She prayed so hard for God to help her through this and she cried like she had done when Michael had gone. Everyone in their own way had left her through no fault of their own; Glenda had gone to live in the North East when she was fourteen then her dad had been killed, her mother died of cancer then Michael had collapsed and died so suddenly, so now her children, grandchildren and John were her life and now her beloved Katherine was moving away too.

On the 21st of August 2018 the house went up for sale. Thomas' childminder went away for a week's holiday and so Kate looked after him for a few days that week. They went to feed the ducks together, looked for diggers and dumper trucks and she thoroughly enjoyed him. He had no idea of her aching heart and she so tried to smile but it wasn't easy. Her heart broke a little bit more when she thought of being so far away from them all.

Katherine and James went to find a new home near to where he would be working. They would live near the Cotswolds one hundred and fifty-eight miles away from them and she just couldn't bear it, but she knew she had to be strong for Katherine's sake. The house soon sold, and they packed all their ornaments and pictures away. Kate looked after some of their clothes as the wardrobes had been taken to the recycling centre and Thomas's teddies were in Kate's study for safe keeping. Katherine did however have some good news; she asked her boss if she could work from home for him and she would come back to Leyland for meetings once or twice a month and he agreed to give it a year and then they would review it.

'I will be seeing you more, Mum,' she said one day, and Kate knew she had done it to make the move easier and also Katherine loved that job and was excellent at it too.

'Oh thank-you,' Kate said, 'I have prayed so hard and He has answered them'

'We can Skype and meet halfway too, Mum, and you can come and stay when John retires in a few months' time. The distance won't change our love for each other you must hang on to that,' she said. 'I don't want you to make yourself ill and you will do if you don't hold on to this.'

The 30th of September 2018 and James set off to his parent's house where he would stay Monday through to Friday and commute to work from there. He was starting his new job at nine a.m. in the morning 1st of October which happened to be Katherine's thirty-seventh birthday and seven years since they had got engaged.

Their new house would not be ready to move into for another two months, so they would alternate the weekends; one weekend James would come up to Leyland and the next Katherine and Thomas would go down to Nanny and Grandad's house in Bromsgrove and in the meantime Kate and John would cherish every second spent with Thomas and Katherine until it was time for them to leave.

Kate realised it was getting nearer every day to the inevitable but today Katherine and Thomas were coming for a birthday treat for her thirty-seventh birthday. Kate went over to their house in the morning whilst the surveyor came to check everything for the new clients. She called at the supermarket to buy a few bits for tea including a birthday cake then came home. She couldn't wait to see them both. Kate had won a voucher for £40 to use at a children's designer shop in Whalley and they were going to have a little spend for Thomas.

It was hard to see beyond the day and she couldn't imagine not seeing them twice a week. She tried to hide her sadness but her face told the story; she was totally gutted but she told Katherine that she loved her enough to let her go. She just wanted her to be happy and she knew it wasn't going to be easy being so far away from her mum either. Never in a million years would she have ever thought of Katherine moving so far away from her. They had been soulmates ever since Michael had died and she adored her so much and little Thomas, it was all so sad. Would he forget her and John, she wondered and all that they had shared? Surely not, she would speak to him every day and go down to see him with John as often as possible and as Katherine said they could meet halfway, maybe just south of Birmingham.

In a few months' time (John and Kate were already counting down the weeks to that day) they will be free and it will be eight years in January 2019 since she had been a stay at home wife. All the grandchildren are growing up fast and Kate is going to really try to be strong for all her beloved family. Richard and Ian are still close by and God willing, Katherine is going to start a lovely new life with her little boy Thomas and husband James in a beautiful newly built home down in the Cotswolds.

**

The whole family had come full circle now; each of the children were happily married and Kate was besotted with John and she knew that she always would be. The way she coped with her nerves was admirable It was only she who knew how she really felt. She still had days when she did not cope well at all, but it was a case of best foot forward. She was eternally grateful for the stoic way in which her parents had instilled in her how to behave, how to cope with the problems in life and although they had died whilst she was young, they had put the ground work in. Places that were very busy like towns, churches and supermarkets were always going to frighten her. Crowds were to be avoided if at all possible. She never went to the grandchildren's school concerts or Christmas parties just in case someone was sick, and it kept her at home an awful lot which in turn had made her life very lonely. In the early days she had missed the company of work more than she had ever let on to her family and friends and most of the days were never-ending unless she was cleaning their home and she did do most of the time. Still, she had absolutely no regrets whatsoever walking out of her job. She would not be treated the way she had been with a colleague.

Kate had been an exemplary employee with twenty-two years' service in the NHS and she knew to have stayed working in that environment would have probably caused her to have a nervous breakdown and no one was worth that. She had had a very eventful life; she had found happiness in abundance with Michael and John, she had known terrible heartache and tragedy far more than she had deserved. Her fear of people being sick never left her and she knew that it never would; it had been sixty-one years now since the episode at Colwyn Bay which had changed her life forever. Her father's death at an early age had also had a profound effect on her and her mother had been hard to live with since he had died. Having lost her first husband at a very early age was the worst time in her life; she had relied on him for everything and when he was gone, she'd had to bring up a family and face the world alone, but she was also very proud of how she had coped and she knew in her heart that if he was looking down on her now, how very, very, proud he would have been of her.

The years at times had left her dejected and yet her faith had given her the strength to endure those desperate times too. Now she would look forward to the rest of her life when John after his retirement on 1st March 2019, and she would then, maybe, not certainly, not need to be so scared of life and when that day arrived he would be the one who would be by her side, Today, Tomorrow and Forever.